Education of Students with an Intellectual Disability

Research and Practice

Education of Students with an Intellectual Disability

Research and Practice

Phil Foreman

IAP
INFORMATION AGE PUBLISHING, INC.
Charlotte, NC • www.infoagepub.com

Library of Congress Cataloging-in-Publication Data

Foreman, Phil.
Education of students with an intellectual disability : research and practice / Phil Foreman.
p. cm.
Includes bibliographical references and index.
ISBN 978-1-60752-214-0 (pbk.) – ISBN 978-1-60752-215-7 (hardcover)
1. Children with mental disabilities–Education–Textbooks. 2. Mental retardation–Textbooks. I. Title.
LC4601.F62 2009
371.92–dc22

2009024392

Printed in the United States of America

To Carolyn

Contents

About the Author

Phil Foreman is Professor of Education at the University of Newcastle, Australia. Following a period as a classroom teacher and school counselor, Dr. Foreman became a teacher educator, specializing in the education of students with intellectual or developmental disabilities. At the University of Newcastle, he served terms as Director of the Special Education Centre, Dean of Students and, from 2002 to 2008, as Dean of Education. He was appointed Chair of the NSW Institute of Teachers in December 2007.

Dr. Foreman has an extensive research and publication record in the area of special education and disability studies. In 2002 the Australian Society for the Study of Intellectual Disability awarded him a Distinguished Service Citation for his contribution to research in special education. He is a Life Member of the Australian College of Educators and of the Royal Institute for Deaf and Blind Children. He is also a member of the Community Services Division of the Administrative Decisions Tribunal. He was Editor of the *Journal of Intellectual & Developmental Disability* for 11 years and is currently on numerous Editorial Boards. He is a Research Advisory Board Member of the National Institute for People with Disabilities Research Institute, New York. In 2000 he was made a Fellow of the Australian Psychological Society.

In addition to research activity, Dr. Foreman has been heavily involved in service provision for people with an intellectual disability. He developed early intervention programs at the University of Newcastle Special Education Centre starting in 1978, leading to similar services in other regions of

Education of Students with an Intellectual Disability, pages xiii–xiv the state. In 1992 he became foundation President of Newcastle & Hunter Community Access, a service for adults with severe disabilities, starting with 2 staff and currently with 70 workers. In 1993 he established Disability Advocacy Service Hunter (DASH). In June 2008 the Chancellor of Macquarie University presented him with the 2007 Alumni Award for Distinguished Service (Professional Category).

Dr. Foreman researches in the area of intellectual disability. His current research focus is on improving the communicative interactions of students with severe and multiple disabilities through training of communication partners.

Preface

This book is designed as a college-level textbook introducing readers to all aspects of intellectual disability in children, from birth to the end of schooling, with an educational focus. The book will be of interest to persons training as special education teachers or who are training as regular teachers with a focus on special education. It will also be relevant reading for parents of children with intellectual disability, for practicing teachers, and for other professionals working with such children (psychologists, social workers, nurses, therapists).

The book is divided into seven chapters. Chapter 1 introduces the concept of intellectual disability and gives a historical perspective. It examines definitional arguments and discusses some of the controversial issues involved in identification of and service provision for people with intellectual disability. Chapter 2 provides an overview of the latest knowledge on genetic, prenatal, perinatal, and environmental causes of intellectual disability. In Chapter 3, issues in identifying and assessing intellectual disability are the focus. This chapter covers different ways of assessing intellectual disability through individual intelligence tests and measures of adaptive behavior. Research and practice concerning early educational intervention for children with intellectual disability is the focus of Chapter 4. Early intervention is examined both as an attempt to change the developmental process and as a regular part of the educational cycle. Chapter 5 covers various aspects of the choices parents make when their child starts formal schooling, and the likely effect of those choices on their children. Chapter 6 provides an

---

Education of Students with an Intellectual Disability, pages xv–xvi

overview of research on best practice in teaching children with intellectual disability. It deals with teaching approaches and their outcomes, and how teaching approaches reflect legislative requirements. The final chapter deals with the options available to teachers and parents when the student is ready to finish with formal schooling.

Because of its comprehensive coverage, the book is not intended to provide an in-depth treatment of all topics related to the education of students with intellectual disability. The book provides a synthesis of the issues and summarizes research that has taken place on each topic, including influential research studies from the past as well as current research findings. Many references are provided for readers who wish to pursue any of the topics in more detail.

The field of special education and intellectual disability practice has been strongly influenced by legislation in the United States. The United States is also the source of most research in the disability field. For this reason, there is an emphasis in this book on research and practice in the United States. However, there is also coverage of research and practice in Australia (where the author is located); the UK, where there are several leading research groups; and other parts of the world.

Instructors may wish to use the book as the basis of a one-semester unit on the education of students with intellectual disability. Each chapter could be treated over 1 or 2 weeks, depending on the focus of the group and the particular interest of the instructor. A group with an early childhood focus would spend more time on early intervention. A secondary-focused group might spend more time on postschool options. Each major chapter section has questions for discussion or reflection, and there are also discussion questions about the case studies provided in each chapter.

The education of students with an intellectual disability has changed greatly over the last 25 years. The next 25 years are likely to produce even greater changes. I would be very happy to be in a situation where positive developments and improvements to the field were so rapid that this book would quickly become out-of-date. To those of you who are embarking on a teaching career or are already working in the profession, I wish you well. I hope that you and the other professionals and parents who read this book find that it provides you with some insights into the extraordinarily important area you are focused on: the education of students with an intellectual disability.

Phil Foreman
Sydney, Australia
March, 2009

1

Understanding Intellectual Disability

Overview: This chapter introduces the concept of intellectual disability and provides a historical perspective on how intelligence has been measured over time. It examines definitional arguments and describes changing terminology. The role of adaptive behavior as part of the definition of intellectual disability is reviewed. The chapter examines some of the controversial issues involved in the classification of people with an intellectual disability and describes different systems of definition.

Intelligence

The concept of intelligence seems to be well understood in the general community. We all understand what is meant when someone is described as an "intelligent" person, and most parents would say that they hope to have intelligent children. High intelligence is seen as being associated with high achievement and success in life, and low intelligence with the opposite. However, the concept is much more complex than may at first be apparent. For example, in everyday conversation we may hear reference to an intelligent baby, an intelligent animal, an intelligent politician, and so on. Surely there must be differing meanings here.

Education of Students with an Intellectual Disability, pages 1–21

The differing meanings derive from the fact that there is always a concept of relativity when intelligence is being discussed. While there is much theoretical debate about how intelligence should be defined and measured and about what factors are included, there is reasonable agreement that assessment of intelligence involves an assessment of an individual's ability to learn, to remember, to understand, and to solve problems, *compared with other similar individuals (or animals)*. The relativity is very important. So the question of how intelligent a person is becomes a question of how well the person can learn, remember, understand, and problem-solve, compared with other people of the same age, in the same culture, and who have had the same opportunities.

Failure to consider these opportunities leads to inappropriate comparisons. For example, if an intelligence test has been developed primarily within one culture, comparisons that are made when the test is used with people from a different cultural group will be meaningless. This issue will be discussed in more detail in Chapter 3.

FOR DISCUSSION AND REFLECTION:

- What do we mean if we describe a 3-year-old as intelligent?
- Provide examples of the concept of relativity when considering intelligence.

Measurement of Intelligence

The quantification or measurement of intelligence has always been a controversial issue. The first psychological scale designed to measure intelligence was developed by a French psychologist Alfred Binet and a collaborator, Théodore Simon, in the very early part of the 20th century. They designed a series of scales that would test average children's ability to acquire particular skills. They looked for items to go in the scale that most children would be able to learn through experience, rather than have to be specifically taught, and they organized the items into age levels. Thus a "6-year-old" item would be one that could be successfully completed by 60%–75% of 6-year-olds (and by 75%+ of 7-year-olds), but was failed by 40%+ of 5-year-olds. Items went down to a 3-year-old level.

Adding up all of the items that the child could complete successfully led to the concept of a "mental age" (MA). Thus, 6-year-olds who performed at an average level should come up with an MA of 6:0, and higher or lower than this if they performed better or worse than average. A further concept that was developed around this time was that of an intelligence quotient, or IQ, as a simple way of stating the relationship between a person's chronological age and their mental age. This was obtained by dividing mental age by chronological age (CA) and multiplying by 100. This was designed to produce an average IQ of 100, if MA and CA were equal, with an IQ of 100+ for students whose MA was higher than their CA, and less than 100 if it was lower. For example a CA of 8:0 with an MA of 4:0 would lead to an IQ of $4/8 \times 100 = 50$.

The first Stanford-Binet Intelligence Scale was published in 1916 by Stanford University psychologist Lewis Terman, based on Binet and Simon's principles. A 1937 edition was published by Terman in association with another Stanford psychologist, Maud Merrill. This was in two forms, the L and the M, which allowed testers to use different editions on retest to avoid practice effects. The scale was widely accepted internationally, and millions of children had their IQs and MAs calculated and, for many, their lives determined, through the Binet formula.

While the concept of a mental age was straightforward and influential, it could also be shown to have some problems. This was particularly so when people were found to have a very low MA. For example, an adult with an intellectual disability may be said to have the mental age of a 7-year-old because of his inability to pass tests beyond the 7-year-old level. However, that person may be functioning in the community at a much higher level than that of a child of 7. He may travel independently, manage his own finances to a moderate level, and work well in supported employment. The concept of an MA of 7:0 years therefore tells us very little about how that person is functioning.

By the time of the 1960 revision of the Stanford-Binet Scale (Terman & Merrill, 1960), it was widely accepted that intelligence could be shown to be "normally distributed." That is to say that most people are in the average band, with fewer and fewer people at each level above and below the mean, fitting a bell-shaped curve. It was no longer considered accurate to use simple MA/CA ratios. The normal curve for intelligence retains an average IQ of 100 for each age level, with a standard deviation of around 15 or 16, depending on which test is used. The 1960 Stanford-Binet produced "deviation IQs." This means that IQ scores were based on how far the child's MA deviated from the mean, rather than on a simple quotient. Other popular individual intelligence tests, such as the Wechsler Intelligence Scale for Children (WISC) (Wechsler, 1949, 1991, 2003) are also based on normal curve statistics and have not used the concept of mental age.

The Binet and WISC intelligence tests are those used most commonly when it is suspected that children may have an intellectual disability. They take about an hour or more per student to administer and must be administered by a trained psychologist. They are therefore an expensive option. For children in regular classes who are not thought to have an intellectual disability, pencil and paper intelligence tests are much more likely to be used.

FOR DISCUSSION AND REFLECTION:

- What is meant by mental age?
- Why is mental age a problematic psychological construct?

Intellectual Disability

Regardless of how intelligence is measured or conceptualized, there will be some people whose ability to learn, to remember, to understand, and to solve problems is significantly impaired, compared with that of other people in their community. It may be that these people have what can be described as an "intellectual disability." However, the term by itself is not very descriptive and tells us very little about how the person is functioning. The definition of intellectual disability has itself been debated over many years, and will continue to be debated. A definition widely accepted as authoritative is that of the American Association on Intellectual and Developmental Disabilities (AAIDD) (Luckasson et al., 2002). This association was known until 2006 as the American Association on Mental Retardation, but the terms "mental retardation" and "mental deficiency" are no longer regarded as acceptable by many people with an intellectual disability and their families, or by disability workers and researchers. "Intellectual disability" is becoming the more widely used term and will be used throughout this book, other than in direct quotes or titles.

The AAIDD's 2002 publication on the definition of intellectual disability was its tenth, the first having been published in 1921. A recent analysis (Schalock, Luckasson, & Shogren, 2007) has shown that all definitions for the last 50 years have contained three important concepts: (1) intellectual limitations, (2) limitations in adapting to environmental demands, and (3) early age of onset during the developmental period. The current (2002) definition is that intellectual disability [mental retardation] is a

> disability characterized by significant limitations both in intellectual functioning and in adaptive behavior as expressed in conceptual, social, and practical adaptive skills. This disability originates before age 18. (Luckasson et al., 2002)

Luckasson et al. list five assumptions that must be taken into account when the definition is applied. These assumptions are discussed in turn.

1. ***Limitations in present functioning must be considered within the context of community environments typical of the individual's age peers and culture.***

Intellectual ability (or disability) cannot be considered in a vacuum. To take an extreme example, a newly arrived immigrant who did not speak English might appear to have an intellectual disability if the assessment was carried out in the English language and contained a large number of verbal items. At a less extreme level, different community environments will be associated with different experiences which, in turn, will impact on the individual's response to an assessment of intelligence. If the assessment used does not take into account the person's typical environment and culture, the results could be misleading.

2. ***Valid assessment considers cultural and linguistic diversity as well as differences in communication, sensory, motor, and behavioral factors.***

Any alteration to a child's environment compared with that of other children could impact on their ability to respond to an intelligence test, but may not mean that they have an intellectual disability. For example, consider a child who was raised on a remote rural settlement, perhaps without access to books, libraries, or television. That child may be a quick learner and problem solver in his own environment. He may be able to identify and track different animals and know about what native fruits can be eaten. He may have learned many skills that are important in his environment. However, when it comes to responding to a test using unfamiliar materials, content, and language, he may be assessed as having an intellectual disability. This assessment would be wrong.

At a more fundamental level, many children have sensory, motor, or other problems that impact on their ability to demonstrate their intelligence. Unless the assessment allows for these factors, the results will be an underestimate of the child's intellectual ability. For example, many intelligent children with severe cerebral palsy have been misdiagnosed as having an intellectual disability for this reason (see Box 1.1).

BOX 1.1 DAVID'S STORY

Soon after David was born, his parents realized that he had substantial problems, and their worries were confirmed when he was diagnosed with spastic quadriplegia, a form of cerebral palsy. He developed very poorly, and although he seemed to be interested in watching what was going on, he had very little purposeful use of his arms or legs and, while he made noises, he was unable to speak. His parents were convinced that he understood them when they spoke to him. For example, he displayed excitement when they told him that his grandparents would be visiting, and he appeared to be looking out for them. He was assessed on an individual intelligence test by a psychologist at age 4:0 and was judged as being TLA (too low to assess). Adaptive behavior was also found to be below the first percentile. He was sent to a special class where a speech pathologist and teacher worked together on his communication skills. He initially used an electronic speech device to communicate simple requests, but eventually started using a computer with a head pointer. By the time he was 7, he was able to write using the computer as well as other children of his age. By grade 3, he had moved into a regular class and was following the general education curriculum, although he continued to need a teacher's aide and technology support. If he had been born 30 years earlier, he may have never been able to demonstrate the intelligence he clearly possessed, and it may have been wrongly believed that he had a severe intellectual disability.

DISCUSSION QUESTIONS

1. What were the early signs that David's intelligence was in the "normal" range?
2. Why did the psychologist's test suggest that his intelligence was too low to assess?
3. How might the psychologist have been able to assess that David's intelligence was as expected for his age level?
4. Why did David's adaptive behavior testing produce such a low result?
5. Which of Luckasson's five assumptions (referred to above) were not taken into consideration when David was first assessed?

3. Within an individual, limitations often coexist with strengths.

The AAIDD definition of intellectual disability makes it clear that the concept is multidimensional. In the past it was often thought that knowing a person's IQ score told you as much as you needed to know about their intellectual and general functioning. An individual's school placement would sometimes be decided solely on the basis of her IQ score. It is now accepted that assessment of intelligence is much more complex than this. An assessment of intellectual functioning may show some skills that are at a similar level to those of typical children of the same age while others are at a much lower level, and it is accepted that intelligence is not a unitary concept. For example, the WISC is divided into verbal and performance scales, with several subscales in each, with considerable research on the implications of various performance profiles. Gardner has produced a model of intelligence suggesting that each person uses multiple intelligences. He postulates that there are at least eight intelligences, including, for example, linguistic, mathematical, musical, and interpersonal intelligences. This is known as the theory of multiple intelligences (Gardner, 1993). Sternberg's theory suggests three interrelated intelligences: analytical intelligence, creative intelligence, and practical intelligence (Sternberg, 1988). Greenspan has also postulated that there are three intelligences, which are identified as conceptual intelligence, practical intelligence, and social intelligence (Greenspan, 1999). These forms of intelligence are recognized as components of adaptive behavior in the 2002 AAIDD definition, which refers to "adaptive behavior as expressed in conceptual, social, and practical adaptive skills" (Luckasson et al., 2002).

Adaptive behavior has been part of the definition of intellectual disability since 1961. The inclusion of this concept should prevent assumptions being made about intellectual disability based on a single assessment using an intelligence test. A diagnosis of intellectual disability must also include an assessment of how well the person operates in their environment, conceptually, functionally, and socially. Thus, a person whose score on an intelligence test suggested that he may have an intellectual disability, but was assessed to have adaptive behavior that was within two standard deviations of population averages, would not be diagnosed as having an intellectual disability (see Box 1.2).

BOX 1.2 SARAH'S ADAPTIVE BEHAVIOR

Sarah's parents are concerned about her school performance. She is aged 7 years 6 months, and although she was slow to learn to talk, she now talks well and has several friends whom she mixes with at school and socially. Sarah's teacher says that she has some concerns about Sarah's language and general development, and would like her to have an individual intelligence assessment by a psychologist. The psychologist finds that Sarah has an IQ of 65 on the WISC-IV (Wechsler, 2003), with better scores on verbal comprehension subscales than on perceptual reasoning subscales. Because this is more than two standard deviations below the mean, it could lead to a classification of "mild intellectual disability," if intelligence testing was regarded as sufficient to determine this. In an earlier era, it could have led to immediate placement in a special class for students with mild intellectual disability. However, the AAIDD definition requires that Sarah can be shown also to have "significant limitations... in adaptive behavior" for a diagnosis of intellectual disability to be made. On the Vineland II Adaptive Behavior Scales (Sparrow, Cicchetti, & Balla, 2005) it is found that in the three scales of Communication, Socialization, and Daily Living, Sarah is functioning with a percentile rank between 10 and 16. She is able to perform many of the tasks that would be expected of a child of her age or a little younger. She can write her own name and read some simple words. She is capable of helping around the house and displays quite good social skills. Although her WISC-IV score places her in the bottom 3% of her age group, her Vineland results are better than this, and throw some doubt on the classification of "intellectual disability." There are a few reasons why this may be so. Sarah may just be a person who has relatively good adaptive skills despite her difficulty in responding to questions on an intelligence test. On the other hand, the IQ test may have been poorly administered and may have produced an erroneous result.

DISCUSSION QUESTIONS

1. Why was it not until she was over 7 years old that Sarah's parents became worried enough about her development to arrange for an assessment?
2. Do Sarah's test results suggest that she can follow a regular class program without further assistance?

*4. **An important purpose of describing limitations is to develop a profile of needed supports.***

In the past, assessment of intellectual functioning has been used primarily for the purpose of classifying children so that they could be placed in a particular type of special school or class. For example, until the 1970s some education systems provided a place in their special classes only for students who had a measurable IQ of 30 or above. Hundreds of thousands of Binet IQ tests were administered for the sole purpose of deciding what type of class a child would be enrolled in. Frequently the extraordinary decision was made that the child's needs were so high that no educational support would be provided.

Fortunately that situation has changed. In the United States, Australia, and most developed countries, the law or government policy requires that an appropriate educational program is provided to all students, regardless of the level of their disability. It is for this reason that the definition of intellectual disability assumes that if you are describing limitations, you should also be assessing the supports needed by the student.

Supports are defined in the 2002 AAMR system as "resources and strategies that aim to promote the development, education, interests, and personal well-being of a person and that enhance individual functioning" (Luckasson et al., 2002, p. 151). These supports may be available through family or friends; through the educational, health or social service system; and through government or community agencies. Determining the type and intensity of support that is required is a very important part of the educational system for people with an intellectual disability and will be discussed in more detail in later chapters.

5. ***With appropriate personalized supports over a sustained period, the life functioning of the person with [intellectual disability] will improve.***

The concept of improvement in life functioning of people with intellectual disability is a very important one for educators. There was a time when children with IQs of 30 to 50 were classified as "trainable," and those with IQs below 30 were classified as "custodial." These were extraordinarily negative classifications with little concept of improvement in life functioning.

Over the last 30 to 40 years, it has become widely accepted that regardless of the level of their disability, all individuals are capable, with support, of improving their life functioning. The way this occurs will be very different for different people. For one person, life functioning will be improved if he learns to read and write sufficiently to manage his own affairs and finances. For another, the objective will be to improve that person's life functioning by teaching her to indicate when she is hungry, thirsty, or uncomfortable. In each case "appropriate personalized supports" will be needed. Despite considerable research, there is little evidence that an underlying intellectual disability is enduringly modifiable through educational or training programs (Hartley, Horrell, & MacLean, 2007). This issue is discussed further under early intervention in Chapter 4. However, there is a great deal of evidence that with appropriate support, children with even the most severe disabilities, can improve their learning and functional behavior.

In 2004 AAIDD [AAMR] published the Supports Intensity Scale (SIS) (Thompson et al., 2004), following 5 years of work led by a team of 10 experts. Accompanying material describes the SIS as "a unique planning tool that enables professionals to assess the daily needs and life goals of a person with an intellectual disability and identify practical support strategies to fulfill them." The SIS was designed to be used with adults, that is, people aged 15+ years old, and includes a Support Needs Scale, a Supplemental Protection, and an Exceptional Medical and Behavioral Support Needs Scale. While the SIS is focused on adults rather than school-age students, it highlights the core importance of identification of support needs when intellectual disability is being diagnosed or identified.

FOR DISCUSSION AND REFLECTION:

- Discuss issues related to changing terminology in intellectual disability.
- What are the advantages of the movement toward a "supports" model in defining intellectual disability?

Why Measure Intelligence?

It is reasonable to ask why we bother measuring intelligence if there are so many problems associated with doing so. Measurement is usually for one or a combination of three purposes: diagnosis, classification, or identification of support needs.

Diagnosis

Parents and teachers are often troubled by a child's difficulty in learning. They want to know whether the child is capable of achieving at a different level. Measuring intelligence will sometimes lead to a diagnosis that helps others to understand the person's difficulty in learning. Often the diagnosis will have positive effects. For example, teachers may have assumed that a child has some form of intellectual disability, but assessment will show that this is not the case. In such circumstances the teacher would need to look for other reasons for the child's difficulty, and the child may benefit from this. It has also been pointed out that a diagnosis of "mental retardation" in the United States can be lifesaving, as people with such a diagnosis cannot be executed for murder in some jurisdictions (Lichten & Simon, 2007).

However, there is a danger that a diagnosis of intellectual disability will be used negatively as the reason why a person is having difficulties, rather than as a reason for supplying further support. Diagnosis of an intellectual disability should only ever be seen as the beginning of an ongoing process of support planning.

Classification

A common purpose of measurement of intelligence is classification. For many years, the results of tests have been used to classify people into various levels of intellectual functioning. At their worst, such classifications have led in the past to people being classified with such terms as "feeble-minded" or "custodial" and not provided with educational services. At their best, classification will assist in the placement of a student in an appropriate educational setting or service where well-planned supports, including an individualized education program, will be provided.

Identification of Supports

The most useful purpose of measurement is to identify the supports needed by the person in order to improve their functioning. Intelligence tests do not usually, by themselves, provide a great deal of information on which supports can be planned. However, some tests such as the Wechsler Preschool and Primary Scale of Intelligence, Version III (WPPSI-III) and Wechsler Intelligence Scale for Children, Version IV (WISC-IV) produce a profile that some researchers and practitioners claim can be used to plan educational programs. Usually the best use of the results of intelligence tests is as just one small part of the set of information that provides a comprehensive picture of the supports the student needs as part of individualized education program. Box 1.3 provides a case study of an assessment process.

FOR DISCUSSION AND REFLECTION:

- See discussion questions in Box 1.3

BOX 1.3 CARL'S ASSESSMENT

Carl is nearly 7 years old and is in his third year in a regular school. Academically, he has achieved very little at school, particularly in reading and in language skills, and is also starting to become a behavior problem, displaying some defiant behaviors in the classroom. With the parents' permission, the school arranges for Carl to have a full educational assessment, including an assessment of intellectual functioning on the WPPSI-III (Wechsler Preschool and Primary Scale of Intelligence, Version III).

The assessment shows that in reading, Carl is about 15 months below the expectation for his age and grade, and he has no phonic skills. Numeracy is better, but is still 6 months below his age expectation. On the WPPSI-III, assessment revealed an IQ of 82–95 on the Verbal Scale (percentile rank 21), 103–116 on the Performance Scale (percentile rank 75), and a full scale IQ of 95–105 (percentile rank 50). The first clear finding from these results is that Carl does not have an intellectual disability, so other reasons need to be found for his learning problems. His verbal skills (vocabulary, comprehension, etc.) are at a lower level than his performance skills (block design, object assembly, etc.). However, his verbal IQ score at the 21st percentile does not fully explain his problems with reading, as his reading scores are below the fifth percentile.

Carl's teacher has observed that his behavior on the playground and in art, craft, and music activities is much better than his behavior in reading and numeracy lessons. She hypothesizes that this is as a result of his awareness of and frustration at the difficulties he is having, particularly in reading. She agrees to arrange a further assessment by a reading specialist, following which she will arrange a meeting of a learning support team, including the reading specialist, the class teacher, and Carl's parents, to plan a detailed program to deal with Carl's reading problems.

DISCUSSION QUESTIONS:

1. Was the WPPSI-III an appropriate assessment for Carl? How important was it to know about his level of cognitive functioning?
2. What difference would it have made if assessment had revealed a full scale IQ of 65? What action might have followed then?
3. Do you think the overall assessment process was positive or negative for Carl? Why?

IQ and Adaptive Behavior "Cut-Offs"

There has been much debate over the years about the upper level "cut-off" for a diagnosis of intellectual disability. If the average IQ is 100, how far below average does the result need to be before it is considered to justify a diagnosis of intellectual disability? Heber's definition (1961) for the AAIDD (then called the American Association on Mental Deficiency) referred to "significantly sub-average general intellectual functioning," which was defined as one standard deviation below the mean of a standardized intelligence test. By this definition, an IQ of 85 was the upper limit for a diagnosis of intellectual disability, although the disability had to be associated with unquantified impairments in adaptive behavior. In 1973 Grossman's revision of the classification and terminology system increased the IQ cut-off to two standard deviations below the mean, or an IQ of about 70 (Grossman, 1973). Through this definition, a theoretical 13.59% of the population, who would previously have been classified as having an intellectual disability, would no longer have this classification. The expected prevalence of intellectual disability dropped from 15.86% to 2.27%!

It was not until the 2002 definition that an attempt was made to quantify limitations in adaptive behavior. The 2002 manual states:

> Significant limitations in adaptive behavior are operationally defined as performance that is at least two standard deviations below the mean of either (a) one of the following three types of behavior: conceptual, social or practical, or (b) an overall score on a standardized measure of conceptual, social, and practical skill. (Luckasson et al., 2002, p. 75)

Lichten and Simon have pointed out that the correlation between IQ and adaptive behavior is relatively low (about 0.2). Using a cut-off of more than two standard deviations for adaptive behavior greatly reduces the number of people who would be diagnosed with intellectual disability. Nearly 40 years ago, Silverstein estimated that if the criterion of two standard deviations was applied both to intelligence test results and to adaptive test results, the number of people identified as having an intellectual disability would drop significantly, perhaps to less than one tenth of the former number, depending on the correlation between the two forms of assessment (Silverstein, 1973). Such a drop could be problematic, as it would lead to lack of identification of many people who may need to be identified for service provision and/or legal reasons. It has been suggested by Lichten and Simon that a more appropriate measure would be a Total Quotient (TQ) that combines the results of both intelligence testing and adaptive behavior testing into one score. Lichten and Simon provide evidence that TQs, while including both intelligence and adaptive behavior, would identify 2.5% of the population as having an intellectual disability, which is the theoretically accepted prevalence (Lichten & Simon, 2007). Whether the concept of a TQ will be found in the next AAIDD definition, due in 2010/2011, remains to be seen.

FOR DISCUSSION AND REFLECTION:

- What is the effect of including adaptive behavior in the definition of intelligence?

Other Systems of Definition, Classification, and Diagnosis

The system of definition emphasized in this chapter has been that provided by the AAIDD (Luckasson et al., 2002). The AAIDD and its predecessors have been defining intellectual disability for 90 years; providing definitions that are generally regarded as authoritative (Schalock et al., 2007) not only in the United States but also in many other parts of the world. However, there are some other systems of definition and classification, which will now be briefly reviewed.

American Psychiatric Association

A very similar definition to that of AAIDD is provided by the American Psychiatric Association in its Diagnostic and Statistical Manual of Mental Disorders, fourth edition (DSM-IV). DSM definitions have tended to parallel those of the AAIDD and its predecessors. The current DSM-IV definition of intellectual disability [mental retardation] appeared first in the 1994 edition of DSM-IV and was unchanged in the 2000 text revision. The definition is virtually identical to the 1992 AAMR definition. The DSM-IV definition is as follows:

> The essential feature of [intellectual disability] is significantly subaverage general intellectual functioning (Criterion A) that is accompanied by significant limitations in adaptive functioning in at least two of the following skill areas: communication, self-care, home living, social /interpersonal skills, use of community resources, self-direction, functional academic skills, work, leisure, health, and safety (Criterion B). The onset must occur before age 18 years (Criterion C). (American Psychiatric Association, 2000)

The age of 18 is accepted by both the APA and the AAIDD as the end of the developmental period. Limitations in intellectual functioning that have their origins after the age of 18 would be due to brain injury arising from accident or illness or, in older persons, from dementia. Causes of intellectual disability are treated in more detail in Chapter 2.

International Classification of Impairments, Disabilities and Handicaps (WHO)

About 30 years ago, the World Health Organization (WHO) provided definitions of "impairments," "disabilities," and "handicaps," which subsequently received wide international acceptance and usage (World Health Organization, 1980). An *impairment* was defined as an irregularity in the way an organ or system functioned. Brain injury, spina bifida, and Down syndrome would be regarded as examples of impairments. The term is generally used to describe a medical or organic condition. A *disability* is a functional consequence of an impairment. For example, as a result of a person's brain injury, she may have speech and language problems. A *handicap* can result from the interaction between a person with a disability and their environment. So, if the person with speech and language problems is not given assistance with their communication, or access to an alternative communication system, they will be handicapped when trying to interact with the world. To provide another example, a person who is very farsighted (impairment) will be unable to read without glasses (disability). However, if appropriate glasses are provided, the person will not have a handicap. Handicaps can therefore be seen, in many cases, as a function of the resources available to the person, and the flexibility and attitudes of others in the society. The focus of this book is on how education can help to reduce the handicapping effects of intellectual disability.

The WHO model was further refined in 1993 by the National Center for Medical Rehabilitation Research (NCMRR). The NCMRR model extended the three domains into five:

- Pathophysiology—cellular, structural, or functional events leading to interference with normal physiological or developmental processes or structures
- Impairment—loss of cognitive, emotional, physiological, or anatomical structure or function
- Functional limitation—inability to perform an action consistent with the purpose of an organ system
- Disability—inability or limitation in performing roles to the level expected within physical and social contexts
- Societal limitations—restriction resulting from social policy or other barriers that prevent the person's ability to participate fully in society (National Institutes of Health, 1993)

It should be noted that these definitions replace the term "handicaps" with another term "societal limitations," emphasizing the impact of society's response to disability. This approach would generally be welcomed by people with a disability who, justifiably, prefer not to be referred to as handicapped.

International Classification of Functioning, Disability, and Health (ICF) (WHO)

The ICF is a framework developed by the World Health Organization (WHO) to measure health and disability, both for individuals and populations. The classification system was endorsed by member states of WHO in May 2001 (World Health Organization, 2001). The ICF attempts new conceptualizations of health and disability. It attempts to mainstream the experience of disability by acknowledging that anyone can experience a disability through illness or accident. Disability is not something that happens only to a minority of humanity. The classification system moves away from seeing disability as a medical or biological dysfunction and focuses rather on the impact of adverse health conditions on a person's functioning. Thus, it becomes a classification of functioning that is applicable to all people, rather than a definition of disability, applicable to particular disadvantaged groups.

The ICF system is a general system for understanding disability and is much broader in concept than intellectual disability. However, it still has some usefulness when planning how services for people with an intellectual disability are provided. Classification will be discussed in more detail in Chapter 3.

International Classification of Diseases (ICD-10)

The World Health Organization's International Classification of Diseases, 10th edition (ICD-10) has a section on "mental retardation" (intellectual disability) within the area of Mental and Behavioural Disorders. Intellectual disability is defined as

> A condition of arrested or incomplete development of the mind, which is especially characterized by impairment of skills manifested during the developmental period, skills which contribute to the overall level of intelligence, i.e., cognitive, language, motor, and social abilities. [Intellectual disability] can occur with or without any other mental or physical condition. (World Health Organization, 1992)

ICD-10 explains that degrees of intellectual disability are conventionally estimated by standardized intelligence tests, which can be supplemented by scales assessing social adaptation in a given environment, that is, adaptive behavior. Four main classification levels are provided: mild, moderate, severe, and profound intellectual disability, with two further classifications of other and unspecified. There is an additional classification that identifies the extent of impairment of behavior. The following are examples of ICD-10 classifications:

F70.1 Mild intellectual disability; significant impairment of behavior
F72.0 Severe intellectual disability; no or minimal behavior impairment
F71.8 Moderate intellectual disability; other impairments of behavior

ICD-10 also deals with the problem of classifying people who have both an intellectual disability and a psychiatric illness. The issue of dual diagnosis will be dealt with in more detail in Chapter 3. A new edition of ICD-10, ICD-11, is due in 2013.

The British Definition

In Britain the term "learning disability" (or "learning disabilities") is used to describe what would be known in the United States, Australia, and many other countries as an intellectual disability. A 2001 Department of Health White Paper defined learning disability as follows:

> Learning disability includes the presence of:
>
> - A significantly reduced ability to understand new or complex information, to learn new skills (impaired intelligence), with:
> - A reduced ability to cope independently (impaired social function); which started before adulthood, with a lasting effect on development....
>
> Learning disability does not include those who have a "learning difficulty" which is more broadly defined in education legislation. (Department of Health, 2001).

The components of the definition are not dissimilar to those of the AAIDD and the DSM-IV, the most striking difference being the change in terminology. To many outside Britain, the terms "learning disability" or "learning disabilities" are used to refer to a difficulty with learning that is independent of general intellectual functioning. There are many examples of people who have difficulties with literacy or numeracy, but whose general intelligence is in the average range or higher. In Britain these people would be referred to as having a learning "difficulty" rather than a learning "disability." In the United States and Australia the terms are usually regarded as interchangeable, but would not generally be used to describe people who have an intellectual disability. Interestingly, one of the leading journals in the field, the *Journal of Intellectual Disability Research* (rather than the *Journal of Learning Disability Research*), is published by a British organization, Mencap, which refers to itself as "the voice of learning disability."

FOR DISCUSSION AND REFLECTION:

- Compare the American Psychiatric Association definition of intellectual disability with the AAMR (AAIDD) definition in the previous section of this chapter. What are the similarities and differences?
- Discuss the statement that handicaps can result from the failure of society to make appropriate provisions for people with a disability

Developmental Delays and Disabilities

Other terminology used in the intellectual disability literature includes reference to "developmental delays" and "developmental disabilities." Developmental delay is sometimes used with young children when it is noticed that aspects of their development are slow, compared with the development of other children their age. The term is relatively nonspecific and avoids the use of other terminology, such as "intellectual disability," which would be seen by many parents as deterministic. Developmental delay was included in the 1997 Individuals With Disability Education Act (U.S. Congress, 1997), and may be used to include a young child who is delayed in physical development, cognitive development, communication development, social or emotional development, or adaptive development, and who, as a result, needs specialized support services. The term is seen as one that usefully describes the current situation without making further unwarranted predictions about the future. However, use of the term has also been criticized as potentially misleading, because it may confuse family members into believing that what is, in many instances, a permanent disability is something that is transient and that the child will eventually "catch up" (Harris, 2006). The term is best used only with very young children, usually below the age of 5, before a clear diagnosis has been made. Developmental delay is currently used to describe the slowed or impaired development of a young child who is at risk of having a developmental disability because of the presence of a syndrome that is generally associated with intellectual or developmental problems (e.g., Fragile X syndrome) and/or because their development has already been observed to be noticeably slower than that of other children of the same age.

The term "developmental disability" was introduced into U.S. legislation in 1970 as a replacement for the term "mental retardation." The definition has evolved over the years but usually includes the following concepts:

- The person has a severe, chronic disability.
- The disability is attributable to an intellectual or physical impairment, or a combination of intellectual and physical impairments.

- The disability occurs before the person reaches adulthood and is likely to continue indefinitely.
- The disability results in substantial functional limitations in three or more of the following areas of major life activity: self-care, receptive and expressive language, learning, mobility, self-direction, capacity for independent living, and economic self-sufficiency.
- The person needs a lifelong combination of special, interdisciplinary, or generic care, treatment, or other services, which are individually planned and coordinated.

A major advantage of the definition of developmental disability is that it includes physical impairments that have a significant impact on how the person functions. There are many situations in which it is unclear whether a child with a physical disability also has an intellectual disability. For example, in Box 1.1, David would be diagnosed as having a developmental disability, which would make him eligible for developmental disability services. The question of whether or not he had an intellectual disability (which he didn't) could be deferred until he was old enough for a valid and reliable assessment to take place. An assessment of intellectual function would be important in due course, but accurate assessments can be very difficult for young children who have substantial physical disabilities. Intellectual disability and developmental disability (or disabilities) are terms often used together to avoid having to artificially separate the populations, which have substantial overlap (e.g., American Association on Intellectual and Developmental Disabilities; *Journal of Intellectual and Developmental Disability*)

FOR DISCUSSION AND REFLECTION:

- Discuss the concepts of "developmental delays," "developmental disabilities," and "intellectual disabilities." How helpful is it to be able to use the differing terminology?

Summary

There has been much discussion and debate about the definition and measurement of intellectual disability. One of the major changes that has occurred since intellectual disability (or mental retardation) was first defined is the inclusion of adaptive behavior in the definition. An important assumption is that the definition will include a consideration of supports needed by the person identified with an intellectual disability. Various changes in the definition have reduced the number of people identified as having an intellectual disability. While there are other systems of definition, classification, and diagnosis, that of the American Association for Intellectual and Developmental Disability has almost certainly been the most influential.

References

American Psychiatric Association. (2000). *Diagnostic and statistical manual of mental disorders* (4th text, Rev. ed.). Washington, DC: Author.

Gardner, H. (1993). *Multiple intelligences: The theory in practice.* New York: Basic Books.

Greenspan, S. (1999). What is meant by mental retardation? *International Review of Psychiatry, 11*, 6–18.

Grossman, H. J. (Ed.). (1973). *A manual on terminology and classification in mental retardation* (Rev. ed.). Washington, DC: American Association on Mental Deficiency.

Harris, J. C. (2006). *Intellectual disability.* New York: Oxford University Press.

Hartley, S., Horrell, S. V., & MacLean, W. E., Jr. (2007). Science to practice in intellectual disability the role of empirically supported treatments. In J. W. Jacobson, J. A. Mulick, & J. Rojahn (Eds.), *Handbook of intellectual and developmental disabilities* (pp. 425–443). New York: Springer.

Heber, R. (1961). *A manual on terminology and classification in mental retardation* (Rev. ed.). Washington DC: American Association on Mental Deficiency.

Lichten, W., & Simon, E. W. (2007). Defining mental retardation: A matter of life or death. *Intellectual and Developmental Disabilities, 45*(5), 335–346.

Luckasson, R., Borthwick-Duffy, S., Buntinx, W., Coulter, D., Ellis, C., Reeve, A., et al. (2002). *Mental retardation: Definition, classification and supports* (10th ed.). Washington, DC: American Association on Mental Retardation.

National Institutes of Health. (1993). *Research plan for the Center For Medical Rehabilitation research. NIH publication no. 93-5309.* Bethesda, MD: Author.

Schalock, R., Luckasson, R., & Shogren, K. (2007). The renaming of mental retardation: Understanding the change to the term intellectual disability. *Intellectual and Developmental Disabilities, 45*(2), 116–124.

Silverstein, A. B. (1973). Note on prevalence. *American Journal of Mental Deficiency, 77*, 380–382.

Sparrow, S., Cicchetti, D., & Balla, D. (2005). *Vineland II Vineland adaptive behavior scales* (2nd ed.). Circle Pines, MN: AGS Publishing.

Sternberg, R. J. (1988). *The triarchic mind: A new theory of human intelligence.* New York: Viking.

Terman, L. M., & Merrill, M. (1960). *The Stanford Binet intelligence scale.* Boston: Houghton Mifflin.

Thompson, J. R., Bryant, B. R., Craig, E., Campbell, E., Hughes, C., Rotholz, D., et al. (2004). *Supports intensity scale.* Washington, DC: American Association on Mental Retardation.

UK Department of Health. (2001). *Valuing people: A new strategy for learning disability in the 21st century.* London: Author.

United States Congress. (1997). *Individuals with Disabilities Education Act, Amendments.* Washington, DC: Author.

Wechsler, D. (1949). *The Wechsler Intelligence Scale for Children.* New York: The Psychological Corporation.

Wechsler, D. (1991). *Wechsler Intelligence Scale for Children* (3rd ed.). San Antonio, TX: Psychological Corporation, Harcourt Brace.

Wechsler, D. (2003). *Wechsler Intelligence Scale for Children* (4th ed.). San Antonio, TX: Psychological Corporation.

World Health Organization. (1980). *International classification of impairments, disabilities and handicaps.* Geneva: Author.

World Health Organization. (1992). *ICD-10. International classification of diseases and behavioural disorders.* Geneva: Author.

World Health Organization. (2001). *International classification of functioning, disability and health (ICF).* Geneva: Author.

2

Causes of Intellectual Disability

Overview: This chapter provides an overview of the various prenatal, perinatal, and environmental causes of intellectual disability, and gives examples of disabilities arising from these causes. The chapter includes a discussion of the interaction between physical, social, and environmental influences, and the impact of these factors on intellectual development. Issues related to prevention of disability are also discussed.

Introduction

When a child is diagnosed with or suspected of having an intellectual disability, one of the first questions many parents will ask is, "What has caused this?" There are many good reasons for asking this question. Many parents will want to know if there is anything they could have done to prevent their child's disability. They will often also wish to know about the prospect of recurrence of the disability in yet-to-be-born children, and whether any such risk can be reduced or overcome.

One way in which the causes (or etiology) of disabilities are frequently conceptualized is in relation to the time of occurrence; that is, prior to birth (prenatal), at about the time of birth (perinatal), or after the child

Education of Students with an Intellectual Disability, pages 23–61

has been born (postnatal). This is the structure used by the AAIDD (Luckasson et al., 2002) and other authors, and it will be followed in this chapter. Examples of causes of intellectual disability arising prenatally, perinatally, or postnatally are shown in Table 2.1. The categories of causes are a method of conceptualization to aid understanding of the range of causes. However, the divisions are not absolute, and there are some disabilities that could fit into multiple categories.

Many myths have come and gone over the years about causes of disability. Some of these have sought to blame parents for their child's disability. In the early 19th century and earlier, disabilities were thought to arise from some evil-doing or misbehavior in the parents, usually of a sexual nature. However, as recently as the 1960s and 1970s, well-regarded authorities were wrongly blaming so-called refrigerator mothers for their children's autism. It is easy to see how this theory developed after first being mentioned by Leo Kanner in the 1940s. Observation of mothers and fathers in interaction

TABLE 2.1 Causes of Intellectual Disability[a]

Time	Nature of Cause	Example/s
Prenatal	Chromosomal disorders	Down syndrome; Turner syndrome
	Inherited disorders	Apert syndrome; PKU; Lesch-Nyhan syndrome; Fragile X syndrome
	Developmental neural/ brain disorder	Spina bifida
	Maternal infection	Rubella
	Maternal toxicity	Fetal alcohol syndrome; drug toxicity
	Other environmental causes	Malnutrition; congenital hypothyroidism; trauma
Perinatal	Gestational disorders	Prematurity; abnormal delivery
	Neonatal disorders	Intracranial hemorrhage; respiratory disorders
Postnatal	Head injury	Accidents or falls; abuse
	Infection	Encephalitis; meningitis
	Degenerative disorder	Rett syndrome
	Seizure disorder	Lennox-Gastaut syndrome
	Toxic-metabolic disorder	Lead poisoning
	Malnutrition	Protein-energy malnutrition (PEM)
	Environmental deprivation	Secondary intellectual disability

[a] Table developed with reference to Luckasson et al. (2002), Harris (2006), and other sources.

with their children who had autism certainly showed poor communication and a lack of typical warm parent-child interrelationships. However, a little reflection would suggest that if babies are unresponsive, resist human interaction, and are distressed at attempts to pick them up or to cuddle them, their parents will tend to back away from normal interactions in order to avoid distressing the child. As a result, even if observations show that the parents' interactions with their child are different from those of most other parents, it is likely that the parents' mode of interaction has been caused by their child's behavior, rather than the other way around.

This does not mean that parental behavior cannot have an impact on children's cognitive development. For example, instances have been described of children who have a secondary intellectual disability that appears to have arisen from living in an abusive or neglectful household. The AAIDD suggests that the etiology (cause) of intellectual disability is indeed multifactorial in nature, and that intellectual disability can result from an interaction between biomedical, social, behavioral, and educational risk factors (Luckasson et al., 2002). This is a marked change from classifying causes as either biological or psychosocial in origin. In many ways, it presents a more optimistic view of disability as, even if it is not usually possible to change the biological origins of the disability, social, behavioral and educational inputs are subject to change. Such changes may lessen or even prevent the disability.

Luckasson et al. (2002, p. 123) suggest that it is important to consider the etiology of intellectual disability for a number of reasons including the following:

1. The etiology may be associated with other health-related problems that may impact on the child's functioning. For example, Down syndrome is known to be associated with heart defects, hypothyroidism, hip displacement, and other medical problems. An alert physician will watch out for any medical conditions that could add to the child's developmental problems.
2. The cause may be treatable. One of the best-known examples of this is phenylketonuria (PKU), which is an inherited error of metabolism caused by an enzyme deficiency. Without a restricted diet, PKU will lead to intellectual disability. However, if PKU is detected at birth, the intellectual disability will be prevented.
3. The cause may be associated with particular behavioral patterns that allow prediction of future support needs. An example is the communicative and other problems that develop in girls with Rett syndrome, which may be better anticipated if the typical patterns

of development associated with the syndrome are known (Kerr & Prescott, 2005).

4. Knowledge of etiology facilitates genetic counseling. Many syndromes associated with intellectual disability have a clearly understood pattern of inheritance. As a result, families can often be given precise information about the likelihood that a particular disability will recur in another child. Some disabilities, however, have a genetic component that interacts with other environmental factors, and the patterns of inheritance are not as clear.
5. Understanding of the various risk factors that are contributory causes of intellectual disability may provide opportunities for prevention of disability. For example, if it can be shown that poverty is a risk factor that exacerbates a potential intellectual disability, understanding how this occurs will suggest ways in which it can be prevented.

A known cause for intellectual disability is more likely if the disability is severe. A biomedical cause is identified in around 70% of individuals with a severe disability and in around 50% of people with a mild disability (McLaren & Bryson, 1987). It is likely that, in time, these percentages will increase, particularly as we come to understand more about the interrelationships between the various risk factors, and also with advances in molecular genetics (MacMillan, 1998). For example, it is known that genetic factors are implicated in the development of autism. In monozygotic twins (who have identical gene patterns), if one of the pair has autism, there is a 60% chance that the other twin will also have the disorder. In dyzygotic twins (who have the similar but not identical genotypes of siblings), the chance of the second twin also having autism is just 5% (Bailey, Palferman, Heavey, & LeCouteur, 1998). Despite this knowledge, the precise pattern of inheritance is not known, nor is it known what, if any, environmental or other factors will trigger the development of autistic behavior, although this question is currently being extensively researched (Dawson, 2008).

The remainder of this chapter will examine some of the prenatal, perinatal, and postnatal causes of intellectual disability, as outlined in Table 2.1. The aim is to provide some examples of how intellectual disability develops, with a focus on one or two illustrative disabilities, rather than to provide a comprehensive coverage of all disabilities and their causes. Readers with an interest in a particular type of disability should consult specialized material on that topic through textbooks and research articles. Most disabilities have associated support organizations that provide excellent information and advice via the Internet. Parents frequently have great expertise in their child's disability and will often have a file of reports that will be useful in planning the child's educational program.

FOR DISCUSSION AND REFLECTION:

- What are the potential benefits of understanding the causes of intellectual disability?
- In what way can the conceptualization of causes as "multifactorial" be considered to be a positive approach?

Prenatal Causes of Intellectual Disability

A prenatal cause for a disability means that it is present by the time the child is ready to be born. It may be a genetic problem, present at conception (e.g., Down syndrome), or it may be that the developmental problem has occurred during the gestational period (e.g., fetal alcohol syndrome, spina bifida). However, "prenatal causes" is not a clear category. For example, girls with Rett syndrome have no disability present at birth and develop normally for the first 6 to18 months of their lives. After this, a dominant gene on the X chromosome, present at conception, causes a progressive degeneration of their cognitive and other abilities. While Rett syndrome is provided as an example of a postnatal degenerative disorder, it could also have been presented as a disorder that is caused prenatally.

Some examples of the mechanisms through which disabilities associated with intellectual disability can occur prenatally are presented below.

Chromosomal Disorders

Almost all people have 23 pairs of chromosomes in each body cell, apart from the sperm cells and the egg cells, which each have just one set of 23 chromosomes. In cells with 46 chromosomes, half of these are inherited from the mother and half from the father. The chromosomes are estimated to carry a total of around 25,000 genes, with the numbers varying from chromosome to chromosome. A disability can be caused by a defect in a single gene, but there are also some disabilities where an entire chromosome is affected. Sometimes there is an additional chromosome in each cell. Sometimes a chromosome is missing from each cell. Many conceptions with the wrong number of chromosomes do not proceed to full-term, and end in miscarriage. However, many healthy children are born with chromosomal abnormalities. Often this will have an impact on their development.

Additional Chromosomes—Down Syndrome

The best known and most common condition involving a whole chromosome and usually leading to an intellectual disability is Down syndrome, occurring about once in 700 to 800 births. Although the syndrome has been known since first identified by John Langdon Down in the 19th century, it was not until the late 1950s that children with Down syndrome were identified by Jerome Lejeune as having an extra 21st chromosome (Lejeune, Gautier, & Turpin, 1959). There are three ways in which cells can divide abnormally, leading to the extra material for chromosome 21. The most common of these is trisomy 21, which occurs when there is abnormal cell division during the development of the sperm cell or the egg cell. This leads to an extra 21st chromosome in the sperm or the egg, resulting in three 21st chromosomes in every cell, a total of 47 chromosomes. This leads to the physical and intellectual characteristics of Down syndrome. There is also a rare form of Down syndrome where the failure of cell division occurs after fertilization. This means that not all cells have the extra chromosome and, in this rare circumstance, referred to as "mosaic Down syndrome," the characteristics of Down syndrome may be less pronounced. Another quite rare form of transmission of the extra chromosome is when part of one the parent's 21st chromosomes becomes attached to another chromosome, before or at conception. In this case children will have the correct two copies of chromosome 21 at the 21st position, but additional chromosome 21 material is found to be "translocated" to another chromosome. This variation is referred to as "translocation 21," and occurs in about 4% of cases of Down syndrome.

Although usually present from the time of conception, Down syndrome is not generally regarded as being *inherited* from parents. It is most commonly an abnormal cell division that can happen to anyone, although it appears more likely to happen in older mothers. An exception to this is in some cases of translocation where the parent is a "balanced carrier." In these cases, the parent has additional chromosome 21 material that has "broken away" and joined a different chromosome. There is a small risk that they will pass on this additional material as well as a regular 21st chromosome to their child, which would lead to a rare inherited form of Down syndrome.

From an educational perspective, expectations for children with Down syndrome have increased significantly over recent years, and there is now a likelihood that many of them will access the general curriculum, including in academic skill area such as literacy and numeracy (Fletcher & Buckley, 2002; Rietveld, 2005). While children with Down syndrome typically display poor muscle tone and delay in development of motor skills, there has been some questioning of the value of intervention programs that focus on motor development, particularly if treated in isolation from other functional skills (Davis, 2008). There has been much research on the education of children with Down syndrome, but there remains a need for more evidence about whether particular classroom practices are more effective than others. In the meantime, teachers should have high expectations of students with Down syndrome, with the knowledge that they are working toward maximum personal independence as adults, with adequate numeracy and literacy skills. Early intervention for babies and preschoolers with Down syndrome is covered in Chapter 4.

Missing Chromosomes—Turner Syndrome

While people with Down syndrome have an *extra* chromosome in every cell (47 instead of 46), there are also syndromes in which problems arise from the *absence* of a chromosome. Turner syndrome occurs in girls when there is a missing X chromosome in each cell or in some cells (mosaicism). Girls normally have two X chromosomes per cell; boys have an X and a Y, so girls with Turner syndrome have 45 chromosomes including just one X chromosome. Turner syndrome occurs in 1:2500 to 1:3000 live female births (Sybert & McCauley, 2004), so is much rarer than Down syndrome. However, it has been estimated that the missing X chromosome occurs in 3% of conceptions but that 99% of conceptions with a missing X chromosome result in spontaneous abortions (Harris, 2006). The most common physical characteristics of Turner syndrome are short stature and loose skin folds on the neck. Unlike Down syndrome, where almost all individuals with the syndrome have some degree of intellectual disability, the majority of girls with Turner syndrome do not have an intellectual disability. Nevertheless, the risk for intellectual disability is much higher in Turner syndrome than in the general population, ranging from 5% in most girls with the syndrome to 30% in some rare forms of the disability (Harris, 2006).

Despite not generally having an intellectual disability, girls with Turner syndrome are likely to have some form of learning difficulty. Among the cognitive problems identified in Turner syndrome are impairments in visual-spatial abilities, mathematical skills, and memory skills (Wodrich & Tarbox, 2008). Girls with Turner syndrome will tend to be in regular classes but will generally need an individualized educational program that takes into account their special learning needs.

Inherited Disorders

The term "inherited disorders" refers to disorders that can be traced to genes carried and passed on to children by their parents, sometimes as a fresh or *de novo* mutation. There are many syndromes associated with intellectual disability that are caused by a single dominant gene or by a pairing of recessive genes. In these cases, it is possible to predict the likelihood of subsequent children or offspring of affected persons also having the disability. Other single gene modes of transmission where the inheritance rate can be clearly predicted are X-linked recessive inheritance and X-linked dominant inheritance.

When a disability is carried by a *dominant* gene, just one copy of the gene is sufficient for the disability to appear. The fact that the other chromosome of the pair does not carry the gene for the disability will not prevent its expression. If the disability is passed on through *recessive* genes, both parents would have to carry the gene *and* pass it on for it to find expression. If only one parent carries a recessive gene for a disability, there is almost no chance that it will have any effect on the child. In the case of an *X-linked recessive* disorder, the gene associated with the disability is carried on one of the mother's two X chromosomes. It will not normally be expressed in the child's mother or in the child's future daughters, even if they receive the affected chromosome. This is because they would normally also have a "good" gene on the other X chromosome, which would counterbalance the effect of the recessive gene. However, as boys have only one X chromosome, the gene for disability will find expression, as there is no counterbalancing nondisability gene.

Dominant Genes—Apert Syndrome

Serious physical or intellectual disabilities caused by dominant genes are relatively rare. Even though a disability caused by a dominant gene would be highly inheritable and would be passed on to 50% of offspring, people with serious disabilities tend not to reproduce, so the gene dies out. Other members of the family who do not have the disability, do not have the gene—if they had the gene they would also have the disability. Disabilities caused by a dominant gene usually arise sporadically because of a fresh mutation (Breuggem, Fitzpatrick, & Verchere, 2008). The exception to this is with some conditions where a gene has variable expression. In these situations, a problem may show up in a very mild form in the parent, but in a more serious form when it is passed on.

An example of a disability caused by a dominant gene is Apert syndrome, which occurs once in around 65,000 live births, so is very rare. Some experts believe it is as rare as 1:200,000 births. First identified in 1906, the syndrome is associated with deformities of the bones of the face and skull, and fusion of the fingers and toes. As with Turner syndrome, Apert syndrome increases the likelihood of intellectual disability, but many people with Apert syndrome have intelligence in the normal range. It is wrong to assume that physical disabilities, whatever the cause, are always associated with intellectual disability. It is preferable to assume normal intelligence unless it can be demonstrated that this is not the case. Because of their many physical and neurological problems, children with Apert syndrome at school will generally need help from a multidisciplinary team comprising a special educator, a physical therapist, an occupational therapist, and a speech pathologist.

Recessive Genes—Phenylketonuria

Inborn errors of metabolism have been recognized for over 100 years, and hundreds of such errors have been identified. In most cases, they are caused by a single gene leading to an enzyme deficiency that affects function and/or development to a greater or lesser degree. An example of an inborn metabolic error that, if untreated, leads to intellectual disability and other behavioral problems is phenylketonuria (PKU), which is an *autosomal recessive* disorder and can occur when *both* parents have a recessive gene for PKU on chromosome 12. Generations can carry a PKU gene without it ever showing up. This is because one recessive gene is insufficient to produce the disorder. Once PKU appears in a family, it can be assumed that each parent is carrying *one* recessive gene for PKU. If the parents carried *two* PKU genes, they would also have PKU. In subsequent pregnancies following birth of a child who tested positive for PKU, the chances of passing on genes would be as follows:

- One chance in four that the child would inherit two PKU genes and therefore would have PKU.
- Two chances in four that the child would inherit one PKU gene and would therefore be an "unaffected carrier"; unless this person's partner also carried a PKU gene, his or her children would not be affected.
- One chance in four of having a child who inherits two non-PKU genes; for this child, PKU is not part of his genetic structure as he can only pass on non-PKU genes.

PKU is an extremely rare cause of intellectual disability in most developed countries. Such countries now provide a simple blood test to newborn babies that identifies PKU in around 1 in 12,000 births. If the disease is identified, the baby will be placed on a phenylalanine-free diet and will not develop the intellectual disability that would otherwise be expected. One of the unexpected outcomes that became apparent in the late 1970s was that women with PKU whose disability had been prevented by diet were likely themselves to have children with severe intellectual disability. This problem has now been largely remedied by use of a phenylalanine-free diet prior to and during pregnancy.

Phenylketonuria is a model case of prevention of a disability through a medically prescribed treatment. It is possible that with further investigation of the genetic and metabolic basis of diseases and disabilities, similar treatments will be developed for other disabilities and disorders. Current research is seeking increasingly sophisticated newborn screening technologies, and it is possible that other disabilities, particularly those associated with inborn errors of metabolism, will be preventable in the future through this process.

X-linked Recessive Disorders—Lesch-Nyhan Disease

Lesch-Nyhan disease (LND) is an example of an inborn error of metabolism that occurs as an *X-linked recessive* disorder. It is associated with faulty purine metabolism. The gene causing the disorder is carried on the X chromosome. This means that girls who inherit the gene will almost always have a "good" gene on the other X chromosome, so they will not be affected by the disability, as it is recessive. Boys do not have a second X chromosome with a "good" gene to counteract the effect of the LND gene, so they are affected even though the gene is recessive. In subsequent pregnancies, once a child with LND had been born, the chances of passing on the disability would be as follows:

- One chance in four that the child would be a boy who inherited the LND gene from his mother and therefore would have LND.
- One chance in four that the child would be a boy who did not inherit the LND gene and therefore would not have LND. For this boy, LND is not part of his genetic structure as he can only pass on a non-LND gene on his X chromosome.
- One chance in four that the child would be a girl who inherited the LND gene from her mother, but would not have LND because of her other X chromosome. She would have a theoretical risk of passing on the faulty chromosome to half of her children, and there would be a risk that half of her sons would be affected by LND.
- One chance in four that the child would be a girl who did not have the LND gene on either of her X chromosomes. For this girl, LND is not part of her genetic structure as she can only pass on a non-LND gene on her X chromosomes.

These are, of course only theoretical possibilities. Just as a mother may have four girls in a row, despite a theoretical prediction that four pregnancies would produce two girls and two boys, she could have one child with LND then four children who were totally clear of the gene, as chance plays a part in each conception.

LND is a very rare disorder, occurring around once in 380,000 live births. People with LND are usually in the mild to moderate range of intellectual disability (Harris, 2006). Many children have to use a wheelchair because of spasticity and other movement problems. Self-mutilation and head banging are among the most consistent behavioral characteristics, and other reported problems include speech problems, depression, and aggression (Wodrich & Tarbox, 2008). There are some variants of the syndrome where the behavioral problems and intellectual disability are less pronounced (Schretlen et al., 2005).

There is limited evidence at this stage as to whether standard behavioral techniques are effective in modifying the very difficult self-mutilation behaviors exhibited by boys with LND. There is evidence that punishment may increase rather than decrease these behaviors (Zilli & Hasselmo, 2008). Olson and Houlihan (2000) reviewed several studies of behavioral interventions for self-injurious behavior. Following a least restrictive model, they suggested that possible procedures could include DRO (differential reinforcement of other behaviors) and DRI (differential reinforcement of incompatible behaviors). They concluded that behavioral interventions can be successful and that long-term maintenance of behavioral changes is possible (Olson & Houlihan, 2000).

The complexity of the behavioral and physical problems requires input from a multidisciplinary team to contribute to educational planning for students with LND. There are some medications to counteract the purine metabolism defect, but these don't appear to change the behavioral symptoms. Some psychotropic medications have been found to reduce aggression. Occupational and physical therapists can make sure that the student's wheelchair is safe and, if the child represents a danger to his own safety, design protective splints or helmets. A psychologist can help to plan a behavior management program, and a special educator can advise on how this can link into the student's educational program.

Fragile X Syndrome

A disorder that was once thought to follow a simple X-linked recessive pattern but has since been shown to be more complex in etiology is Fragile X syndrome. Fragile X syndrome is associated with a microscopically observable fragile site on one of the X chromosomes in girls, and on the single X chromosome in boys. Although unknown until about 40 years ago, Fragile X syndrome is now described as the most common form of *inherited* intellectual disability in males, while it also occurs to a lesser extent in females (Cornish, Turk, & Hagerman, 2008). Prevalence estimates are 1 in 4,000 for boys, and 1 in 8,000 for girls (Schwarte, 2008). The identification of Fragile X syndrome occurred in 1969 when it was observed by clinicians that when intellectual disability of unknown origin ran in families, it was boys rather than girls who were most likely to be affected. This led to the hypothesis that there was an unidentified disorder associated with intellectual disability originating on the X chromosome, which, if it followed normal X-linked inheritance patterns would, like hemophilia or LND, affect only or primarily boys.

Chromosomal analysis of the cells of brothers with intellectual disability of unknown origin showed an apparent break or "fragility" in the X chromosome. The disorder is now believed to be caused by the inactivation of a single gene, identified as the Fragile X Mental Retardation -1 (FMR-1) gene (Cornish et al., 2008). This chromosomal abnormality, combined with certain physical and behavioral characteristics, became know as Fragile X syndrome. Subsequent research has shown that the pattern of inheritance is much more complicated, and that girls can not only be carriers, but may also be affected by the syndrome, but usually to a lesser extent than boys. Fragile X is now identified through an alteration to the FMR-1 gene (molecular genetics) rather than by identification of the fragile site on the X chromosome (cytogenetics) (Harris, 2006).

A great deal of research is taking place on the molecular basis of Fragile X syndrome (Lombroso & Ogren, 2008), which may, in due course, lead to specific medical treatments. In the meantime, educational interventions need to focus on the behavioral aspects of the syndrome, which vary among children, but include autistic behaviors, self-injurious behavior, ADHD, and communication difficulties (Cornish et al., 2008; Schwarte, 2008). Teachers and parents of children with Fragile X syndrome are referred to Web sites such as http://www.fragilex.org and to the academic literature for extensive information on the topic.

Multifactorial Transmission

Some disabilities have what is referred to as *multifactorial* transmission. This means that several genes are implicated, sometimes in association with environmental factors. The most common form of multifactorial transmission is what is known as "cultural-familial" intellectual disability. This is usually associated with a mild degree of intellectual disability and occurs when parents who have a mild intellectual disability have a child who also has a mild disability. The reason it is regarded as multifactorial is that intelligence, like many other human characteristics, is known to be highly heritable. So, just as tall parents will tend to have tall children, intelligent parents will tend to have intelligent children, and parents with a mild intellectual disability will tend to have children with a mild intellectual disability. However, in the case of cultural-familial mild disability, this will often be exacerbated by social and environmental factors. The parents may have had a poor education, may live in a deprived environment, and may have difficulties with parenting. Thus, the disability will arise from a combination of prenatal (genetic) and postnatal (environmental) factors (see Box 2.1). Some early intervention programs have been aimed at reducing the impact of the environmental factors (see Chapter 4). Another example of a disability with apparent multifactorial transmission is *spina bifida*, discussed under the heading "Developmental neural/brain disorder" in the next section of this chapter.

BOX 2.1 KAYLAH'S STORY

Kaylah is the third child of Marianne, a single mother who lives in a trailer park on the outskirts of a large city. Marianne's two older children are being cared for in foster homes, but Marianne has expressed a strong desire to keep Kaylah at home and "give her a chance." Marianne was in a special education program as a child and was diagnosed as having a mild intellectual disability. She finished school before her 15th birthday. Her reading ability is at around a second grade level and she has very basic numeracy skills. Marianne smokes around three packs of cigarettes a week and meets friends at the local tavern once a week. She also drinks beer occasionally at home.

Marianne did not see a doctor until she was 6 months pregnant, and Kaylah was born at 35 weeks, weighing 1700 grams (3.75 lbs.). Kaylah's 1 minute and 5 Apgar scores were 4 and 5, respectively. She was in a incubator for 2 weeks and was allowed home from the hospital at 4 weeks. Marianne is having difficulty with breastfeeding and is thinking of putting Kaylah on formula.

Before she took Kaylah home from the hospital, the pediatric social worker organized a meeting with Marianne to plan various forms of support to help her care for Kaylah at home. It was decided that the following initial forms of assistance would be provided:

- A community nurse will visit Marianne at home to help her organize a feeding and general care routine. If possible,

Marianne will continue with breastfeeding. If not, the nurse will help to set up a formula feeding routine. The nurse will also help Marianne to move onto a "healthy living" program, the number one objective of which is to provide a smoke-free environment for Kaylah.

- The social worker will arrange for Marianne's name to go on a priority list for public housing and will check that she is receiving any benefits she is entitled to.
- An early childhood special educator will visit Marianne to discuss ways of making the environment more interesting and stimulating for Kaylah as she grows. She will encourage Marianne to attend a local mothers' group/playgroup so that she has good models of mother-baby interaction. If Marianne is interested, the special educator will return on a regular basis to monitor and advise on Kaylah's progress and will organize for Marianne and Kaylah to start in an early intervention program when Kaylah is 6 months old.

DISCUSSION QUESTIONS:

1. What are the risk factors that make it likely that Kaylah will have a mild intellectual disability?
2. Research "Apgar Scores" on the Internet. What is the significance of Kaylah's scores?
3. Consider the plan that has been developed for Marianne and Kaylah. How helpful do you think it will be? Is there anything else that could be done to reduce the likelihood that Kaylah will have similar problems to her mother?

Developmental Neural/Brain Disorders

Spina bifida is an example of a congenital disorder (i.e., disorder present at birth) that results from developmental neurological problems and is believed to be *multifactorial* in origin (Volcik et al., 2002). It is one of a number of *neural tube defects.* Other neural tube defects are *anencephaly,* where most of the brain is absent, and *encephalocele,* where part of the brain protrudes from the skull. Anencephaly will almost always lead to a spontaneous abortion, stillbirth, or neonatal death. The presence of an encephalocele is associated with a variety of developmental problems that can include spasticity and severe intellectual disability.

There are various forms of evidence that suggest that neural tube defects are caused by the interaction of a number of factors. Some of this evidence comes from prevalence information and risk data. The prevalence of spina bifida in the general population is around 1:1000. In subsequent pregnancies, a mother who has a child with spina bifida has an increased risk of having another child with a neural tube defect. The risk increases from around 0.1% if there is no prior history to around 2% in subsequent pregnancies after a child with a neural tube defect has been born. While this risk is therefore about 20 times higher than for the general population, it is still much lower than the risks described earlier in the chapter for single-gene causes arising from dominant genes, recessive genes, or X-linked transmission. These types of risk could be up to 50% if, for example, a person with a dominant gene for a disability, such as a person with Apert syndrome, were to reproduce.

In the case of neural tube defects, it is believed that several genes could be involved (Davidson et al., 2008), and that these genes may lead to a susceptibility for the developmental problem to occur during pregnancy. This genetic susceptibility appears to be affected by environmental factors, the most significant of which is the absence of folic acid in the mother's diet at the time of conception. Other risk factors are believed to include maternal obesity, insulin dependent diabetes, and certain medications.

Spina bifida (meaning bisected spine) occurs when the neural tube enclosing the spinal cord fails to close on the 28th day of gestation. There are four types of spina bifida. *spina bifida occulta* (hidden spina bifida) is the mildest form, and may be so mild that it is never discovered, or discovered only when the person happens to have a back x-ray for other reasons. One or two of the vertebrae are not properly formed, but there is no nerve damage and little or no external evidence of a problem. With a *meningocele,* part of the spinal cord covering, the meninges, protrudes from the back as a sac containing cerebrospinal fluid. The nerves and spinal cord are not usually affected, so once the sac is removed, there are no continuing problems. A *lipomeningocele* is another relatively mild form of spina bifida where the protruding sac contains fatty tissue. There may be some nerve damage and consequent urinary problems.

The most complex and serious form of spina bifida is *myelomeningocele.* In this case, the spinal cord and associated nerves and protective covering protrude from the back. The protrusion has to be removed and repaired, and there will be damage to the nerves and spinal cord, leading to problems that can include paralysis, urinary and bowel incontinence, and deformities of the lower limbs. When a person is described as having spina bifida, it usually means that they have a myelomeningocele, and this convention will be used for the remainder of this discussion.

Most people with spina bifida (i.e., myelomeningocele) have a blockage that prevents drainage of cerebrospinal fluid from the brain. If untreated, this results in hydrocephalus; there may also be other abnormalities of the brain. Most children with spina bifida will have a shunt inserted to drain off the fluid, and some children will have a mild degree of intellectual disability, poor mathematical skills, and problems in visual and tactile perception (Mataro, Junque, Poca, & Sahuquillo, 2001).

Nowadays, children with spina bifida will often attend regular schools, even if they use wheelchairs and have associated medical problems. Most of these students will have intelligence that is in the lower end of the normal range and are likely also to have some learning difficulties and attention problems (Burmeister et al., 2005). Barron and Obringer (1987) found average WISC IQs for children with spina bifida to be 76, with average verbal IQs at 82 and performance IQs at 74. An IEP for a student with spina bifida will need to carefully consider the student's physical needs and any assistance needed for mobility around the school and general self-care. This will involve consultation with an occupational therapist and/or physical therapist. There will also need to be careful consideration of the student's learning needs, as it is likely that the student will need an individualized program to facilitate access to the general education curriculum. Planning of individual educational programs is covered in more detail in Chapter 6.

Maternal Infection

Rubella (or German measles) is a dramatic example of how a relatively mild viral infection in the early part of pregnancy can have catastrophic effects on the developing infant. As well as intellectual disability, congenital rubella syndrome (CRS) can lead to vision or hearing impairment, heart defects and/or impaired growth. There is some evidence that exposure to rubella can lead to health problems in adulthood for children who, at birth, do not appear to have been affected by the syndrome (Penner & Brown, 2007). The risk of some form of problem for fetuses exposed to rubella in the first trimester is as high as 90%.

In the past, outbreaks of rubella were followed by the birth of large cohorts of children with sensory or intellectual problems, for whom special services had to be provided. Since the late 1960s vaccination of teenage girls has prevented such outbreaks and has greatly reduced the incidence of CRS in most developed countries, and most teachers will now never see a child with CRS. However, rubella and its consequences remain an eminently preventable problem in some developing countries.

There are other maternal infections that have been shown to be associated with a variety of disabilities, including intellectual disability, in children. Accounts of the possible effects of *toxoplasmosis* have been published since the 1930s. A study published in 1988 followed nearly 23,000 mothers and their children, and reported on outcomes when the child was 7 years old. The study found that women with high levels of exposure to toxoplasmosis had increased risk of having a child who was deaf, who had microcephaly, or who had an intellectual disability (Sever et al., 1988). Cats are believed to be the main source of the infection, which may also come from touching or eating undercooked meat products, so women who may be pregnant are usually advised to exercise caution in these areas. The infection is detectable and treatable prenatally, although there is debate about the viability of doing so (Ledger, 2008).

Cytomegalovirus is a very common infection that usually causes only a flu-like illness. However, if it occurs in pregnant women, it is known to produce risk of vision or hearing loss and/or intellectual disability in their children (Ledger, 2008). It has been described as the main cause of such disabilities that are related to congenital infections (Benoist, Jaquemard, Leruez-Ville, & Ville, 2008).

A recent study of 400 children with cerebral palsy found that nearly 40% of their mothers had had a significant infection of some type during pregnancy (Bax, Tydeman, & Flodmark, 2006). The cerebral palsy may occur because the damage caused by the infection limits the ability of the fetus to adapt to the labor process (Gunn & Bennet, 2008). The authors of the study of children with cerebral palsy concluded that there was need for a more systematic approach to the identification and treatment of maternal infections during pregnancy (Bax et al., 2006).

Maternal Toxicity

Fetal alcohol syndrome provides a clear demonstration of the way in which exposure to toxic substances *in utero* can damage the developing fetus. For many years it has been noted that babies born to alcoholic mothers have developed less well than other children. However, it was assumed that this was because alcoholic mothers would tend to be less well educated, have poorer prenatal care, and have inferior nutrition, when compared with the general population. It was not until 1973 that a number of children of chronically alcoholic mothers were identified as having a "pattern of malformation," which was named fetal alcohol syndrome (Jones & Smith, 1973; Jones, Smith, Ulleland, & Streissguth, 1973). Ethanol is now acknowledged to be the most significant teratogenic substance affecting the fetus (Harris, 2006).

The earliest detailed case report of eight children born to alcoholic mothers showed them to have developmental delay and growth deficiency, and seven of the eight children had microcephaly (Jones et al., 1973). Later research has defined the syndrome as a triad of signs comprising characteristic facial abnormalities, growth deficiency, and disorders of the central nervous system, associated with high maternal alcohol intake (Ryan & Ferguson, 2006). Fetal alcohol spectrum disorder (FASD) is now recognized as the most common cause of intellectual disability in the United States, with prevalence estimates of up to 1% of live births (Harris, 2006), with the likelihood that many cases are unidentified (Niccols, 2007).

Not all children of mothers who have consumed high levels of alcohol in pregnancy are born with developmental problems. There are suggestions that this may be another area where genetic susceptibility is involved. Streissguth and Dehaene (1993) studied 16 sets of twins born to alcoholic mothers, 5 pairs of which were monozygotic (MZ) and 11 pairs dizygotic (DZ). MZ twins have identical genotypes while DZ twins have similar genotypes, like any pair of siblings. However, all twins have identical prenatal environments such that they will have equal exposure to their mother's intake of alcohol. The researchers found that the concordance rate for MZ twins was 100%; that is, they either both had FASD or neither did. For DZ twins, the concordance rate was 64%, meaning that there were situations where they were differently affected. This suggests that genes may affect the extent to which alcohol impacts on the developing fetus (Streissguth & Dehaene, 1993)

There is also variability in the extent to which affected children display the developmental problems and physical characteristics of fetal alcohol syndrome, with some children of high-alcohol-using mothers clearly having the defined syndrome, some children displaying a different pattern of problems, and some apparently being unaffected. It is for this reason that the condition is now frequently referred to as fetal alcohol *spectrum*, suggesting the variability of outcome, which can be on any part of the spectrum. Apart from genetic predisposition, referred to above, maternal age, amount of alcohol consumed, poor nutrition, drug use, poverty, obstetric medication, stage of pregnancy when alcohol is consumed, and paternal alcohol consumption are all factors that may affect the risk and manner of the fetus being affected by maternal alcohol intake (Niccols, 2007).

There have been some efforts to separate the impact of the syndrome from the impact of the deprived environment into which many of these children are born. This research has suggested that the developmental problems will continue even for children adopted into a normal environment

(Streissguth & LaDue, 1985). Testing from various studies has shown that individuals with fetal alcohol syndrome are likely to have a degree of intellectual disability ranging from mild to moderate, and occasionally severe, although some have average or above average intellectual ability. However, even those who do not have an intellectual disability may have other cognitive problems such as difficulties in executive function: planning, sequencing and reasoning (Kerns, Don, Mateer, & Streissguth, 1997). In addition to intellectual disability and problems with cognitive functions, students with fetal alcohol syndrome often have speech and language difficulties, memory deficits, and problems with visuo-spatial functioning (Green, 2007). They are also likely to have attention deficit disorder, social and behavioral problems, and mental health challenges.

The pattern of possible problems described above makes it clear that students with FASD will have difficulties at school. Green (2007) suggests that for interventions to be effective, account must be taken of the interaction between the neuropsychological effects of the syndrome and the behavioral symptoms. For example, a child's challenging behavior in the classroom may be a direct result of his difficulties with executive function. Unable to reason his way through a problematic situation, he responds with an outburst of disruptive, challenging behavior. Green (2007) recommends the use of positive behavior supports (see Chapter 6), visual cues and schedules, teaching of self-directed problem solving, and cognitive modeling. She recommends structure and consistency in routines, and concrete rules for behavior. Because of the complexity and variety of their problems, students with FASD would benefit from a multidisciplinary team approach. If the student is still with his birth parents, there will be additional sensitivities to be observed, as FASD is one of the very few situations where a child's developmental problems can be directly linked to particular behaviors on the part of a parent.

Since the dramatic teratogenic effects of the prescribed drug thalidomide became apparent in the 1960s, there has been a heightened awareness of the need for caution in drug use in pregnancy. Meador et al. (2009) recently reported significantly lower IQs in 309 children whose mothers had taken the anti-epileptic medication valproate during pregnancy. The children's IQS were seven points lower on average at age 3 than those of children whose mothers took other forms of anti-epileptic medication. The most commonly reported effects of the use of recreational drugs and tobacco are premature birth and low birth weight. The general advice given to women who are or may be pregnant is to avoid alcohol, tobacco, and recreational drugs, and to seek medical advice about the safety of prescribed drugs.

Other Prenatal Environmental Causes

While there are many good reasons for pregnant women to follow a healthy diet (Fowles, 2004), there is very little evidence that maternal malnutrition will impact significantly on the intellectual development of the unborn child, except in the most extreme of circumstances. Changes to the maternal hormonal system during pregnancy ensure that the fetus receives sufficient nutrients, regardless of maternal diet (Osteria, 1982). The outcome may be different if an individual is on a starvation diet or if malnutrition occurs at particular stages of pregnancy (Read, 1982), but in general, maternal malnutrition is not a major cause of intellectual disability. However, one disability that can be shown to be related to maternal diet is congenital hypothyroidism.

Congenital hypothyroidism results in inadequate production of thyroid hormone in the newborn infant. It is detectable by a blood test at birth. While it can be caused by a defect in the child's thyroid gland, it can also result from a lack of iodine in the pregnant woman's diet. This cause has largely been eliminated by the iodization of salt, although there are still some countries where diet-related endemic hypothyroidism occurs. If hypothyroidism is detected in the newborn, the child can be treated, and the intellectual disability that would have developed can be prevented. Congenital hypothyroidism was previously known as "cretinism," but this term is no longer in use. It is now very rare to see children with this condition in developed countries, as it is prevented through diet or they are detected through newborn thyroid hormone screening.

If a pregnant woman suffers prenatal trauma, such as an accident or fall, or a violent incident, this can obviously lead to injury to or even the death of the unborn infant. As might be expected, more severe injuries usually lead to more serious outcomes for the child (Klinich et al., 2008), although even a minor injury can lead to fetal loss (Leroy-Malherbe, Bonnier, Papiernik, Groos, & Landrieu, 2006). Life-threatening injuries have been estimated to lead to fetal loss in 40% to 50% of cases, whereas for mild injuries, fetal loss is estimated at 1% to 5%. However, as minor injuries are much more prevalent than life-threatening injuries, minor injuries are the major cause of fetal loss through accident (Hill & Pickinpaugh, 2008).

Although there is some debate about the extent to which the fetus is protected from injury, most pregnancies continue in the normal way, and there is no systematic follow-up of children whose mothers suffer an injury during pregnancy (Leroy-Malherbe et al., 2006). Depending on the circumstances, Leroy-Malherbe and colleagues suggest various forms of post-traumatic monitoring of the fetus, including heart monitoring, ultrasound examination, and MRI of the fetal brain. They recommend careful follow-up of the child once it is born, particularly if there are signs of neurological problems (Leroy-Malherbe et al., 2006).

FOR DISCUSSION AND REFLECTION:

- Draw up a 2 × 2 grid and see if you can use it to demonstrate how simple recessive inheritance occurs, and another 2 × 2 grid to demonstrate simple dominant inheritance.
- Why are girls usually less affected than boys in X-linked inheritance?
- Discuss the concept of multifactorial causes.

Perinatal Causes of Intellectual Disability

Prematurity

Perinatal refers to the period immediately before and immediately after birth. It is usually defined as starting around a week before birth and finishing around 1to 4 weeks after birth. The most common and widely researched problem associated with the perinatal period is prematurity, which usually refers to a gestation period of 36 weeks or less. The degree of prematurity can be further classified either by birth weight or by weeks of gestation; most of the research is based on birth weight, this being the most objective measure. The usual definitions of low birth weight (LBW) are as follows:

- Extremely Low Birth Weight (ELBW): <1000 g (2.2 lbs.)
- Very Low Birth Weight (VLBW): 1000–1500 g (2.2–3.3 lbs.)
- Moderately Low Birth Weight (MLBW): 1500–2500 g (3.3–5.5 lbs.)

Babies can also be categorized on the basis of whether their weight is appropriate for the length of their gestation. Those below the 10th percentile or above the 90th percentile would be classified as small for gestational age (SGA) or large for gestational age (LGA), respectively.

As gestational age increases, so does the chance of survival. There have been increases in recent years both in the number of children born prematurely and in the survival rate for such births. The increased number of premature births is related to reproductive technology, which has increased the number of multiple births, and to the overall increase in survival rate. An infant weighing less than 1000 g who survives the birth process is classified as ELBW, but previously might have been a stillbirth or miscarriage.

The increased survival rate results from improvements in medical technology and processes that have led to children surviving at weights that would have been regarded as nonviable 20 or 30 years ago.

The increasing survival rate for children with ELBW is an area of some controversy. This is because survival of these children is associated with very high rates of disability. For example, up to 15% of such children will have cerebral palsy, and up to 50% will have significant neurobehavioral problems (Thompson et al., 2007). These rates are very much higher than for the general population. This has led some to argue that we should not regard infants born with a birth weight of less that 1000 g as viable until the risk of serious disability greatly diminishes. The counterargument is that even if 50% of surviving ELBW children have a disability, 50% will not have disabilities; we cannot improve this situation without continuing research into how ELBW children develop after birth. The debate will, no doubt, continue as medical science lowers the barriers for life outside the womb.

Another complicating factor in examining the effect of LBW on later disability is the question of whether the disability is a cause or an effect of the premature birth. Gunn and Bennet (2008) point out that preterm infants have far higher rates of brain injury and perinatal hypoxia than infants born at term. However, they suggest that some acute injuries may occur well before birth or may compromise the ability of the fetus to adapt to labor, thus leading to perinatal brain damage. It is possible that antenatal problems may predispose the child to be born prematurely, and that the premature birth exacerbates the existing problem. It may therefore be an interactive process we are looking at rather than a simple cause-and-effect.

While premature birth combined with ELBW may cause intellectual disability in some children, it is likely that the impact of birth weight on intelligence is not huge on average. For example, a study of an African American cohort compared children who had a birth weight of less than 2000 g with children of normal birth weight. The average difference was 7 IQ points, which, while significant, does not constitute intellectual disability, although it could have had a substantial impact in individual cases. In the 2000–2500 g group, the difference was even less—around 3 points (Dombrowski, Noonan, & Martin, 2007). These results confirmed early studies suggesting that overall IQ differences between LBW children and other children may be statistically significant but are not necessarily clinically significant for most children (Shenkin, Starr, & Deary, 2004). On the other hand, a population study of nearly 1 million children born in Florida over a 5-year period found gestational age of less than 37 weeks to be the highest population-level risk factor for later developmental delay. The highest individual risk factor was birth weight below 1500 g (Delgado, Vagi, & Scott, 2007). Other risk indicators included low Apgar scores, multiple births, and labor complications.

Other Perinatal Problems

Children born at full term may still experience perinatal problems that can impact on later development. Looney and colleagues (2007) reported a study in which magnetic resonance imaging was used to detect intracranial hemorrhage (ICH) in a sample of 97 newborns. They found ICH in 26% of vaginal births and concluded that, while it was likely that the majority of these would resolve quickly without ill-effects, it was possible that some may have long-term neurocognitive consequences. Perinatal infection has also been associated with brain damage in the infant (Rees, Harding, & Walker, 2008), and perinatal hypoxia-ischemia (lack of oxygen leading to insufficient blood flow to cells and organs) is possibly the most important cause of brain injury in the newborn infant (du Plessis & Volpe, 2002) with subsequent cognitive problems. Hypothermia therapy (cooling treatment) has been shown to decrease the amount of later disability arising from hypoxic-ischemic encephalopathy (brain injury) (Shankaran et al., 2008).

Dean and Davis (2007) found that it was possible to predict a high risk for later educational difficulty on the basis of a combination of perinatal complications, referred to by Dean and Davis as a "synergistic effect" or interaction between factors. They found that even if perinatal factors did not lead to major physical or intellectual disability, they placed children at increased risk of learning disabilities, autism, and attention difficulties. From a teacher's perspective, there are no specific educational approaches that apply to children whose disabilities arise from perinatal causes. They will be as varied and diverse as any other groups of children, and educational programs will need to be planned on an individual basis. Dean and Davis suggest that the use of structured measures of perinatal risk factors could help school psychologists to identify children who are at risk for developmental problems. While there are dangers in labeling children as "at risk," there can also be benefits from early identification, and subsequent provision of educational intervention and other forms of support (see Chapter 4).

FOR DISCUSSION AND REFLECTION:

- Discuss the arguments for and against using technology to help babies survive at lower birth weights.
- Discuss the suggestion that disability could be a cause or effect of premature birth.

Postnatal Causes of Intellectual Disability

Head Injury

Motor vehicle accidents, sporting injuries, falls, abuse, and gunshot wounds are the major causes of severe traumatic brain injury (TBI) in children in the United States (McDermott, Durkin, Schupf, & Stein, 2007). Abusive head trauma (shaken baby syndrome) has become a recognized cause of disability, with outcomes including vision or hearing impairment, intellectual disability, and in severe cases, death. It is the most common form of nonaccidental head injury affecting the developing brain (Bonnier, Mesples, & Gressens, 2004).

In the United States the National Center for Injury Prevention and Control estimates that among children aged birth to 14 years, there are 435,000 emergency room visits annually for TBI, leading to 37,000 hospitalizations and around 2,600 deaths. Falls are the major cause of TBI in children aged birth to 14 years. The number of children with abusive head trauma is not known. Many of these are undiagnosed because identification is likely to lead to criminal charges.

Traumatic brain injury in children is among the most preventable of causes of intellectual disability. The compulsory use of well-designed baby carriers and car seats has reduced the number of injuries from motor vehicle accidents in developed countries. Most parks and playgrounds now have soft-fall material around climbing equipment to reduce injury from falls, a major cause of hospitalization in children. There are now programs to reduce the incidence of shaken baby syndrome through parent education and other forms of guidance. It is very unlikely that any parent would wish to harm their own child, but some parents need assistance and support in coping with the frustration that can result when babies are difficult to settle.

The consequences of TBI are highly variable and can range from little or no discernible impact, through short-term impact, to severe lifelong impact or death. There is considerable debate about and research into the functional plasticity of the young brain (Ewing-Cobbs, Barnes, & Fletcher, 2003). Some researchers have argued that young children are more likely to recover from a TBI as their brains will be sufficiently plastic for undamaged parts to "take over" damaged functions. However, a study by Anderson and colleagues has suggested that children who suffer a severe injury at a younger age (3 to 7 years) are less likely than older children (8 to12) to show later improvement in their cognitive performance. As expected, the severity of injury has been shown to be related to the degree of intellectual disability (Anderson, Catroppa, Morse, Haritou, & Rosenfeld, 2005). A follow-up study of Anderson's younger group after 5 years found the severity of the injury to be the best predictor of later educational performance. Pre-injury functioning was the best predictor of adaptive behavior (Catroppa, Anderson, Morse, Haritou, & Rosenfeld, 2008). This is an area of considerable complexity, with other variables including whether the injury is focal, diffuse or both and, if focal, the nature and location of the lesion (Ewing-Cobbs et al., 2003).

Surprisingly, TBI is not regarded as a major cause of moderate and severe intellectual disability. This is probably because injuries that are sufficient to cause a significant intellectual disability in children are likely to be fatal (McDermott et al., 2007). Teachers are more likely to come across children whose brain injury has led to problems in the basic skills of arithmetic and reading, behavioral and mood challenges, and problems with memory (McDermott et al., 2007). However, occasionally they will also come across children whose TBI has led to multiple severe intellectual and physical disabilities.

Infections

Infections of the brain during childhood can lead to brain damage and consequent serious intellectual and sensory disability, or even death. Until the 1970s meningitis arising from haemophilus influenza type B (Hib) was a leading cause of postnatally acquired intellectual disability. Meningitis is an infection of the membrane covering the brain (the meninges) and can also arise from mumps, measles, or polio. In developed countries, meningitis from Hib and other childhood diseases has been virtually eliminated through vaccination, and meningitis is now an extremely rare cause of disability. Vaccination against meningococcal infection is also recommended for young children as an additional precaution to prevent other forms of meningitis.

Encephalitis is another infection of the brain that can have very serious consequences, including severe intellectual disability, sensory disability, and seizures. It is fatal in up to 20% of cases (Lazoff, 2007). For around 1:1000 patients who have measles, this disease will be followed by encephalitis. Because of the very serious potential outcomes of encephalitis, vaccination against measles is highly recommended by public health authorities. Meningitis and encephalitis are examples of preventable causes of intellectual disability.

Degenerative Disorders

Rett syndrome is an example of a degenerative disorder that appears in girls after they have been developing normally for 6 to 18 months. It is a disability that could logically have been listed under "prenatal causes" as an inherited disorder, but is described here as an example of a degenerative disorder, manifested after a period of typical development. As an X-linked *dominantly* transmitted disorder, mutation of a single gene on just one of a girl's two X chromosomes is sufficient for the disability to appear. If a male has the mutated gene on his single X chromosome, this will usually result in a spontaneous abortion or death in infancy. There have been some reported cases of males with Rett syndrome, and in most cases this leads to severe intellectual disability, but it is primarily a disorder affecting girls (Harris, 2006). Estimates of prevalence vary from 1 in 8500 to 1 in 23,000 live female births, so it is a relatively rare cause of disability.

Although the mutated gene is present from the time of conception, almost invariably as a fresh mutation, the characteristics of Rett syndrome in girls do not appear until between the ages of 6 months and 18 to 24 months, after the infant has been developing normally. Characteristics of Rett syndrome include regression and loss of hand skills, stereotypic hand movements, severe language impairment, seizures, and severe intellectual disability. Although around 85% of children with Rett syndrome are found to have a mutation of the gene, the diagnosis is usually made through the distinctive clinical symptoms.

Until Rett syndrome was identified as a distinct neurodevelopmental disorder in 1983, individuals with the disorder were often given a primary diagnosis of autism (Mount, Charman, Hastings, Reilly, & Cass, 2003). Autism is now recognized as one of the likely behavioral characteristics of Rett syndrome and, indeed, of many other syndromes associated with intellectual disability. In Rett syndrome, autism is estimated to occur in 80% to 100% of cases (Cohen et al., 2005).

There is some evidence from mouse models that reversibility of the neurological defects of Rett syndrome is possible (Guy, Gan, Selfridge, Cobb, & Bird, 2007). However, medical science is currently a long way from this situation in humans; present treatment involves medical management of seizures and other physical problems, together with a carefully planned program to improve physical, behavioral, and communication skills. There is evidence that improvements in these areas can occur through intervention by a multidisciplinary team (Baptista, Mercadante, Macedo, & Schwartzman, 2006; Pizzamiglio et al., 2008). Teachers will play a key role as team members in helping families to deal with the behavioral, social, and communication problems experienced by children with Rett syndrome.

Seizure Disorders

There are a number of seizure disorders that appear during childhood, often in children who have been developing normally. While mild epilepsy typically has no adverse intellectual or behavioral outcomes, more frequent or severe seizures can be associated with later intellectual disability and other behavioral and/or cognitive problems. An example of such a disorder is Lennox-Gastaut syndrome (LGS). The usual age of onset is from 2 to 8 years, often following a history of infantile spasms (MacAllister & Schaffer, 2007). The prevalence rate is around 2 per 10,000. There is no specific cause for LGS. Some children develop LGS following perinatal hypoxic-ischemic encephalopathy (brain injury) or following one of the brain infections referred to under "Infections" above. In some cases the disability is idiopathic; that is, of unknown cause.

Children with LGS have frequent seizures of different forms that are very difficult to manage and control. Having more than one type of seizure is characteristic of LGS: both generalized tonic-clonic seizures and absence seizures; many also have prolonged seizures (status epilepticus). Children with LGS are susceptible to injury through sudden falls and often have to wear a protective helmet. In addition to progressive intellectual disability, students with LGS are likely to have behavioral problems such as attention disorders, perseveration, and autistic or psychotic behaviors (Besag, 2006). Some of these behavioral problems may result from the heavy and multiple medications used in an attempt to control the seizures.

When students with LGS attend school, priority will usually need to be given to management of the seizure disorder and its associated problems. Students with LGS will often be enrolled in special schools. Some will be enrolled in mainstream classes, but they will tend to need additional support from a nurse or special aide to assist with administration of medication or the management of seizures.

Lennox-Gastaut syndrome is at the very serious end of seizure disorders, and the prospect of remission is not good (Camfield & Camfield, 2007). However, many students with epilepsy will have their seizures largely controlled by medication and will not suffer any adverse cognitive effects from their disability. Teachers may need to know how to respond in the event that the student has a seizure at school or to remind the student about taking medication. If there are additional learning problems, these will need to be planned for in the same way as for any other student with learning problems. Teachers will occasionally be asked to observe children who are having trials with different medications. Physicians will be aiming for a medication that controls the seizures without causing drowsiness or attention problems. Teacher observations will be very important in such situations.

Toxic-Metabolic Disorders

For hundreds of years environmental toxins have been recognized as having a potentially damaging impact both on the fetus and on the young child. Perhaps the best known of these toxins is lead, which has, over the years, been found domestically in paint, toys, water, food, industrially contaminated soil, cans, and of course, gasoline. While lead poisoning was first described by the Greeks in the second century BC (Gloag, 1980), the first scientific case reports of lead encephalopathy occurred in the late 1800s (Norman, 1995). Examination of the behavioral, cognitive, and health effects of various blood-lead levels has continued since then. The relationship is not a simple one, as some of the factors associated with higher blood-lead levels (e.g., living close to industrial areas and factories, living in older properties that contain lead-based paint, being more exposed to ingested dirt) are also factors that are likely to be associated with poverty, and poverty is known to be associated with lower levels of intellectual functioning. A further confounding factor is nutritional status, which may alter susceptibility to lead toxicity (Mahaffey, 1990).

Despite these difficulties, it is now possible to demonstrate that lead has a significant impact on the health and cognitive functioning of the young child (Fewtrell, Pruss-Ustun, Landrigan, & Ayuso-Mateos, 2004). On the basis of data from 14 geographical regions, Fewtrell et al. estimated that exposure to lead amounts to nearly 1% of the "global burden of disease" when mild intellectual disability and cardiovascular outcomes are considered. They point out that while differences between exposed and nonexposed children on a population basis may be just a few points, these differences may be functionally significant and could mean that some children who would not otherwise be diagnosed as having an intellectual disability would fall into the category of mild intellectual disability (Fewtrell et al., 2004). Attention and memory problems have also been reported (McDermott et al., 2007).

Lead exposure is a highly preventable cause of mild intellectual disability and other health problems. The main environmental change that has reduced blood-lead levels in developed countries has been the introduction of unleaded gasoline. It has been estimated that 90% of children with raised blood-lead levels are in developing countries, particularly those that are still using leaded gas (Fewtrell et al., 2004). It is expected that understanding of the adverse impacts of lead and other environmental chemicals will, in due course, bring about a cleaner and healthier environment.

Malnutrition

There has been much debate and research on whether malnutrition in young children can impact on their intellectual development. Much of the research has taken place in underdeveloped countries, as chronic undernutrition and acute malnutrition are relatively rare, although not unknown, in developed countries. From an early study in Uganda, it was concluded that while there were relationships between malnutrition and intellectual disability, it was chronic undernutrition rather than acute malnutrition that was the crucial factor in determining the level of disability (Hoorweg, 1976). A report by Read (1982) concluded that severe malnutrition during the third trimester of pregnancy and the first six months of life can decrease the cellularity of the brain and impair learning ability. However, the relationship is complicated by the fact that malnutrition almost invariably occurs in impoverished and unstimulating environments (Read, 1982). Yaqoob and colleagues (2004) found social deprivation and malnutrition to be the apparent causes of mild intellectual disability in 28% of 40 children identified as having mild disability in a longitudinal study of 649 children in Lahore, Pakistan.

A recent report on children with chronic protein-energy malnutrition (PEM) in Bangalore, India, found deficits in various aspects of cognitive functioning, including working memory, visual perception, and cognitive flexibility, in malnourished children compared with a group with adequate nutrition. The researchers concluded that chronic PEM can result in long-lasting cognitive impairments (Kar, Rao, & Chandramouli, 2008). Although differences in intelligence were not measured in this study, the reported cognitive processing deficits were in areas similar to the cognitive processes measured in tests of intelligence.

While much of the research on malnutrition has taken place in developing countries, PEM is not totally unknown in developed countries, including the United States. A recent study of severe malnutrition in the state of Georgia reported a review of hospital records over a 30-month period and identified 29 cases of children hospitalized with severe PEM. However, most of these cases were associated with known metabolic disorders or diseases, and only three were believed to be associated with primary nutritional deficiency (Carvalho, Tomashek, Powell, & Mellinger-Birdsong, 2001). Carvalho et al. estimated the number of children hospitalized with severe PEM at 2 per million. Extrapolating from the other reported figures, the number of children in the United States whose PEM resulted from nutritional rather than metabolic reasons would be 0.2 per million, an insignificant number by world standards. By contrast, the World Health Organization estimates that there are 20 million children worldwide suffering from severe malnutrition, the vast majority of these in developing countries.

Environmental Deprivation

At an extreme level, it is obvious that a child who was totally deprived of all normal human interaction would acquire few of the developmental tasks of childhood such as learning to speak and to interact with the world and would present as a child with a severe intellectual disability. The question is, at what level does environmental deprivation begin to impact on intellectual development? How much deprivation is too much, and how long do the effects last? Skeels and Dye (1939) provided evidence that being in the nonstimulating environment of an institution could have a negative impact on intellectual functioning. Subsequent studies have shown the enduring emotional impact of long-term institutional care (Tizard & Hodges, 1978). At a less extreme level, even children living at home could be experiencing a deprived environment if they have inadequate emotional and physical care. How might this affect development?

One of the difficulties in studying the effect of environmental deprivation on later development is separating the impact of different risk factors. If a child is born into a highly impoverished environment, the chances are that multiple factors could impact on his development. It is possible that his mother would have had less than optimal medical care during pregnancy and childbirth. Diet during pregnancy may have been inadequate, and tobacco and alcohol may have been used. There may be increased risk of a preterm birth. As a newborn, he may be more likely to have been exposed to inadequate nutrition, environmental toxins, limited medical care, and other forms of abuse or neglect. There may also be familial genetic factors predisposing him to a lower IQ. A child who is institutionalized will not be breastfed and may have a limited alternative diet, and certainly will not have the one-on-one attention of a normal mother-child relationship. Given the number of interacting risk factors, how is it possible to determine their impact on later development?

An interesting series of studies has been conducted by Michael Rutter and his colleagues in the UK, known as the English Romanian Adoptees (ERA) study. Following the fall of the Ceauscescu regime in Romania in1989, many babies who had been living in very deprived conditions in Romanian orphanages were adopted by English families. These children had previously spent most of their time in their cots with few playthings, poor nutrition, and very limited human interaction (Rutter et al., 1998). In their first report, the development at age 4 years of children who had been aged less than 6 months when adopted was compared by Rutter's team with the development of those children who were aged 6 to 24 months on adoption. Good records were kept of height, weight, and head circumference upon the children's arrival in the UK, and adoptive parents made a retrospective assessment of the child's level on the Denver Developmental Scales, based on their memory and records of what the child was like when first adopted.

Rutter et al. found that by the age of 4, both groups had made up most or all of the earlier developmental deficit. The group of children under 6 months on adoption had gone from a mean Denver quotient of 77 to a mean of 116, and those of 6 to 24 months old had gone from a mean of 48 to a mean of 97. In other words, both groups had moved from well below average to an average or above average level of functioning. Using weight on arrival as a measure of nutritional status, Rutter concluded that psychological privation was probably a more important factor than nutritional privation. The results suggested that developmental problems could be overcome if adverse circumstances are changed early enough in a child's life.

In the most recent report from the ERA team, further detailed analysis was undertaken of the impact of subnutrition at age 11 (Sonuga-Barke et al., 2008). It was found that the Romanian children who were adopted at less than 6 months had a mean WISC IQ at age 11of 112 if there was no evidence of subnutrition on adoption, and a mean IQ of 94 if there was subnutrition evident, as judged by weight at adoption. For older adoptees, mean WISC IQs were close to identical for the groups with and without subnutrition. In both cases the mean IQs of older adoptees, at 86 and 84, were lower than those of the younger adoptees. Rutter's team also observed autistic-like symptoms in 9% of the Romanian adoptees at aged 11, compared with 0% in a group of UK adoptees (Rutter et al., 2007).

In summary, it is clear that early environmental deprivation can affect later cognitive and intellectual development, but that some of this impact may be mitigated by a positive change in the environment. Other risk factors are likely to interact with the environmental deprivation. The earlier the child moves to a nondeprived environment, the greater the likelihood that the effects of deprivation will be lessened.

FOR DISCUSSION AND REFLECTION:

- What adaptations would you need to make for a student in your class with Lennox-Gastaut syndrome?
- Why is it difficult to assess the effects of environmental deprivation on intellectual development?

Prevention of Intellectual Disability

There is a strong movement in modern health care toward prevention of disease and disability wherever possible. This is because prevention is not only economically preferable, but it also greatly reduces the impact of disease and disability on the individual, the family, and society. Some examples have already been given of the prevention of the adverse effects of PKU and hypothyroidism through newborn screening. Vaccination against rubella, measles, and meningococcal disease has largely eliminated disabilities arising from these infections. The strong movement away from institutionalization of young babies with disabilities has prevented the exacerbating effects of early environmental deprivation.

There are also increasingly sophisticated ways of detecting disability prenatally. Amniocentesis to detect Down syndrome has been available since the 1970s and chorionic villus sampling (CVS) since the 1980s. During amniocentesis, a sample of amniotic fluid is removed from the uterus by inserting a thin needle through the abdomen. CVS is performed by removing a small sample of the placenta from the uterus with either a catheter or a needle. These are invasive procedures and carry with them the risk that they will induce a spontaneous abortion, even if there is nothing wrong with the fetus. The amount of risk depends on when the investigation takes place and the skill and experience of the person conducting the procedure. The risk of a spontaneous loss with amniocentesis has recently been estimated at around 1:50 at 13 weeks of pregnancy or less, and at 1:300 at 16 to 20 weeks (Evans & Andriole, 2008). Evans and Andriole recommend the use of CVS for early diagnosis, with procedure-induced loss from CVS at 10 weeks gestation or later being around the same as for midtrimester amniocentesis (i.e., around 1:300).

In order to reduce the risk of loss of an unaffected fetus, screening tests can now be used as an indication that the mother is likely to be carrying a fetus with Down syndrome. In most cases, amniocentesis or CVS will be performed for confirmation only when an ultrasound and maternal blood test, combined with consideration of the mother's age, indicate a high likelihood that the child has Down syndrome. Amniocentesis or CVS is then used for final diagnosis. Various studies have shown that 70% to 90% of mothers will elect to have their pregnancy terminated if Down syndrome is diagnosed (Perry, Woodall, & Pressman, 2007).

Although it stands as an example of an effective method of preventing disability, prenatal diagnosis for Down syndrome and other disabilities is not an uncontroversial procedure. One aspect of the controversy relates to the number of spontaneous abortions of unaffected fetuses that will occur because of the procedure. In addition, from a disability rights perspective, many people would argue that using the presence of Down syndrome as a reason for termination denies the very humanity of the hundreds of thousands of men, women, and children who have Down syndrome and implies that their lives are not worth living. The counterargument is that for any pregnancy, women have the right to decide whether they are able to carry the child to full term and to provide the time and resources necessary to raise it.

With increasingly sophisticated diagnostic processes, the debates are likely to become more rather than less complex. Michael Kirby (2001), a former judge of the High Court of Australia, has pointed out that the success of the Human Genome Project is likely to make it possible to detect a huge number of characteristics prenatally. Already there are debates arising from preimplantation genetic diagnosis (PGD) as part of *in vitro* fertilization. Issues have arisen in this field both in relation to attempts to eliminate disability and in attempts to produce a child with a specific disability. For example, parents who have dwarfism or are deaf may request an embryo that has the same disability as they have, so that their child will be better able to fit into their family and community. Others will want all forms of disability to be excluded. Kirby extends the debate by posing the interesting question of whether some parents might, in the future, seek to abort a fetus because it was prenatally diagnosed, for example, to be homosexual or susceptible to male-pattern baldness. He argues that while relief of pain of suffering is a worthwhile objective, difference and disability are sometimes in the "eye or ear or mind or heart of the beholder" (Kirby, 2001). This debate will no doubt continue.

Regardless of where the debate on prevention through prenatal diagnosis progresses to, many children with intellectual disability will continue to be born. Early in this chapter, reference was made to the fact that intellectual disability can result from an interaction between biomedical, social, behavioral, and educational risk factors (Luckasson et al., 2002). All of these factors need to be considered if we are to provide an optimal environment for all citizens. In addition to good medical and social care, a civil and just society has an obligation to provide children who have an intellectual disability with an accurate and informative diagnosis and appropriate educational and therapeutic programs, starting at the earliest possible time, and continuing through to adulthood. An educational focus on how this should occur is the topic of the following chapters.

FOR DISCUSSION AND REFLECTION:

- Discuss arguments for and against the use of prenatal diagnosis to prevent intellectual disability.

Summary

The causes of intellectual disability are frequently conceptualized in terms of their time of origin: prenatal, perinatal, or postnatal. Prenatal causes include chromosomal problems, inherited disorders, developmental neural/brain disorders, maternal infection, and maternal toxicity. Perinatal causes of intellectual disability tend to be those related to prematurity and associated low birth weight. Postnatal causes can include head injury, infections, degenerative disorders, seizure disorders, toxic metabolic disorders, malnutrition, and environmental deprivation. Prevention of some disabilities through prenatal diagnosis is becoming increasingly possible. This is an area in which strong ethical debates exist and are likely to continue.

References

Anderson, V., Catroppa, C., Morse, S., Haritou, F., & Rosenfeld, J. (2005). Functional plasticity or vulnerability after early brain injury? *Pediatrics, 116*(6), 1374–1382.

Bailey, A., Palferman, S., Heavey, L., & LeCouteur, A. (1998). Autism: The phenotype in relatives. *Journal of Autism and Developmental Disorders, 28*, 369–392.

Baptista, P. M., Mercadante, M. T., Macedo, E. C., & Schwartzman, J. S. (2006). Cognitive performance in Rett syndrome girls: A pilot study using eye-tracking technology. *Journal of Intellectual Disability Research, 50*(9), 662–666.

Barron, M. L., & Obringer, S. J. (1987, November 11–13). *The intellectual functioning of children with myleomenigocele.* Paper presented at the annual meeting of the Mid-South Educational Research Association, Mobile, AL.

Bax, D. M., Tydeman, C., & Flodmark, O. (2006). Clinical and MRI correlates of cerebral palsy: The European cerebral palsy study. *Journal of the American Medical Association, 296*, 1602–1608.

Benoist, G., Jaquemard, F., Leruez-Ville, M., & Ville, Y. (2008). Cytomegalovirus (CMV) congenital infection. *Gynecologie, Obstetrique & Fertilite, 36*(3), 248–260.

Besag, F. M. C. (2006). Cognitive and behavioral outcomes of epileptic syndromes: Implications for education and clinical practice. *Epilepsia, 47*(Suppl. 2), 119–125.

Bonnier, C., Mesples, B., & Gressens, P. (2004). Animal models of shaken baby syndrome: Revisiting the pathophysiology of this devastating injury. *Pediatric Rehabilitation, 7*(3), 165–171.

Breuggem, C. C., Fitzpatrick, D. F., & Verchere, C. (2008). Monozygotic twins with Apert syndrome. *Cleft Palate & Craniofacial Journal, 45*(1), 101–104.

Burmeister, R., Hannay, H. J., Copeland, K., Fletcher, J. M., Boudousquie, A., & Dennis, M. (2005). Attention problems and executive functions in children with spina bifida and hydrocephalus. *Child Neuropsychology, 11,* 265–283.

Camfield, P., & Camfield, C. (2007). Long-term prognosis for symptomatic (secondary) generalized epilepsies: A population-based study. *Epilepsia, 48*(6), 1128–1132.

Carvalho, N., Tomashek, K., Powell, K., & Mellinger-Birdsong, A. (2001). Severe malnutrition among young children—Georgia, January 1997–June 1999. *Journal of the American Medical Association, 285*(20), 2573–2574.

Catroppa, C., Anderson, V. A., Morse, S., Haritou, F., & Rosenfeld, J. V. (2008). Outcome and predictors of functional recovery 5 years following pediatric traumatic brain injury (TBI). *Journal of Pediatric Psychology, 33*(7), 707–718.

Cohen, D., Pichard, N., Tordjman, S., Baumann, C., Burglen, L., Excoffier, E., et al. (2005). Specific genetic disorders and autism: Clinical contribution towards their identification. *Journal of Autism and Developmental Disorders, 35*(1), 103–116.

Cornish, K., Turk, J., & Hagerman, R. (2008). The fragile X continuum: New advances and perspectives. *Journal of Intellectual Disability Research, 52*(6), 469–482.

Davidson, C. M., Northrup, H., King, T. M., Fletcher, J. M., Townsend, I., Tyerman, G. H., et al. (2008). Genes in glucose metabolism and association with spina bifida. *Reproductive Sciences, 15*(1), 51–58.

Davis, A. S. (2008). Children with Down syndrome: Implications for assessment and intervention in school. *School Psychology Quarterly, 23*(2), 271–281.

Dawson, G. (2008). Early behavioral intervention, brain plasticity, and the prevention of autism spectrum disorder. *Development and Psychopathology, 20,* 775–803.

Dean, R. S., & Davis, A. S. (2007). Relative risk of perinatal complications in common childhood disorders. *School Psychology Quarterly, 22*(1), 13–25.

Delgado, C. E. F., Vagi, S. J., & Scott, K. G. (2007). Identification of early risk factors for developmental delay. *Exceptionality, 15*(2), 119–136.

Dombrowski, S. C., Noonan, K., & Martin, R. (2007). Low birth weight and cognitive outcomes: Evidence for a gradient relationship in an urban, poor African American birth cohort. *School Psychology Quarterly, 22*(1), 26–43.

du Plessis, A. J., & Volpe, J. J. (2002). Perinatal brain injury in the preterm and term newborn. *Current Opinion in Neurology, 15,* 151–157.

Evans, M. I., & Andriole, S. (2008). Chorionic villus sampling and amniocentesis in 2008. *Current Opinion in Obstetrics and Gynecology, 20,* 164–168.

Ewing-Cobbs, L., Barnes, M. A., & Fletcher, J. M. (2003). Early brain injury in children: Development and reorganization of cognitive function. *Developmental Neuropsychology, 24*(2/3), 669–704.

Fewtrell, L. J., Pruss-Ustun, A., Landrigan, P., & Ayuso-Mateos, J. L. (2004). Estimating the global burden of diseases of mild mental retardation and cardiovascular diseases from environmental lead exposure. *Environmental Research, 94,* 120–133.

Fletcher, H., & Buckley, S. (2002). Phonological awareness in children with Down syndrome. *Down Syndrome Research and Practice, 8,* 11–18.

Fowles, E. R. (2004). Prenatal nutrition and health outcomes. *Journal of Obstetric, Gynecologic and Neonatal Nursing, 33,* 809–822.

Gloag, D. (1980). Is low-level lead pollution dangerous? *British Medical Journal, 281,* 1622–1625.

Green, J. H. (2007). Fetal alcohol spectrum disorders: Understanding the effects of prenatal alcohol exposure and supporting students. *The Journal of School Health, 77*(3), 103–108.

Gunn, A. J., & Bennet, L. (2008). Timing of injury in the fetus and neonate. *Current Opinion in Obstetrics and Gynecology, 20,* 175–181.

Guy, J., Gan, J., Selfridge, J., Cobb, S., & Bird, A. (2007). Reversal of neurological defects in a mouse model of Rett syndrome. *Science, 315*(5815), 1143–1147.

Harris, J. C. (2006). *Intellectual disability.* New York: Oxford University Press.

Hill, C. C., & Pickinpaugh, D. O. (2008). Trauma and surgical emergencies in the obstetric patient. *Surgical Clinics of North America, 88,* 421–440.

Hoorweg, J. (1976). *Protein-energy malnutrition and intellectual abilities: A study of teenage Ugandan children.* Paris: Mouton S. Gravenhage.

Jones, K. L., & Smith, D. W. (1973). Recognition of the fetal alcohol syndrome in early infancy. *Lancet, 2*(7836), 999–1001.

Jones, K. L., Smith, D. W., Ulleland, C. N., & Streissguth, A. P. (1973). Pattern of malformation in offspring of chronic alcoholic mothers. *Lancet, 1*(7815), 1267–1271.

Kar, B. R., Rao, S. L., & Chandramouli, B. A. (2008). Cognitive development in children with chronic protein energy malnutrition. *Behavioral and Brain Functions, 4*(31), e1–12.

Kerns, K., Don, A., Mateer, C. A., & Streissguth, A. P. (1997). Cognitive deficits in nonretarded adults with fetal alcohol syndrome. *Journal of Learning Disabilities, 30*(6), 685–693.

Kerr, A., & Prescott, R. J. (2005). Predictive value of the early clinical signs in Rett disorder. *Brain Development, 27*(Suppl. 1), 20–24.

Kirby, M. (2001, June 24). *Living with the genome.* Address to the Queensland Academy of Arts and Sciences, Brisbane, AUS.

Klinich, K. D., Flannagan, C. A. C., Rupp, J. D., Sochor, M., Schneider, L. W., & Pearlman, M. D. (2008). Fetal outcome in motor-vehicle crashes: Effects of crash characteristics and maternal restraint. *American Journal of Obstetrics and Gynecology, 198*(4), 450e1–450e9.

Lazoff, M. (2007). Encephalitis. *eMedicine: The Medscape Journal* (pp. 1–13).

Ledger, W. L. (2008). Perinatal infection and fetal/neonatal injury. *Current Opinion in Obstetrics and Gynecology, 20,* 120–124.

Lejeune, J., Gautier, M., & Turpin, R. A. (1959). Mongolisme: Une maladie chromosomique (trisomy). *Bulletin de l'Academie Nationale de Medecine, 143,* 256–265.

Leroy-Malherbe, V., Bonnier, C., Papiernik, E., Groos, E., & Landrieu, P. (2006). The association between developmental handicaps and traumatic brain injury during pregnancy: An issue that deserves more systematic evaluation. *Brain Injury, 20*(13–14), 1355–1365.

Lombroso, P. J., & Ogren, M. P. (2008). Fragile X syndrome: Keys to the molecular genetics of synaptic plasticity. *Journal of the American Academy of Child and Adolescent Psychiatry, 47*(7), 736–739.

Looney, C. B., Smith, J. K., Merck, L. H., Wolfe, H. M., Chescheir, N. C., Hamer, R. M., et al. (2007). Intracranial hemorrhage in asymptomatic neonates: Prevalence on MR images and relationship to obstetric and neonatal risk factors. *Radiology, 242*(2), 535–541.

Luckasson, R., Borthwick-Duffy, S., Buntinx, W., Coulter, D., Ellis, C., Reeve, A., et al. (2002). *Mental retardation: Definition, classification and supports* (10th ed.). Washington, DC: American Association on Mental Retardation.

MacAllister, W. S., & Schaffer, S. G. (2007). Neuropsychological deficits in childhood epilepsy syndromes. *Neuropsychology Review, 17,* 427–444.

MacMillan, C. (1998). Genetics and developmental delay. *Seminars in Pediatric Neurology, 5*(1), 39–44.

Mahaffey, K. R. (1990). Environmental lead toxicity: Nutrition as a component of intervention. *Environmental Health Perspectives, 89,* 75–78.

Mataro, M., Junque, C., Poca, M. A., & Sahuquillo, J. (2001). Neuropsychological findings in congenital and acquired hydrocephalus. *Neuropsychology Review, 11*(4), 169–178.

McDermott, S., Durkin, M. S., Schupf, N., & Stein, Z. A. (2007). Epidemiology and etiology of mental retardation. In J. W. Jacobson, J. A. Mulick, & J. Rojahn (Eds.), *Handbook of intellectual and developmental disabilities* (pp. 3–40). New York: Springer.

McLaren, J., & Bryson, S. E. (1987). Review of recent epidemiological studies of mental retardation: Prevalence, associated disorders, and etiology. *American Journal of Mental Retardation, 92,* 243–254.

Meador, K. J., Baker, G. A., Browning, N., Clayton-Smith, J., Combs-Cantrell, D., Cohen, M., et al. (2009). Cognitive function at 3 years of age after fetal exposure to antiepileptic drugs. *New England Journal of Medicine, 360*(16), 1597–1605.

Mount, R. H., Charman, T., Hastings, R. P., Reilly, S., & Cass, H. (2003). Features of autism in Rett syndrome and severe mental retardation. *Journal of Autism and Developmental Disorders, 33*(4), 435–442.

Niccols, A. (2007). Fetal alcohol syndrome and the developing socio-emotional brain. *Brain and Cognition, 65*, 135–142.

Norman, E. H. (1995). Lead toxicity intervention in children. *Journal of the Royal Society of Medicine, 88*(March), 121–124.

Olson, L., & Houlihan, D. (2000). A review of behavioral treatments used for Lesch-Nyhan syndrome. *Behavior Modification, 24*(2), 202–222.

Osteria, T. S. (1982). Maternal nutrition, infant health and subsequent fertility. *Philippine Journal of Nutrition, 35*(3), 106–111.

Penner, J. D., & Brown, A. S. (2007). Premorbid anomalies and risk of schizophrenia and depressive disorders in a birth cohort exposed to prenatal rubella. *School Psychology Quarterly, 22*(1), 58–73.

Perry, S., Woodall, A. L., & Pressman, E. K. (2007). Association of ultrasound findings with decisions to continue Down syndrome pregnancies. *Community Genetics, 10*, 227–230.

Pizzamiglio, M. R., Nasti, M., Piccardi, L., Zotti, A., Vitturini, C., Spitoni, G., et al. (2008). Sensory-motor rehabilitation in Rett syndrome. *Focus on Autism and Other Developmental Disabilities, 23*(1), 49–62.

Read, M. S. (1982). Malnutrition and behavior. *Applied Research in Mental Retardation, 3*(3), 279–291.

Rees, S., Harding, R., & Walker, D. (2008). An adverse intrauterine environment: Implications for injury and altered development of the brain. *International Journal of Developmental Neuroscience, 26*, 3–11.

Rietveld, C. (2005). Classroom learning experiences of mathematics by new entrant children with Down syndrome. *Journal of Intellectual and Developmental Disability, 30*(3), 127–138.

Rutter, M., Andersen-Wood, L., Beckett, C., Bredenkamp, D., Castle, J., Dunn, J., et al. (1998). Developmental catch-up, and deficit, following adoption after severe global, early privation. *Journal of Child Psychology and Psychiatry, 39*(4), 465–476.

Rutter, M., Kreppner, J., Croft, C., Murin, M., Colvert, E., Castle, J., et al. (2007). Early adolescent outcomes of institutionally deprived and non-deprived adoptees. III. Quasi-autism. *Journal of Child Psychology and Psychiatry, 48*(12), 1200–1207.

Ryan, S., & Ferguson, D. L. (2006). On, yet under, the radar: Students with fetal alcohol syndrome disorder. *Exceptional Children, 72*(3), 363–379.

Schretlen, D., Ward, J., Meyer, S. M., Yun, J., Puig, J. G., Nyhan, W., et al. (2005). Behavioral aspects of Lesch-Nyhan disease and its variants. *Developmental Medicine and Child Neurology, 47*(10), 673–677.

Schwarte, A. R. (2008). Fragile X syndrome. *School Psychology Quarterly, 23*(2), 290–300.

Sever, J. L., Ellenberg, J. H., Ley, A. C., Madden, D. L., Fuccillo, D. A., Tzan, N. R., et al. (1988). Toxoplasmosis: Maternal and pediatric findings in 23,000 pregnancies. *Pediatrics, 82*(2), 181–192.

Shankaran, S., Pappas, A., McDonald, S. A., Ehrenkranz, R. A., Tyson, J. E., Walsh, M., et al. (2008). Outcomes of safety and effectiveness in a multicenter randomized, controlled trial of whole-body hypothermia for neonatal hypoxic-ischemic encephalopathy. *Pediatrics, 122*(4), e791–798.

Shenkin, S. D., Starr, J. M., & Deary, I. J. (2004). Birth weight and cognitive ability in childhood: A systematic review. *Psychological Bulletin, 130*(6), 989–1013.

Skeels, H., & Dye, H. (1939). A study of the effects of differential stimulation on mentally retarded children. *Proceedings of the American Association on Mental Deficiency, 44,* 114–136.

Sonuga-Barke, E. J. S., Beckett, C., Kreppner, J., Castle, J., Colvert, E., Stevens, S., et al. (2008). Is sub-nutrition necessary for a poor outcome following early institutional privation? *Developmental Medicine and Child Neurology, 50*(9), 664–671.

Streissguth, A. P., & Dehaene, P. (1993). Fetal alcohol syndrome in twins of alcoholic mothers: Concordance of diagnosis and IQ. *American Journal of Medical Genetics, 47*(6), 857–861.

Streissguth, A. P., & LaDue, R. A. (1985). Psychological and behavioral effects in children prenatally exposed to alcohol. *Alcohol Health and Research World, 10,* 6–12.

Sybert, V. P., & McCauley, E. (2004). Turner's syndrome. *New England Journal of Medicine, 351*(12), 1227–1238.

Thompson, D. K., Warfield, S. K., Carlin, J. B., Pavlovic, M., Wang, H. X., Bear, M., et al. (2007). Perinatal risk factors altering regional brain structure in the preterm infant. *Brain, 130*(667–677).

Tizard, B., & Hodges, J. (1978). The effect of early institutional rearing on the development of eight-year-old children. *Journal of Child Psychology and Psychiatry, 19,* 99–118.

Volcik, K. A., Blanton, S. H., Kruzel, M. C., Townsend, I. T., Tyerman, G. H., Mier, R. J., et al. (2002). Testing for genetic associations in a spina bifida population: Analysis of the HOX gene family and human candidate gene regions implicated by mouse models of neural tube defects. *American Journal of Medical Genetics, 110*(3), 203–207.

Wodrich, D. L., & Tarbox, J. (2008). Psychoeducational implications of sex chromosome anomalies. *School Psychology Quarterly, 23*(2), 301–311.

Yaqoob, M., Bashir, A., Zaman, S., Ferngren, H., von Dobeln, U., & Gustavson, K.-H. (2004). Mild intellectual disability in Lahore, Pakistan: Aetiology and risk factors. *Journal of Intellectual Disability Research, 48*(7), 663–671.

Zilli, E. A., & Hasselmo, M. E. (2008). A model of behavioral treatments for self-mutilation behavior in Lesch-Nyhan syndrome. *NeuroReport, 19*(4), 459–462.

3

Identification, Assessment, and Classification

Overview: Issues in identifying and assessing intellectual disability are the focus of this chapter. The chapter examines classification issues and covers different ways of assessing intellectual disability through individual intelligence tests, measures of adaptive behavior, and assessment of support needs. The issue of identification of persons with the dual diagnosis of intellectual disability and psychiatric illness or behavioral disturbance is also discussed.

Identifying and Classifying Intellectual Disability

The term "intellectual disability" is a very broad descriptive term, covering individuals with a wide and varied range of functional abilities. The term tells us very little about the person so described. Indeed, in many instances there will be more differences between two people, both of whom are classified as having an intellectual disability, than between a person with and a person without a disability. One person with an intellectual disability may be indistinguishable on general observation from the general population; another person's disability may be apparent to all on first meeting.

Education of Students with an Intellectual Disability, pages 63–96

Other people may appear, superficially, to have an intellectual disability, despite the fact that they are very intelligent.

Intellectual disability is not a medical diagnosis, nor does it tell us anything about the cause of the disability, of which there are some hundreds. It describes a very heterogeneous group of people. It is because intellectual disability is such an amorphous term that various classification systems have been used in an attempt to provide a more precise description of a person's functioning. Such classification systems can have either positive or negative outcomes. Positive outcomes can result when a person's classification leads to them receiving the health, educational, physical, and other forms of support they need. The outcome will be negative if the classification leads others to underestimate the person's capabilities, to treat them as less human than a person without a disability, or simply to set limits on what the person can achieve.

Terminology describing people with an intellectual disability tends to acquire a negative meaning over time. It was explained in Chapter 1 that intellectual disability is the term currently preferred by many, although like other previously acceptable terminology, this may also eventually fall from favor. There are many terms that were once regarded as neutrally descriptive that are no longer used because of their negative connotations, such as *mentally deficient, subnormal,* and *mentally retarded.* About 100 years ago, an organization that was a forerunner of the American Association for Intellectual and Developmental Disability (AAIDD) adopted the classifications *feebleminded, moron, imbecile,* and *idiot* as ways of categorizing people with a disability, based on medical classifications current in the 1870s. So negative and offensive have these terms become that it is hard to believe that they were at one time used objectively by medical and educational professionals.

The classification terms referred to above were, in due course, replaced with other terms that have also since fallen from favor. These terms classified people with intellectual disability as *educable, trainable,* or *custodial,* based on the results of IQ tests. Again, these classifications came, in due course, to be seen as negative and unhelpful terms. In this case it wasn't so much the nature of the words but rather the deterministic effect they had on people's lives. On the basis of perhaps one IQ test on one day, a decision was made about whether a person was able to be educated or trained or needed custodial care. It is little wonder these terms are no longer widely used.

The next classification system grew out of the previous one, but with revised terminology. This system classified people as having a mild, moderate, severe, or profound degree of intellectual disability. These classifications, as described in the World Health Organization's International Classification of Diseases (ICD-10) (World Health Organization, 1992), are shown in Table 3.1. As can be seen from the foregoing discussion, they have direct links to classification systems of the mid-19th century, when the Massachusetts School for Idiotic and Feebleminded Youth was opened in 1848.

The classification of intellectual disability as "mild," "moderate," or "severe" has been found to be useful by service providers and is still in wide use today. Many school systems have organized their special education programs around these classifications, with different forms of service being provided depending on whether a student is classified as having a mild, moderate, or severe intellectual disability. For example, classes for children with mild disability may have more students and higher student:staff ratios than classes for children with moderate or severe intellectual disability.

TABLE 3.1 ICD-10 Classification of Intellectual Disability (Mental Retardation)

F70 Mild mental retardation

Approximate IQ range of 50 to 69 (in adults, mental age from 9 to under 12 years). Likely to result in some learning difficulties in school. Many adults will be able to work and maintain good social relationships and contribute to society.

Includes: Feeblemindedness, mild mental subnormality

F71 Moderate mental retardation

Approximate IQ range of 35 to 49 (in adults, mental age from 6 to under 9 years). Likely to result in marked developmental delays in childhood, but most can learn to develop some degree of independence in self-care and acquire adequate communication and academic skills. Adults will need varying degrees of support to live and work in the community.

Includes: Moderate mental subnormality

F72 Severe mental retardation

Approximate IQ range of 20 to 34 (in adults, mental age from 3 to under 6 years). Likely to result in continuous need of support.

Includes: Severe mental subnormality

F73 Profound mental retardation

IQ under 20 (in adults, mental age below 3 years). Results in severe limitation in self-care, continence, communication, and mobility.

Includes: Profound mental subnormality

Source: World Health Organization. (1992). *ICD-10. International classification of diseases and behavioural disorders.* Geneva: Author.

The term "profound" applied to intellectual disability has been abandoned by some education authorities because of its negative connotations and because of the difficulty of making accurate assessments of IQs below 30. On the other hand, some people working with students who have a very severe intellectual disability, combined with serious physical and sensory impairments, use the *term profound intellectual and multiple disabilities* (PIMD) to describe this group. The International Association for the Scientific Study of Intellectual Disability (IASSID) has a special interest research group that describes this group of people as follows:

> Individuals with profound intellectual and multiple disabilities form a heterogeneous group. The "core group" consists of individuals with such profound cognitive disabilities that no existing standardized tests are applicable for a valid estimation of their level of intellectual capacity and who often have profound neuromotor dysfunctions for example, spastic tetraplegia. In addition to profound intellectual and physical disabilities, it has been demonstrated that they also frequently have sensory impairments. Individuals with PIMD form a physically very vulnerable group of persons with a high dependence on personal assistance for every day tasks, 24 hours a day. (IASSID Special Interest Research Group on PIMD, 2008)

Those who work with students who have this level of disability argue that these students need to be considered as a distinct group because the level, complexity, and multiplicity of their needs means that they are unlikely to benefit from programs and services designed for children who have less complex or less severe disabilities. Because of the nature of their disabilities, the usual assessment processes will provide little useful information about students with PMID, and they may need to be assessed by a multidisciplinary team using specialized assessment processes (Carnaby, 2007). The person's sensory and physical impairments are likely to interact in unpredictable ways with their cognitive impairments, and all of these areas will need to be considered in planning an optimal educational program. Indeed, there is an increasing focus on research and practice aimed at providing appropriate educational programs for students with PIMD in order to improve their lives and their ability to participate in classroom and life activities. As a result, students who were once regarded as needing only custodial care, who spent their lives in bed, in a wheelchair, or perhaps sitting on a beanbag chair, may now be found in a specially designed standing frame in a classroom, communicating with their teachers and peers through the use of a choice board or other augmentative and alternative communication (AAC) device (see Chapter 6).

FOR DISCUSSION AND REFLECTION:

- What impact does terminology have on the way we think about people with an intellectual disability?
- What are the advantages and disadvantages of the use of systems to classify people into categories of intellectual disability?

Changes to Classification Systems

Beyond changes in language, the first major change in classification of intellectual disability in nearly 100 years came in 1992 with the ninth edition of the then American Association on Mental Retardation's definitional manual (Luckasson et al., 1992). The change was a positive move away from classification by severity of the person's disability to a description of the extent of the supports the person needed. This was a major paradigmatic change, as it moved away from describing intellectual disability as a problem within the person toward describing the nature of the supports that are required for the person to function optimally, noting that the intensity of support needs is dynamic and changes across time. Thus it was not a simple substitute for the IQ-based system. A description of the supports needed is a description of the environment that must be provided if the student is to function optimally. Consequently, any failure can be seen as a failure of the system to provide an optimal environment rather than a failure within the student.

The use of a system to classify intensity of supports will be described in more detail later in this chapter. However, there are some who argue that the usual system of identifying and classifying people with an intellectual disability is a socially constructed myth. Smith (2003, p. 361), writing about the "myth of mental retardation," states that "The most positive paradigm shift might be the deconstruction of mental retardation. The best definition of mental retardation may be no definition." Smith argues for the use of the broader term *developmental disabilities,* suggesting that the "plurality of the term" (p. 361) would provide a better description of the heterogeneity of people classified as mentally retarded; that is, having an intellectual disability. However, as pointed out in Chapter 1, developmental disability includes physical impairments that have a significant impact on how the person functions. As a result, there are many people, for example with cerebral palsy, who would be described as having a developmental disability according to most definitions, but who do not have an intellectual disability. Whether the distinction between an intellectual disability and a developmental disability is useful is a matter for debate, and it may be that Smith's suggestion of a much broader term may in due course be taken up. It certainly would obviate the need to classify people as having an intellectual disability and could move the focus to the intensity of their support needs.

Arguing from the perspective of discursive psychology, Rapley (2004, p. 208) suggests that intellectual disability is a "disreputable moral status socially constructed, by psy [psychology/psychiatry] as a speakable truth about such persons." He argues that we should replace explanation with description and abandon typological thinking which, as Smith (2003) points out, implies that there is an "essence" of intellectual disability that denies the heterogeneity of the population it attempts to categorize. Rapley (2004, p. 208) recommends a respectful and helpful account of the competences and capacities of the person, free from "empty diagnostic categories and pseudo-science."

There is no doubt that many horrific acts have been committed as a result of the assessment and classification of people with intellectual disability (or mental retardation, mental deficiency, subnormality, or feeble-mindedness, to use previous terminology). As evidence that a disability can be socially constructed, the Grossman (1973) revision of the classification and terminology system, which increased the IQ cut-off from one to two standard deviations below the mean, changed the expected prevalence of intellectual disability from 15.86% to 2.27%. Suddenly, millions of so-called "borderline retarded" people no longer had this classification. Yet there are many stories of people who were classified in this way who ended up spending their lives in institutions as a result of behavioral problems that were unrelated to their intellectual ability. Tens of thousands of men, women, and children were sterilized as part of a eugenics movement, designed to eliminate genetic disorders. The fact that they met a particular classification or typology, however imperfectly assessed, removed their basic human rights and allowed them to be treated in a way that would be considered objectionable by most people.

Many of the decisions that are now looked on as totally unacceptable were made, at the time, by people who believed that they were doing the right thing by the people concerned and their families. With hindsight, we know how wrong they were, and we need to ensure that the same mistakes are not made again.

Despite the potential pitfalls in the assessment of levels of intelligence, it is difficult not to acknowledge that there are large variations in cognitive functioning, and that some people have physical, intellectual, and/or sensory impairments that necessitate specialized teaching, medical, therapy, and other services. Assessment of intelligence and associated adaptive functioning has been one way of ensuring that services go to those who are most in need, and are appropriately allocated. We need to ensure that any assessment that is done must be only for the person's benefit and is not used to restrict them in any way. The recent focus on assessment of support needs rather than a focus on intellectual level may help to ensure that this is so.

FOR DISCUSSION AND REFLECTION:

- What evidence is there that intellectual disability is, at least in part, socially constructed?

Assessing Intelligence

Despite the AAIDD's move away from classification by IQ, the definition of intellectual disability still contains reference to intellectual functioning, with explanatory notes referring to an IQ cut-off that is at least two standard deviations below the mean on "an appropriate assessment instrument" (Luckasson et al., 2002). On most current assessment instruments, this means an IQ of 70 or below. In addition, many professionals regard an accurate assessment of the child's intellectual functioning to be an essential part of understanding the child's cognitive problems, and planning for their needs.

Some of the problems involved with intelligence testing were highlighted in Chapter 1 and in the earlier part of this chapter. It is essential to realize that an IQ test result is simply that: the result of testing on a particular instrument on a particular day. We would not accept a numeracy test done when a child was 5 years old as something that defined his "mathematical ability" for the rest of his life—his "MQ"! Neither should we see an IQ result as something that is fixed, immutable, or even necessarily accurate. Intelligence is not measured directly by an intelligence test in the same way that we can use a test to measure blood pressure or cholesterol. At best, we infer someone's intelligence from how they perform on a test. Some critics of traditional tests suggest that intellectual ability should be assessed dynamically by observing how children learn in response to teaching rather than by how they respond in a static test (Borkowski, Carothers, Howard, Schatz, & Farris, 2007).

In the case of children who are thought to have an intellectual disability, an individually administered intelligence test, suitable for the child's age, will usually be selected. The test will need to be administered by a child psychologist or similar professional who is trained in test administration and who is skilled in assessing children who may have an intellectual disability. Such children will have problems with attention and concentration, and unless the test administrator is able to maximize the child's engagement with the test, the result will become a measure of the child's attention rather than a measure of their intelligence. This is particularly the case when children have serious disabilities or associated behavioral problems or attention deficits. A result obtained from a child who is not engaged or is uncooperative or inattentive will usually be meaningless as an assessment of the child's intellectual functioning. Children who have a neuromotor disorder such as cerebral palsy, which affects their speech and movement, can easily be misdiagnosed as having an intellectual disability. In order to be able to produce a valid assessment of a child with a severe disability and/or associated behavioral or sensory problems, a psychologist would normally need to specialize in assessing children with a disability.

Another example of the way test results can be misinterpreted is given by Rosenbaum (1998), who tells of a young boy with cerebral palsy and developmental delays whose mother was told, following a reassessment on a developmental scale, that her son's functioning was "deteriorating." In fact the child was continuing to develop and could do more than he had done on his previous assessment. However, because his development was at a much slower rate than other children, his centile rank had dropped (Rosenbaum, 1998), and this had been interpreted as deterioration in functioning.

Various instruments that are commonly used to assess intellectual functioning are discussed below. All of the instruments described in detail have been demonstrated to have good psychometric properties. That is to say that the design of the instrument, its content, and the procedures used to obtained population norms are such that, within the limitations that all such instruments possess, the instrument can be regarded as being both valid and reliable. If it is valid, it is measuring what it claims to measure—intelligence and/or its components. If it is reliable, it will yield similar results on different occasions and with different assessors. However, even instruments that have good validity and reliability and are administered by experts still provide results that may be affected by a statistic referred to as the Standard Error of Measurement (SEM). For example, the WISC IV (see later in this Chapter), a widely used intelligence test for school-aged children, has a reported SEM for its full-scale IQ (FSIQ) of 3 points. This means that if a child receives an FSIQ score of 70, there is a 95% chance that the correct IQ score is in the range of 67 to 73. There is also a 5% chance that it is outside this range.

Assessing Babies and Toddlers

Assessing intellectual and developmental functioning in infants is a very difficult task for a number of reasons. The problems referred to above related to attention and engagement are multiplied in infants and very young children. We all know instances of babies who can "wave bye-bye" or "clap hands" at home, but who refuse to do so when their parents try to get them to show off for relatives or friends. And we have all seen toddlers who take an hour or so to "warm up" before they will talk in front of strangers. If the assessment process takes an hour, the child may not have warmed up by the time the assessment is finished. In the hands of a skilled and experienced assessor, some of these barriers will be quickly broken down, but the assessment of very young children is a particularly challenging task, likely to lead to unreliable results in many cases.

Another problem in accurately assessing young children is that development does not occur in a smooth, linear fashion. An assessment of a child who is about to undergo a developmental spurt will be a poor predictor of future development and is likely to underestimate the child's potential. Again, we have all seen situations in which a child has little or no oral language at 18 months but is talking fluently by 2 years of age. Another child may have started to talk at 18 months but has made little further progress by age 2. Assessments of very young children should generally be regarded more as descriptions of current functioning than predictors of future performance.

The Bayley Scales of Infant Development (BSID) is an instrument that is widely used to assess the developmental level of children aged from 1 month to 42 months. Other widely used developmental tests are the Gesell Developmental Schedules and the Denver Developmental Screening Test. The BSID has been in wide use for 40 years, the first edition being published in 1969, the second in 1993, and the latest (BSID-III) in 2005 (Bayley, 2005). The BSID-III comprises five scales. The cognitive scale, motor scale, and language scale are completed through direct interaction with the child. The social-emotional scale and adaptive behavior scale are completed through parent interview.

Although developmental tests for infants are normally designed to provide a description of the child's current development, they often include standard scores, which have been interpreted by some as similar in nature to IQ scores, predictive of future intellectual development. The BSID-II for example, produced a Mental Developmental Index (MDI) and Psychomotor Developmental Index (PDI). In the BSID-II, the MDI and PDI were reported as standard scores with means of 100 and standard deviations of 15, as for IQ tests. It would be easy to interpret the MDI as an IQ measure, but there is evidence that this should be done with caution. For example, Hack and her colleagues (2005) followed a group of children with extremely low birth weight (ELBW) who had been assessed on the BSID-II at 20 months and on the Kauffmann Assessment Battery for Children at 8 years. They found that 80% of children who scored an MDI at a level suggestive of intellectual disability at 20 months had scores *above* this level by age 8. Hack et al. acknowledged that the Bayley scores may be a good indicator of children in need of special education services, but cautioned against their use to make decisions about medical treatment or policy. Alfonso and colleagues were critical of the inability of the BSID-II to provide MDI scores below 50, making it difficult to interpret scores for children with more severe disabilities (Alfonso, Russo, Fortugno, & Rader, 2005).

Perhaps for reasons related to the criticisms outlined above, the BSID-III no longer contains an MDI, although it does contain a Cognitive Composite Score. As it is a relatively new instrument, there are not yet any studies of its long-term predictive validity. Spittle, Doyle, and Boyd (2008) reviewed the "clinimetric" properties of the BSID-III and eight other infant assessment instruments and found the BSID-III to be clinically useful in assessing the neuromotor development of preterm infants in their first year. All tests that purport to measure cognitive performance or predict later performance need to be treated with caution. The younger the child, the greater the caution that is needed.

Most of the instruments used to assess babies and toddlers provide developmental evaluations that are based on normative comparisons with expected development. Heffelfinger and Koop (2009) have recently pointed to the need for instruments to be developed that could be used for neuropsychological assessments of young children with suspected disabilities. Such instruments would assess neuropsychological domains not normally included in developmental assessments, such as attention, executive functioning, and spatial skills. Heffelfinger and Koop suggest that accurate neuropsychological assessment could lead to an intervention plan that might help to ameliorate the long-term outcomes of particular neuropsychological problems.

Assessment of Intellectual Ability in Early Childhood

Individual assessment of intellectual ability of young children will usually be with the Wechsler Preschool and Primary Scale of Intelligence, Version III (WPPSI-III) (Wechsler, 2003b) or the Stanford Binet Intelligence Scales, Version 5 (SB-5) (Roid, 2003). Some of the 100-year history of the Binet scales was presented in Chapter 1. Although developed more recently, the Wechsler scales have a 60-year history. The use of the WPPSI-III and the Wechsler scale for older children, the Wechsler Intelligence Scale for Children version IV (WISC-IV) (Wechsler, 2003a), will be discussed later in this chapter.

Stanford Binet Intelligence Scales, Version 5 (SB-5)

Unlike the Wechsler scales, which have a preschool, child, and adult version, the SB-5 covers the age range from 2 years to 85+ years. The SB-5 covers five cognitive ability factors: fluid reasoning, knowledge, quantitative processing, visual-spatial memory, and working memory. Unusually, there are both nonverbal and verbal items for each of the five cognitive factors. For example, working memory is assessed by nonverbal items including block span, and verbal items including memory for sentences. Results are reported as a full-scale IQ, a verbal IQ and a nonverbal IQ, and as five factor-index scores, all having a mean of 100 and a standard deviation of 15.

A feature of the SB-5 is that while it has returned to the use of functional age levels, the separation of verbal and nonverbal items provides flexibility in the use and interpretation of the test results. For example, the nonverbal scales can be used by themselves for a child who has difficulties with expressive language, for whatever reason. This will give an estimate of the child's cognitive functioning, independent of expressive language. An interpretive manual allows psychologists and educators to consider whether the pattern of cognitive functioning revealed by the assessment has implications for the child's educational program or for teaching methodology. For example, the child's demonstrated learning strengths may be emphasized, and measures could be put into place to help overcome the effects of particular weaknesses.

The standard range of full-scale IQ scores on the SB-5 is from 40 to 160. However, an additional "Extended IQ" measure can be used to assess IQs as low as 10 (or as high as 225). This could prove useful when assessing very young children who may have an intellectual disability, particularly if scores below 40 can be shown to be valid and reliable estimates of cognitive functioning. Another advantage for young children with an intellectual disability is that assessment on the SB-5, which can take up to 75 minutes to administer in full, can be broken into sections administered over several days.

There was some dissatisfaction with the fourth edition of the Stanford Binet. Some practitioners were unhappy with its structure and format, while others had issues with the validity and reliability of the outcomes. For example, Couzens, Cuskelly, and Jobling (2004) provided evidence that some individuals with Down syndrome scored progressively lower IQs on the fourth edition when tested over a period of some years, with some people even moving from the mild range to the severe range of intellectual disability. Couzens and colleagues were concerned that these outcomes may have been an artifact of the test, rather than a reflection of deteriorating cognitive function. So far, the SB-5 has been well received by practitioners. It will be some time before it is known whether any issues such as those raised by Couzens et al. are associated with the fifth edition. With its toy-based items and capacity to start at a very early level, it is currently considered a useful instrument for assessing preschool-aged children suspected of having an intellectual disability.

Wechsler Preschool and Primary Scale of Intelligence, Version III (WPPSI-III)

The first WPPSI was published in 1967 as a downward extension of the highly successful Wechsler Intelligence Scale for Children (WISC). The WPPSI-III is designed for children aged 2 years 6 months to 7 years 3 months, which is a younger starting age than the previous two editions. The second edition (WPPSI-R) was published in 1989, and the third edition (WPPSI-III) in 2003 (Wechsler, 2003b). The WPPSI produces a full scale IQ and, for children aged 4 years and older, separate verbal and performance IQs. In addition, the WPPSI-III provides scores for processing speed and general language.

Until separate scales became available on the Stanford-Binet, the WPPSI was the preferred instrument for practitioners who wished to separate verbal and performance IQs, for example for children with aphasia or whose English language facility was limited. However, some studies of earlier editions have found performance IQ to be a poorer predictor of later academic performance than verbal IQ or full scale IQ (Kaplan, 1996). Other studies have suggested a 4-factor model as the best explanation of intelligence as measured by the WPPSI (Ottem, 2003). Ottem described these as two knowledge-dependent factors ("knowing how" and "knowing that") and two processing-dependent factors ("seeing how" and "seeing that"). The "knowing" factors made up the verbal scale of the WPPSI and the "seeing" factors formed the performance scale.

The 2003 WPPSI-III contains substantial changes from the previous edition, the WPPSI-R. Two subtests in the verbal scale, Arithmetic and Sentences, were discontinued, and three new subtests have been added: Receptive Vocabulary, Word Reasoning, and Picture Reasoning. In the performance scale, Geometric Designs, Mazes, and Animal Pegs were discontinued and four subtests were added: Coding, Matrix Reasoning, Picture Concepts, and Symbol Search. Interestingly, the discontinued subtests were mainly those described by Ottem (2003) as processing-dependent rather than knowledge dependent.

The decision on whether to use a WPSSI-III or the SB-5 will be made by a psychologist, based usually on observation of how the child is functioning, and the assessor's personal preferences. For example, if the child is very young and is likely to have a moderate or severe disability, the WPPSI may produce scores of zero on several subtests. The resulting IQ would not be a valid assessment of the child's intellectual functioning; the WPPSI-III is not usually recommended for children who may have a more severe intellectual disability. Sometimes, a school system, psychology service, or similar organization will have policy that determines the instrument to be used in particular circumstances. A review of the child's adaptive behavior ratings may help guide the decision as to whether the WPPSI-III is an appropriate instrument to use (Tylenda, Beckett, & Barrett, 2007). Veronica's story (Box 3.1) highlights some of the issues involved in assessing young children.

BOX 3.1 VERONICA'S ASSESSMENT

Veronica is aged 3 years 3 months and has been attending the neighborhood childcare center since she turned 3. Her teachers are worried about her, as she seems to be functioning more like a child of 18 to 20 months old than a 3-year-old. She is not yet toilet trained and needs assistance with eating. She uses only single words without putting them into sentences. She has difficulty playing simple games with other children, who are constantly complaining that Veronica has taken their toys or spoiled their game. The senior teacher talks to Veronica's mother, Mrs. T, who advises that she has consulted her family doctor who says that Veronica is just a "slow developer" and will probably soon have a developmental spurt. Mrs. T says that her mother-in-law has always said that Veronica's father, now a warehouse manager, was also a slow developer and that Veronica will "grow out of it." Mrs. T says that she has been worried about Veronica but has been discouraged by her mother-in-law from taking any action. The teacher suggests that Mrs. T discuss with her husband the possibility of arranging for Veronica to be assessed. Mr. & Mrs. T agree to the assessment, and the teacher refers Veronica to the center's visiting psychologist. Because of her age, Veronica is assessed using the Wechsler Preschool and Primary Scale of Intelligence, Version III (WPPSI-III). The psychologist finds that Veronica is very difficult to engage, and she loses concentration after about 10 minutes. The psychologist is unable to record a full-scale IQ in which she has any confidence. She seeks Mr.

and Mrs. T's permission to refer Veronica to a psychologist who specializes in assessing young children, with a request that Veronica be assessed on the Bayley Scales of Infant Development, Third Edition.

DISCUSSION QUESTIONS:

1. What indications were there that Veronica has developmental problems?
2. Why hadn't she been assessed before this?
3. Was the WPPSI-III an appropriate instrument to use? Why or why not?
4. Why was the BSID-III selected as an alternative assessment instrument?
5. Assuming the BSID-III indicated a possible intellectual disability, what would happen next?

Detailed information is available to assist with interpretation of various patterns of scores on the WPPSI-III (Lichtenberger & Kauffman, 2004). In the hands of a skilled assessor and interpreter of results, the WPPSI-III may provide an indication of areas that need attention in an educational program. For example, a child who had relatively good performance scores but had a much lower verbal IQ and general language scores might be given a program that was designed to help to develop his verbal and language skills, while at the same time giving him the opportunity to experience success through activities more related to those on the performance scale. However, as is explained in the next section, caution needs to be exercised to avoid overinterpreting the implications of various clinical profiles.

Assessing Intelligence in School-Aged Children

As indicated previously, the Stanford-Binet Fifth Edition (SB-5) can be used to assess people of all ages, and it is certainly a popular choice for assessing children of school age, particularly if they are suspected of having an intellectual disability. An alternative assessment instrument is the Wechsler Intelligence Scale for Children, Fourth Edition (WISC-IV) (Wechsler, 2003a).

The first Wechsler Intelligence Scale for Children (WISC) was published in 1949 (Wechsler, 1949). At that stage, the Stanford-Binet Scales were the individual intelligence test of choice for most psychologists, but the WISC provided an interesting alternative, with its division into full-scale IQ, verbal IQ and performance IQ outcomes, and the provision of subtest scores showing possible patterns of strengths and weaknesses. A revision (the WISC-R) was published in 1974, and a third edition (the WISC-III) in 1991. The current edition, WISC-IV, was published in 2003.

A major difference between the WISC-IV and the previous version is the movement away from the reporting of three main scores (verbal IQ, performance IQ, and full-scale IQ), plus four factor scores. These were replaced in the WISC-IV by the full-scale IQ score and four indices, similar to the previous factor scores:

- Verbal Comprehension Index: vocabulary, comprehension, and similarities subtests;
- Perceptual Reasoning Index: block design, picture concepts, and matrix reasoning subtests;
- Processing Speed Index: coding and symbol search subtests; and
- Working Memory Index: digit span and letter-number sequencing subtests.

Some of the subtests in WISC-IV were carried over from the WISC-III, while others were developed specifically for the fourth edition. It has been suggested that the change away from reporting verbal and performance IQ scores will be helpful in preventing possible misinterpretation of the implications of significant differences between verbal and performance results (Baron, 2005). Indeed, there is continuing debate about the interpretation of factor scores in the WISC and its successors. Experienced clinicians often find profile analysis to be diagnostically helpful, while statisticians seeking relationships between variables are more likely to be skeptical about such relationships (Charter, 2003; Stanton & Reynolds, 2000). A recent study by Freberg and colleagues has suggested that the full-scale IQ is the best predictor of later academic achievement in a special-education population, even in the presence of discrepant factor scores (Freberg, Vandiver, Watkins, & Canivez, 2008). The Freberg study was based on an archival data set of WISC-III results, but Freberg et al. believe that similar outcomes would result with the WISC-IV because of the consistency between the two versions of the test in the abilities being assessed. The debate will no doubt continue as more evidence on the WISC-IV becomes available (Baron, 2005; Mayes & Calhoun, 2004).

The WISC-IV has been generally welcomed by psychologists and is likely to receive wide usage for school-aged children. As it covers the age range 6–16 years, a choice can be made to use the WPPSI-III for children aged between 6 and 7 years, which would be preferred for children who are thought to have an intellectual disability. Like the WPPSI, the WISC-IV is not usually recommended for children suspected of having a moderate or severe intellectual disability. There is evidence that the WISC-IV may overestimate the IQ of some children, due to floor effects. This happens when children who score zero on subtests still end up with a measurable IQ score. There is also evidence of systematic underestimation of IQ scores in some groups (Whitaker, 2008). As a result, like any IQ scores, WISC-IV scores need to be treated with caution. They are the results on a particular test at a particular time. They may be helpful and informative, but they can also be misleading and inaccurate.

Assessing Students with Severe or Profound Multiple Disabilities

The instruments referred to above are unlikely to provide useful information about students described earlier in this chapter as having PIMD (profound intellectual and multiple disabilities). Following results on standard assessment instruments, such students will often have their IQs recorded as TLA (too low to assess), although occasionally, because of floor effects, a higher IQ will be recorded that bears no relation to the student's cognitive level. Neither of these outcomes is helpful in understanding the child's functioning or in preparing an educational program.

Some assessment devices have been designed specifically for students with more severe disabilities. For example, the Developmental Assessment for Students with Severe Disabilities, Second Edition (DASH-2), is designed to assess people with severe disabilities who are functioning developmentally between birth and 11 years (Dykes & Erin, 1999). According to its authors, the DASH-2 focuses on the person's strengths and can be used as an initial assessment instrument, a basis for curriculum planning, and as a means of monitoring progress. The DASH-2 does not fit neatly under any of the general headings for assessment devices used in this Chapter (intelligence, adaptive behavior, and support needs), and contains elements of each form of assessment, geared toward students with more severe disabilities. The DASH-2 (Dykes & Erin, 1999) should not be confused with the Diagnostic Assessment for the Severely Handicapped–II (DASH-II) (Matson, 1995)—see under Dual Diagnosis later in this chapter.

FOR DISCUSSION AND REFLECTION:

- Why are individual tests used if a child is thought to have an intellectual disability?
- Why is it difficult to assess the intelligence of very young children and children with multiple disabilities?
- Discuss the statement that a person's IQ may be just the result of one test on one day and therefore unreliable.

Assessing Adaptive Behavior

As explained in Chapter 1, the assessment of adaptive behavior has been part of the definition of intellectual disability provided by the American Association for Intellectual and Developmental Disability and its predecessors since 1961. The current AAIDD definition refers to "significant limitations both in intellectual functioning and in adaptive behavior as expressed in conceptual, social, and practical adaptive skills" (Luckasson et al., 2002). In other words, to be identified as having an intellectual disability, a person must not only score more that two standard deviations below the mean on an assessment of intelligence, but must also have significant problems in everyday functioning.

The measurement of adaptive behavior is conceptually quite different from the assessment of intelligence. In assessing intelligence, we are trying to form an indirect estimate of a person's cognitive functioning from their response to various items designed to measure factors that are thought to indicate how intelligent the person is. For example, we may obtain an indication of the capacity of their working memory by testing the length of the number span they can remember. However, we cannot be 100% certain that this estimate will be valid if the person needs to use their working memory under different conditions. By contrast, measurement of adaptive behavior is a process of assessment of how the child currently functions in everyday life. Adaptive behavior is more directly observable than intelligence. Measurement of adaptive behavior is based on information about how the child operates in his environment.

Another difference between assessing intelligence and adaptive behavior is that an intelligence test requires the child to be present, to cooperate with the tester, and to complete tasks within a particular time slot. From the child's performance, an inference is made about her *current* cognitive functioning, which is regarded as predictive of her *future* cognitive functioning. Typically, information on adaptive behavior is gathered from informants who are familiar with the child, so there is no need for the child to be present when this occurs or to cooperate in any way with the process. The informant is usually a parent or primary caregiver, but for some instruments it can be a teacher or other professional who knows the child well. The informant will be asked questions such as, "Does she talk to someone she knows on the phone?" "Does she turn on a TV set?" "Does she drink from a glass without assistance?" From the responses to dozens of questions such as these, organized into behavioral domains and age-related sequences, an estimate is made of the child's current level of adaptive functioning, compared with that of other children of a similar age, and a picture is built up of the child's current functional level.

The use of an informant or rater makes some assumptions about the ability and willingness of the informant to provide accurate information. The child is not being directly observed, so there is nothing to prevent the informant from exaggerating (or underestimating) the child's adaptive functioning. However, the instruments discussed below report high reliability scores and are regarded as having satisfactory psychometric properties.

The current AAIDD definition of intellectual disability refers to three dimensions of adaptive behavior: *conceptual* skills (e.g., communication skills, language, academic skills), *social* skills (e.g., social interaction, social problem solving, leisure skills) and *practical* skills (e.g., personal care, self-help, daily living skills, safety, travel). Luckasson et al. (2002) point out that these are not the only factors that have emerged from factor-analytic studies of adaptive behavior, but argue that they are generally supported by research on the construct of adaptive behavior. The earlier (1992) AAMR definition of intellectual disability included 10 areas of adaptive behavior (Luckasson et al., 1992), while others have suggested that the number of factors could be as few as just one (Bruininks, McGrew, & Maruyama, 1988). Schalock suggests that there are "most likely" five factors: personal independence, responsibility, cognitive/academic performance, physical/developmental competencies, and vocational/community skills (Schalock, 2004). Evidence from the normative data of the Adaptive Behavior Scales (Second Edition) (Lambert, Nihira, & Leland, 1993) suggests a 2-factor model (Watkins, Ravert, & Crosby, 2002) (see discussion of ABS-IIS, below).

To meet the AAIDD definition of significant limitations in adaptive behavior, a child must be assessed as being at least two standard deviations below the mean in one of the three dimensions (conceptual, social, or practical) or in overall adaptive behavior. This means their adaptive behavior would be in the bottom 3%, or below the third percentile, for their age. If the instrument provides standard scores with a mean of 100 and standard deviation of 15, the adaptive behavior score would be below 70.

Adaptive behavior will tend to be highly correlated with intelligence for most people, as adaptive behavior is an indication of how well the person has learned the skills of everyday living, and the ability to learn is correlated with results on intelligence tests. This is likely to be particularly so for conceptual skills, which is the aspect of adaptive behavior most closely related to intellectual ability. However, there are some people whose adaptive behavior is much better than would be predicted by a result on an intelligence test (see Box 1.2 in Chapter 1). Such people should not be identified as having an intellectual disability if their everyday functioning suggests that they don't have one. Adaptive behavior measurement is intended to act as a "fail-safe" provision for people whose intelligence is incorrectly assessed or whose ability to function in society is better than their IQ would predict. It is most crucial for people whose measured IQ is around the 60 to 70 mark, as these are the people whose identification as having an intellectual disability is most likely to be contradicted by their adaptive behavior.

Several different instruments have been developed to measure adaptive behavior. Some of the most frequently used measures will be discussed below.

FOR DISCUSSION AND REFLECTION:

- Discuss the statement that measures of adaptive behavior are more direct measures than measures of intelligence.
- What could lead to discrepancies between adaptive behavior scores and IQ scores?

Adaptive Behavior Measures

AAMR—Adaptive Behavior Scales

The development of the Adaptive Behavior Scales (ABS) is reflective of changing terminology in intellectual disability. The first version was produced by the American Association on Mental Deficiency in 1969, the second by the American Association on Mental Retardation in 1993, and the third is due to be released by the American Association on Intellectual and Developmental Disabilities in 2010. The current edition (ABS-II) has two versions: a residential and community version, and a school version (Lambert et al., 1993). The residential version does not have comparative norms for people without a disability, so cannot be used as part of the diagnosis of intellectual disability. The school edition does have comparative norms, so it can be used to determine whether a person has "significant limitations" in adaptive behavior, when compared with the rest of the population. The school version (ABS-IIS) will be the focus of the discussion in this chapter.

The ABS-IIS is designed to be completed by the teacher, parent, or other person who knows the child well. Assessment yields results for 16 subtests across five domains in two parts. This structure is outlined in Table 3.2. However, factor analytic research by Watkins and colleagues on the normative data of the ABS-IIS led to the suggestion that, rather than the five factors outlined in Table 3.2, the outcomes are best understood as two factors: personal independence and social behavior (Watkins et al., 2002).

TABLE 3.2 Domains and Factors of the AAMR Adaptive Behavior Scales, Second Edition (School Version) (1993)

PART 1: Personal Independence			PART 2: Personality/Behavior		
	Factors			Factors	
Domains	Lambert	Watkins	Domains	Lambert	Watkins
Independent functioning Physical development	Personal self-sufficiency	Personal independence	Social behavior Conformity Trustworthiness	Social adjustment	Social behavior
Economic activity Language development Numbers and time	Community self-sufficiency		Stereotyped and hyperactive behavior Self-abusive behavior	Personal adjustment	
Prevocational/vocational activity Self-direction Responsibility Socialization	Personal-social responsibility		Social engagement Disturbing interpersonal behavior	Other	

The factors comprise the two parts of ABS-IIS, as shown in Table 3.2. Thus, Watkins et al. are not arguing against the structure of the instrument but rather against the subdivision into factors. This means that in interpreting the results for educational or programming purposes, it may be wiser for teachers to consider the child's performance in the two broad areas of personal independence and social behavior, rather than basing programs on differences among the five factors shown in Table 3.2, as these may not be unidimensional domains. However, functional difficulties that show up in particular items or subtests may still provide useful indications of areas that need attention in curriculum or programming, either for the child or the class. For example, if children were showing more difficulty relative to other tasks at items relating to handling or understanding money, this might suggest an area to which classroom attention could be directed.

Diagnostic Adaptive Behavior Scale

The AAIDD is in the final stages of development of the Diagnostic Adaptive Behavior Scale (DABS), which is due for release in 2010 (Bersani et al., 2008). The DABS will replace the ABS-II and is designed to measure the AAIDD adaptive behavior dimensions of conceptual, social, and practical skills from the 2002 definition of intellectual disability (Luckasson et al., 2002). Like most other adaptive behavior scales, the DABS will use information from a respondent who is very familiar with the person, and will translate raw scores into a developmental level based on population norms. The instrument will take into account cultural differences in adaptive behavior and will allow clinicians to make a judgment about whether factors unrelated to intellectual disability have limited the child's ability to learn or to demonstrate adaptive behavior typical of their age. Adaptive behavior needs to be recognized as a culture-specific construct (Schalock, 2004). For example, if a child is part of a culture where the expectation is that she won't leave the house unaccompanied, she may have less opportunity to display skills of practical independence, such as travel skills. Other personal factors will also impact on adaptive behavior. A child who has a speech impairment unrelated to intellectual disability may not use the telephone, but this is not because he lacks the conceptual ability to do so.

The developers of the DABS are very clear that the purpose of the instrument is specifically to assist in the diagnosis of intellectual disability and not as a basis for planning interventions or for assessing the effectiveness of interventions (Bersani et al., 2008). It will therefore focus primarily on the IQ range where differential diagnosis is crucial (around 70 IQ) and is being designed as a brief and precise test that can differentiate between the adaptive behavior of people with and without an intellectual disability to determine eligibility for specific services. It will involve a "tailored testing" approach that allows items to be selected that, while still based on normative sampling, are relevant to the person's life situation. The instrument is currently (2009) in its final developmental stages.

Vineland II—Adaptive Behavior Scales

The Vineland Adaptive Behavior Scales, Second Edition (V-II) were developed from the Vineland Social Maturity Scale, which was produced by Edgar A. Doll of the Vineland Training School, and was first published in 1935. Doll's instrument was designed to determine the "fitness of patients" for training courses. The Social Maturity Scale was replaced in 1984 by the Vineland Adaptive Behavior Scales, Interview Edition (VABS-I) (Sparrow, Balla, & Cicchetti, 1984). The Classroom Edition (VABS-C) was published in 1985. The VABS-I and VABS-C were replaced in 2005 by the V-II, which, in its various forms, is the current edition (Sparrow, Cicchetti, & Balla, 2005). A table showing the age ranges for the V-II compared with the previous edition is provided in Table 3.3.

The V-II is available in a variety of formats. The Expanded Interview Form is the most in-depth form and is recommended for use when assessing very young children and those suspected of having a more severe disability. The Survey Interview Form requires a semistructured interview with a parent or caregiver. The Survey Parent/Caregiver Rating Form requires the parent or caregiver to complete a rating scale and does not require face-to-face contact with the informant. The Teacher Rating Form can be completed independently by the child's teacher.

TABLE 3.3 Age Range and Domains of the Vineland Adaptive Behavior Scales (1984/5; 2005)

	VABS (1984/5)		V-II	
	• Interview Edition • Survey Form • Expanded Form	• Classroom Edition	• Survey/ Interview • Expanded Interview • Parent/ Caregiver Rating Form	• Teacher Rating Form
Ages	0–18 years, 11months	3–12 years, 11months	0–90 years	3–21years, 11months
Domains	Communication, Daily Living Skills, Socialization, Maladaptive Behavior (optional)			

The Vineland Scales are well-regarded by professionals and are among the most popular of the adaptive behavior scales. As well as being used to identify the adaptive component of intellectual disability, they are often used for program planning and research (Dixon, 2007). For example, as suggested with the ABS-IIS, a teacher or psychologist may use the outcomes of the Vineland to suggest areas of adaptive behavior that could be the focus of the child's Individualized Educational Plan. "Teaching to the test" is not considered to be a problem here, as items on adaptive behavior scales are the sorts of behaviors that are regarded as valuable to learn, and teachers would generally broaden them from the items on the scale. If the child is unable, for example, to name the current day of the week (a task normally accomplished by 7-year-olds), but is able to do other tasks at around that age level or just below, it may suggest that items related to the calendar and knowing what day it is could become learning goals. If the child subsequently does better at "days of the week" items on an adaptive behavior assessment, this cannot be considered to be a bad thing.

The 1984 Vineland has been used extensively in research on people who have autism associated with intellectual disability. The findings are generally that people with autism have greater impairment in adaptive behavior than other people with a similar level of intellectual disability (Carpentieri & Morgan, 1996; Kraijer, 2000). Measurement of adaptive behavior may therefore assist in the diagnosis of autism. A microanalysis of Vineland scores by Paul and her colleagues(2004) suggested that subtests of the Vineland were able to distinguish between children with autism and children with what is known as Pervasive Developmental Disorder Not Otherwise Specified (PDD-NOS). People with PDD-NOS have problems with communication and stereotypical behavior, but do not meet diagnostic criteria for autism. Their identification is therefore difficult and Paul et al. suggest that analysis of Vineland scores could not only assist with diagnosis, but could provide suggestions for intervention.

The research by Paul et al. predated the latest edition of the Vineland—the V-II. The V-II has not yet been extensively researched but appears to have been improved by additional items to measure facility with spoken language and ability to maintain social relationships (Dixon, 2007). The extended age range for the Teacher Rating Form—up from 12 years 11 months to 21 years 11 months—will be helpful for educators working with older students or young adults.

Scales of Independent Behavior, Revised

Along with the Adaptive Behavior Scales-IIS and the Vineland II, the Scales of Independent Behavior-Revised (SIB-R) is among the most widely used instruments for assessing the adaptive behavior of people suspected of having an intellectual disability. The original version was published in 1984, and the revised version appeared in 1996 (Bruininks, Woodcock, Weatherman, & Hill, 1996). The SIB-R can be used from infancy through to old age.

Unlike the forthcoming DABS, which makes a virtue of having a single purpose (diagnosis of intellectual disability), the SIB-R claims usefulness in program development and evaluation, individual monitoring of progress, and in research classification, as well as in identifying the level of adaptive behavior for diagnostic purposes. For example, the available materials include an Individual Plan Recommendation form, which is designed to be used to track a person's support and service needs and goals. A summary of the 14 adaptive behavior clusters of the SIB-R is provided in Table 3.4. Luckasson et al. (2002) regard the SIB-R's Social Interaction & Communication Skills, Personal Living Skills, and Community Living Skills clusters as appropriate for assessing the social, practical, and conceptual domains of adaptive behavior, according to the 2002 AAIDD (AAMR) definition. There is also a separate checklist for problem behavior.

The SIB-R is available in interview and checklist form, and there is also an early development form, which makes provision for special circumstances that impact on the ability to demonstrate adaptive behavior, such as physical disability or the use of adaptive and alternative communication systems. The SIB-R provides norms that allow comparison with the general population and is regarded as having good psychometric properties (Dixon, 2007). Like other currently available scales, computer-based systems are available to assist with scoring, analysis, and report writing.

TABLE 3.4 Adaptive Behavior Clusters for the Scales of Independent Behavior, Revised (1996)

Motor Skills	Social Interaction & Communication Skills	Personal Living Skills	Community Living Skills
• Gross motor • Fine motor	• Social interaction • Language • Comprehension • Language expression	• Eating and meal preparation • Toileting • Dressing • Personal self-care • Domestic skills	• Time and punctuality • Money and value • Home/ community orientation

Battelle Developmental Inventory, Second Edition

Practitioners who are seeking an instrument that assesses adaptive behavior more directly in young children could use the Battelle Developmental Inventory, Second Edition (BDI-II) (Newborg, 2004). This is suitable for children up to the age of 8 years and requires the assessor to observe the child responding to instructions and performing tasks on request. Some information is also obtained from the parent/s. Because it involves direct assessment, the BDI-II is quite time-consuming and can take from 1 to 2 hours to administer, although a briefer screening version is also available. Direct assessment overcomes problems of informant reliability, and the BDI-II has been evaluated as having good psychometric properties (Dixon, 2007). Shevell and his colleagues studied a cohort of children who had been assessed using the BDI at age 3 as having a global developmental delay, and were then reassessed at age 7. They found that children who had an early diagnosis of developmental delay tended to continue to have functional and developmental problems at age 7 (Shevell, Majnemer, Platt, Webster, & Birnbaum, 2005).

FOR DISCUSSION AND REFLECTION:

- Why are the results of adaptive behavior tests more likely to be used in children's educational programs than the results of IQ tests?
- How might cultural differences impact on adaptive behavior outcomes?
- Choose a particular age level relevant to your teaching. What are some adaptive behaviors that would indicate typical achievement for a child or student of that age?

Assessing Support Needs

Earlier in this chapter it was mentioned that a paradigmatic change occurred in 1992 when the AAMR (now AAIDD) moved toward classifying a person's disability by a description of the extent of the supports the person needed, rather than by a description of their deficits. In order to assist with the assessment of support needs, the AAIDD published the Supports Intensity Scale (SIS) (Thompson et al., 2004), which had been developed by a team of 10 experts in the field of intellectual disability. In describing the development of the SIS, Thompson and his colleagues defined support needs as

> Resources and strategies that promote the interests and welfare of individuals and that result in enhanced personal independence and productivity, greater participation in an interdependent society, increased community integration and or improved quality of life (p. 390).

The SIS can be used as a planning tool to assess the daily needs and longer-term goals of a person with an intellectual disability and to identify the supports that will help the person achieve those goals. Thompson et al. (2002, p. 391) suggest a 4-stage process in dealing with support needs:

1. Identify desired life experiences and goals;
2. Determine the intensity of support needs;
3. Develop the individualized support plan; and
4. Monitor progress.

While the SIS was designed to be used with adults, that is, people aged 15+ years, there is no reason for a similar model not to be used with school-aged students. Indeed, the support-needs approach has been advocated in schools for some years. For example, as long ago as 1995, David Mitchell, a special educator from New Zealand, outlined a 5-level support system for children with additional educational needs. The various levels described the supports the child needed in order to function optimally in an educational environment (Mitchell, 1995). Such supports could include curriculum modification, small group teaching, therapy support, assistive technology, and other teaching adaptations. A more detailed explanation of the range of classroom supports that might be provided to a student with an intellectual disability is included in Chapter 6.

A problem with the assessment of support needs is that there is room for considerable subjectivity on the part of the assessor. Support-needs assessments tend to involve value judgments by raters. Assessment of support needs is often associated with the provision of funding so that those needs can be met, and there is some evidence that students will be rated as having higher support needs if higher ratings lead to higher funding (Guscia, Harries, Kirby, & Nettlebeck, 2006). Some might argue that this doesn't matter, as the more funding received the better, but resources are always limited and, in the long run, if one student receives more than their entitlement, another will receive less. Better rater reliability will normally occur if raters are trained and experienced (Thompson, Tasse, & McLaughlin, 2008).

The concept of support needs as the focus of assessment is one that is viewed positively by people with a disability and their advocates. There is still some debate about whether the measurement of adaptive behavior and measurement of support needs are reciprocals of the same construct (Harries, Guscia, Nettlebeck, & Taplin, 2005). In other words, do low scores on adaptive behavior scales always mean high support needs, and vice versa? However, regardless of the answer to this question, it is likely that the supports model will continue to develop. Luckasson et al. (2002) point out that the supports paradigm reflects a shift in thinking in education and rehabilitation that is characterized by

- a focus on person-centered planning, which emphasizes personal growth and development, choices, decisions, and empowerment;
- an ecological approach to disability that stresses the power of person-environmental interactions . . . ;
- a quality revolution that emphasizes personal well-being, quality of life and valued outcomes; and
- the provision of services and supports in natural environments, based on the principles of inclusion and equity (p. 146).

FOR DISCUSSION AND REFLECTION:

- What are the potential benefits of focusing on support needs as part of assessment?

Dual Diagnosis

People with an intellectual disability are as susceptible to psychiatric or mental illness and behavioral disturbances as other members of the community, possibly more so. Sometimes psychiatric problems will be masked by the syndrome that has led to intellectual disability. For example, David, a 15-year-old with Down syndrome, has become reluctant to participate in family activities, spends a large amount of time in bed, and is generally unhappy and difficult to get along with. It would be easy to attribute his change in mood and behavior to his syndrome—"That's what happens when you have Down syndrome." However, if he didn't have Down syndrome, it is quite likely that David would be diagnosed as having depression, which would probably be treated through reference to an appropriate psychological or psychiatric service. In David's case, it appears that he has the *dual diagnosis* of Down syndrome and depression; it is just as important to treat his depression as it would be if he didn't have Down syndrome.

There are various causes of psychiatric or behavioral problems in people with an intellectual disability. Sometimes psychiatric problems will arise from the person's experiences as a person with a disability. People with a mild or moderate disability are particularly likely to be aware of functional and life experience differences between themselves and the general population and to be sensitive to feelings of loneliness and rejection that may lead to depression. Some people with an intellectual disability have difficulty dealing with stressors in the environment and may respond aggressively if they are teased by others about their disability or suffer other disappointments. In other cases, the particular disability predisposes the person to certain behavioral problems (Einfeld, 2005). For example, people with Fragile X syndrome sometimes develop self-injurious or autistic behaviors. If a person's intellectual disability has been caused by abuse or maltreatment, this abuse may also predispose them to later psychiatric illness. And people with intellectual disability have at least the same risk as other people in the general population of having a genetic or biochemical abnormality that will lead to a psychiatric illness such as anxiety disorder, clinical depression, or schizophrenia.

Prevalence and Diagnosis

Estimations of the prevalence of psychiatric illness in populations with an intellectual disability are difficult, for some of the reasons mentioned above. Many such illnesses are undiagnosed or masked by the disability. Kerker and her colleagues have conducted a large-scale review of studies of mental health disorders of people with an intellectual disability in the United States (Kerker, Owens, Zigler, & Horwitz, 2004). They found prevalence difficult to estimate because of methodological limitations in research and because of the difficulties experienced by health care providers in diagnosing psychiatric illness. However, there appeared to be a consensus in the studies they reviewed that there is a higher prevalence of some mental health disorders in people with intellectual disability than in the general population. For example, children with intellectual disability are more likely than the general population to have anxiety disorders, and adults with intellectual disability have a greater chance than the general population of being diagnosed with a psychotic disorder.

There has been a large amount of professional interest over recent years in the identification and treatment of people with the dual diagnosis of intellectual disability and psychiatric disorder, mental illness, or behavioral disturbance. For example, in the United States, the National Association for the Dually Diagnosed has developed supplementary criteria to assist health care professionals to more accurately diagnose mental illness in people with an intellectual disability, based on the 2000 revision of DSM-IV. In Australia, an instrument in the form of a checklist for assessment of behavioral and emotional disturbance in people with an intellectual disability has received wide acceptance (Einfeld & Tonge, 1995). A short form of this checklist has recently been published (Taffe et al., 2007). In the UK, the Royal College of Psychiatrists has produced diagnostic criteria to assist in the identification of adults who have a psychiatric disorder associated with an intellectual disability (Royal College of Psychiatrists, 2001). There are also many checklists and rating scales for the assessment of self-injurious and aggressive behavior in students with an intellectual disability (Rojahn, Whittaker, Hoch, & Gonzalez, 2007). Other scales that are more likely to be used with older persons or adults thought to have a dual diagnosis include the Mini Psychiatric Assessment Schedule for Adults with Developmental Disability (Mini PAS-ADD) (Prosser et al., 1998), the Diagnostic Assessment for the Severely Handicapped-II (DASH-II) (Matson, 1995), and the Assessment of Dual Diagnosis (ADD) (Matson & Bamburg, 1998).

The Teacher's Role in Dual Diagnosis

Teachers are certain to play a significant role when one of their students is thought to have a dual diagnosis of intellectual disability and psychiatric or behavioral disturbance. It is likely to be the teacher who observes behaviors in the classroom that are causing concern or is contacted by a parent who is worried about their child's behavior or emotional state. The teacher would make a referral to the school psychologist or other health care professional so that further assessment can take place. It is probable that the teacher will be involved in the diagnostic process. She may be asked to observe the child in the classroom and make anecdotal notes or keep a running record of his behavior. She may be asked to undertake structured observations, such as counting or timing the number of aggressive outbursts that occur on a daily basis. She may even be asked to complete a diagnostic checklist such as the Reiss Scales for Children's Dual Diagnosis (Reiss & Valenti-Hein, 1990).

Once the diagnosis has been made, the teacher will also be part of the follow-up program. This might involve checking that the child is taking his medication, if appropriate; monitoring any changes that have occurred in his behavior or mood; and participation in a program of positive behavior support (see Chapter 6). Psychotropic medications (medicines prescribed to change behavior) often have unwanted side effects. Teachers are well-positioned by their experience, training, and intensity of contact with the child to watch for such side effects and report them to the child's parents or doctor. In most cases, the child's dual diagnosis will impact on his individualized educational program (IEP). Ideally, the child's mental health professional/s and parents will be part of the support team that develops his program.

FOR DISCUSSION AND REFLECTION:

- Why are psychiatric illnesses often undiagnosed in people with an intellectual disability?
- What is the teacher's role in dual diagnosis?

Summary

The identification, assessment, and classification of students with an intellectual disability are important but controversial processes. In the past such processes have produced negative outcomes for many children, some of which have lasted a lifetime. Professionals involved in the assessment process need to ensure that the purpose and outcome of any assessment is to benefit the person being assessed. To assess suspected intellectual disability, an individual intelligence test such as the Stanford-Binet, Fifth Edition or Wechsler Intelligence Scale for Children, Fourth Edition will be administered by a trained and experienced psychologist. If the results suggest intellectual disability, this needs to be confirmed by an assessment of the child's adaptive behavior using an instrument such as the Vineland-II or the Scales of Independent Behavior, Revised. There has also been a recent focus on assessment of a person's support needs as an important component of diagnosis and classification. Teachers should also be alert to the possibility that their students who have an intellectual disability may also have a psychiatric illness or behavioral disturbance that requires careful assessment and intervention.

References

Alfonso, V. C., Russo, P. M., Fortugno, D. A., & Rader, D. E. (2005). Critical review of the Bayley Scales of Infant Development–second edition: Implications for assessing young children with developmental delays. *The School Psychologist, 2005*(Spring), 67–73.

Baron, I. S. (2005). Test review: Wechsler Intelligence Scale for Children–fourth edition (WISC-IV). *Child Neuropsychology, 11*, 471–475.

Bayley, N. (2005). *Bayley Scales of Infant and Toddler Development.* San Antonio, TX: The Psychological Corporation.

Bersani, H., Tasse, M. J., Schalock, R., Balboni, G., Duffy, S. A., Scherba de Valenzuela, J., et al. (2008). The development of the Diagnostic Adaptive

Behavior Scale, *IASSID World Congress on Intellectual Disability*. Cape Town: IASSID.

Borkowski, J. G., Carothers, S. S., Howard, K., Schatz, J., & Farris, J. R. (2007). Intellectual assessment and intellectual disability. In J. W. Jacobson, J. A. Mulick, & J. Rojahn (Eds.), *Handbook of intellectual and developmental disabilities* (pp. 261–278). New York: Springer.

Bruininks, R., McGrew, K., & Maruyama, G. (1988). Structure of adaptive behavior in samples with and without mental retardation. *American Journal of Mental Retardation, 93*, 265–272.

Bruininks, R., Woodcock, R. W., Weatherman, R. F., & Hill, B. K. (1996). *Scales of independent behavior–revised*. Itasca, IL: Riverside.

Carnaby, S. (2007). Developing good practices in the clinical assessment of people with profound intellectual disabilities and multiple impairment. *Journal of Policy and Practice in Intellectual Disabilities, 4*(2), 88–96.

Carpentieri, S., & Morgan, S. B. (1996). Adaptive and intellectual functioning in autistic and nonautistic retarded children. *Journal of Autism and Developmental Disorders, 26*(6), 611–620.

Charter, R. A. (2003). A cautionary note on deviation scores for the WISC-III and WAIS-III. *Journal of Clinical Psychology, 59*(7), 787–790.

Couzens, D., Cuskelly, M., & Jobling, A. (2004). The Stanford Binet fourth edition and its use with individuals with Down syndrome: Cautions for clinicians. *International Journal of Disability, Development and Education, 51*(1), 39–56.

Dixon, D. R. (2007). Adaptive behavior scales. In J. L. Matson (Ed.), *Handbook of assessment in persons with intellectual disability*. London: Academic Press.

Dykes, M. K., & Erin, J. (1999). *DASH-2: An assessment and programming instrument for individuals with severe disabilities* (2nd ed.). Austin, TX: ProEd.

Einfeld, S. (2005). Behaviour problems in children with genetic disorders causing intellectual disability. *Educational Psychology, 25*(2–3), 341–346.

Einfeld, S., & Tonge, B. J. (1995). The developmental behaviour checklist: The development and validation of an instrument to assess behavioural and emotional disturbance in children and adolescents with mental retardation. *Journal of Autism and Developmental Disorders, 25*, 81–104.

Freberg, M. E., Vandiver, B. J., Watkins, M. W., & Canivez, G. L. (2008). Significant factor variability and the validity of the WISC-III full-scale IQ in predicting later academic achievement. *Applied Neuropsychology, 15*, 131–139.

Grossman, H. J. (Ed.). (1973). *A manual on terminology and classification in mental retardation* (Rev. ed.). Washington, DC: American Association on Mental Deficiency.

Guscia, R., Harries, J., Kirby, N., & Nettlebeck, T. (2006). Rater bias and the measurement of support needs. *Journal of Intellectual and Developmental Disability, 31*(3), 156–160.

Hack, M., Taylor, H. G., Drotar, D., Schluchter, M., Cartar, L., Wilson-Costello, M. D., et al. (2005). Poor predictive validity of the Bayley Scales of Infant

Development for cognitive function of extremely low birth weight children at school age. *Pediatrics, 116*(2), 333–341.

Harries, J., Guscia, R., Nettlebeck, T., & Taplin, J. (2005). Support needs and adaptive behavior. *American Journal on Mental Retardation, 110*(5), 393–404.

Heffelfinger, A. K., & Koop, J. I. (2009). A description of preschool neuropsychological assessment in the PINT clinic after the first 5 years. *The Clinical Neuropsychologist, 23*, 51–76.

IASSID Special Interest Research Group on PIMD. (2008). Special Interest Research Group: Profound Intellectual and Multiple Disabilities: http://seocura.org/IASSID/Index.html. Accessed February 2, 2009.

Kaplan, C. (1996). Predictive validity of the WPPSI-R. *Psychology in the Schools, 33*(3), 211–220.

Kerker, B., Owens, P. L., Zigler, E., & Horwitz, S. M. (2004). Mental health disorders among individuals with mental retardation: Challenges to accurate estimates. *Public Health Reports, 119*, 409–417.

Kraijer, D. (2000). Review of adaptive behavior studies in mentally retarded persons with autism/pervasive developmental disorder. *Journal of Autism and Developmental Disorders, 30*(1), 39–47.

Lambert, N., Nihira, K., & Leland, H. (1993). *AAMR Adaptive Behavior Scale-School and Community*. Austin TX: Pro-Ed.

Lichtenberger, E. O., & Kauffman, A. S. (2004). *Essentials of WPPSI-III assessment.* Hoboken, NJ: John Wiley & Sons.

Luckasson, R., Borthwick-Duffy, S., Buntinx, W., Coulter, D., Ellis, C., Reeve, A., et al. (2002). *Mental retardation: Definition, classification and supports* (10th ed.). Washington, DC: American Association on Mental Retardation.

Luckasson, R., Coulter, D., Polloway, E. A., Reiss, S., Schalock, R., Snell, M., et al. (1992). *Mental retardation: Definition, classification and systems of supports* (9th ed.). Washington, DC: American Association on Mental Retardation.

Matson, J. L. (1995). *The Diagnostic Assessment for the Severely Handicapped–II.* Baton Rouge, LA: Scientific Publishers.

Matson, J. L., & Bamburg, J. W. (1998). Reliability of the assessment of dual diagnosis (ADD). *Research in Developmental Disabilities, 19*, 89–95.

Mayes, S. D., & Calhoun, S. L. (2004). Similarities and differences in Wechsler Intelligence Scale for Children–third edition (WISC-III) profiles: Support for subtest analysis in clinical settings. *The Clinical Neuropsychologist, 18*, 559–572.

Mitchell, D. (1995). New Zealand special education policies and systems. In D. Fraser, R. Moltzen, & K. Ryba (Eds.), *Learners with special needs in Aotearoa/New Zealand.* Palmerston North, NZ: Dunmore Press.

Newborg, J. (2004). *Battelle Developmental Inventory–II.* Scarborough, ON: Thomas Nelson.

Ottem, E. (2003). Confirmatory factor analysis of the WPPSI for language impaired children. *Scandinavian Journal of Psychology, 44*, 433–439.

Paul, R., Miles, S., Cicchetti, D., Sparrow, S., Klin, A., Volkmar, F., et al. (2004). Adaptive behavior in autism and Pervasive Developmental Disorder-Not Otherwise Specified: Microanalysis of scores on the Vineland Adaptive Behavior Scales. *Journal of Autism and Developmental Disorders, 34*(2), 223–228.

Prosser, J., Moss, S., Costello, H., Simpson, M., Patel, P., & Rowe, S. (1998). Reliability and validity of the Mini PAS-ADD for assessing psychiatric disorders in adults with intellectual disability. *Journal of Intellectual Disability Research, 42,* 264–272.

Rapley, M. (2004). *The social construction of intellectual disability.* Cambridge, UK: Cambridge University Press.

Reiss, S., & Valenti-Hein, D. (1990). *Reiss scales for children's dual diagnosis: Test manual.* Orlando Park, IL: International Diagnostic Systems.

Roid, G. H. (2003). *Stanford Binet Intelligence Scales* (5th ed.). Itasca, IL: Riverside Publishing.

Rojahn, J., Whittaker, K., Hoch, T. A., & Gonzalez, M. L. (2007). Assessment of self-injurious and aggressive behavior. In J. L. Matson (Ed.), *Handbook of assessment in persons with intellectual disability.* London: Academic Press.

Rosenbaum, P. (1998). Screening tests and standardized assessments used to identify and characterize developmental delays. *Seminars in Pediatric Neurology, 5*(1), 27–32.

Royal College of Psychiatrists. (2001). *The diagnostic criteria for psychiatric disorders for use with adults with learning disabilities/mental retardation.* London: Gaskell Press.

Schalock, R. (2004). Adaptive behavior: Its conceptualization and measurement. In E. Emerson, C. Hatton, T. Thompson, & T. Parmenter (Eds.), *The international handbook of applied research in developmental disabilities* (pp. 369–384). Chichester, UK: John Wiley & Sons.

Shevell, M., Majnemer, A., Platt, R. W., Webster, R., & Birnbaum, R. (2005). Developmental and functional outcomes at school age of preschool children with global developmental delay. *Journal of Child Neurology, 20*(8), 648–654.

Smith, J. D. (2003). Abandoning the myth of mental retardation. *Education and Training in Developmental Disabilities, 38*(4), 358–361.

Sparrow, S., Balla, D., & Cicchetti, D. (1984). *Vineland Adaptive Behavior Scales.* Circle Pines, MN: American Guidance Service.

Sparrow, S., Cicchetti, D., & Balla, D. (2005). *Vineland II-Vineland Adaptive Behavior Scales* (2nd ed.). Circle Pines, MN: AGS Publishing.

Spittle, A. J., Doyle, L. W., & Boyd, R. N. (2008). A systematic review of the clinimetric properties of neuromotor assessments for preterm infants during the first year of life. *Developmental Medicine and Child Neurology, 50,* 254–266.

Stanton, H. C., & Reynolds, C. R. (2000). Configural frequency analysis as a method of determining Wechsler profile types. *School Psychology Quarterly, 15,* 434–448.

Taffe, J. R., Gray, K. M., Einfeld, S., Dekker, M. C., Koot, H. M., Emerson, E., et al. (2007). Short form of the Developmental Behaviour Checklist. *American Journal on Mental Retardation, 112*(1), 31–39.

Thompson, J. R., Bryant, B. R., Craig, E., Campbell, E., Hughes, C., Rotholz, D., et al. (2004). *Supports Intensity Scale.* Washington, DC: American Association on Mental Retardation.

Thompson, J. R., Hughes, C., Schalock, R., Silverman, W., Tasse, M. J., Bryant, B., et al. (2002). Integrating supports in assessment and planning. *Mental Retardation, 40*(5), 390–405.

Thompson, J. R., Tasse, M. J., & McLaughlin, C. A. (2008). Interrater reliability of the Supports Intensity Scale. *American Journal on Mental Retardation, 113*(3), 231–237.

Tylenda, B., Beckett, J., & Barrett, R. P. (2007). Assessing mental retardation using standardized intelligence tests. In J. L. Matson (Ed.), *Handbook of assessment in persons with intellectual disability* (pp. 27–97). London: Academic Press.

Watkins, M. W., Ravert, C. M., & Crosby, E. G. (2002). Normative factor structure of the AAMR Adaptive Behavior Scale–school, second edition. *Journal of Psychoeducational Assessment, 20,* 337–345.

Wechsler, D. (1949). *The Wechsler Intelligence Scale for Children.* New York: The Psychological Corporation.

Wechsler, D. (2003a). *Wechsler Intelligence Scale for Children* (4th ed.). San Antonio, TX: The Psychological Corporation.

Wechsler, D. (2003b). *Wechsler Preschool and Primary Scale of Intelligence* (3rd ed.). San Antonio TX: The Psychological Corporation.

Whitaker, S. (2008). WISC-IV and low IQ: Review and comparison with the WAIS-III. *Educational Psychology in Practice, 24*(2), 129–137.

World Health Organization. (1992). *ICD-10. International classification of diseases and behavioural disorders.* Geneva: Author.

4

Early Intervention

Overview: This chapter deals with research and practice concerning early educational and therapeutic intervention for children with intellectual disability, either from the time of diagnosis or as a preventative measure. Model programs are described, and research on the efficacy of early intervention is discussed. Early intervention is examined both as an attempt to change the developmental process and as a regular part of the educational cycle. The chapter also covers transition to school.

Background

Until around 40 years ago, it was commonplace for some children with intellectual disability to start formal education later than other children. For example, in some Australian state education systems, the general school starting age was 5 years, but government special school services for children with intellectual disability did not start until children were aged 6. The rationale for this difference was that, as these children were "delayed" in their development, they would have greater "readiness" to participate in educational programs if the start of their schooling was also delayed. In some jurisdictions, special services for children with mild intellectual disability were delayed until they were aged 8.

Education of Students with an Intellectual Disability, pages 97–124

Early intervention is based on the opposite rationale. Any observer of child development will conclude that the first months and years of a child's life are the time when development is occurring faster than at any other time thereafter. Between birth and the age of 6, children will typically learn to walk, talk, sing, skip, run, and manage most aspects of their own personal care. Many will have developed skills of literacy and numeracy. Over the second 6 years these skills will be further refined and extended, but never again will there be a period of such extraordinary development and change as occurs in the first 6 years of life. Early intervention programs attempt to capitalize on the potential of the early developmental years by providing educational, therapeutic, and related services from the earliest possible time, sometimes from birth or even during pregnancy.

In broad terms, there have been three different target groups for early intervention programs. One target group has been the children referred to in Chapter 2 as being at risk of having "cultural-familial intellectual disability" and whose environment is less likely to promote educational success. The second target group is children who are identified as having a disability or a syndrome or condition associated with intellectual or other disability. A third group is those children whose development has been identified as being delayed, regardless of whether a cause has been identified. The second and third groups tend to be catered to in the same programs, and a child could be a member of all three groups. For example, a child could be from a deprived background, have an identified disability, and be identified as having a developmental delay. Early intervention programs also aim to assist children who do not have an intellectual disability but have a language, emotional, behavioral, sensory, or physical problem.

While government policy and practice have been supportive of the wide-scale provision of early intervention programs, there remains considerable debate about their impact on children and families (Dunst, 2007). For example, Dunst provides evidence suggesting that early intervention that is service centered rather than family centered is unlikely to have a substantial impact on the child and may even have negative outcomes. Research on early intervention will be discussed later in this chapter.

FOR DISCUSSION AND REFLECTION:

- Why has there been a change in attitudes toward the optimal age to begin educational programs for children who are likely to have developmental delays?

Overcoming Environmental Disadvantage

In the 1960s there was increasing acknowledgement of the importance of the early developmental years, as referred to above, and a recognition that environmental circumstances could impact either positively or negatively on development. It was recognized that children who were living in poverty were sometimes multiply disadvantaged by the time they started school. In addition to having possibly inherited a lower-than-average potential level of intelligence, they may have lived in a household that contained no books, where no stories had been read to them, and where their diet and nutrition were less than optimal. In addition, they almost certainly would not have had access to a high quality preschool program. They may have had poorer access to medical services, and their parents would have been less likely to be knowledgeable about child development. The cycle of poverty was therefore destined to continue as, other than in extraordinary circumstances, these children were unlikely to succeed at school and to proceed to college.

Large-Scale Government Programs: Head Start

A program that was specifically aimed at overcoming the negative effects of poverty on children was Head Start, which began in 1965 in the United States as part of President Lyndon Johnson's War on Poverty. The program was designed to provide comprehensive child development services for children aged 3 to 5 years from low-income families, and continues to operate. In 1994 the reauthorization of the Head Start Act extended the program downwards to infants and toddlers through the Early Head Start program (Fenichel & Mann, 2001). Families are provided with a range of educational, health, nutritional, and psychological services. The cost of the Head Start program in 2008 was $7 billion, and almost a million children were involved in the program. The average annual cost of the program per child per year is around $7000 to $9000 (Ludwig & Phillips, 2008).

A recent study of the long-term effects of the Head Start program by public policy analysts concluded that the program is effective, from a benefit to cost perspective (Ludwig & Phillips, 2008). Ludwig and Phillips argue against making major changes to the program; debates nevertheless remain about its content, form, and outcomes. For example, since a primary objective of Head Start is prevention of reading failure, it has been suggested that Head Start teachers may need to have more training in the teaching of emerging literacy skills including phonological awareness (Hawken, Johnston, & McDonnell, 2005). Another recent study suggests that children's cognitive capacities could be improved by teaching them specific executive function skills, including utilization of working memory, inhibitory control, and attention set shifting (Bierman, Nix, Greenberg, Blair, & Domitrovich, 2008). They suggest that if instructional strategies in Head Start focus too narrowly on memorization of discrete content, they may "miss the mark, developmentally" (p. 822).

Head Start provides a Child Outcomes Framework, which is designed to guide staff in their assessment of children's development and progress. The outcomes are organized into eight general domains, with 27 elements and 100 indicators of development and accomplishment. Sample domains, elements, and indicators are outlined in Table 4.1. While there is general support for children from disadvantaged backgrounds having the benefit of high quality early childhood programs, there is no clear evidence that the Head Start program has prevented disability in a systematic way. Differences in IQ found in early studies comparing children in Head Start programs with children in control groups tend to have dissipated by the time the children are of school age. However, it is likely that many children have received a better educational start, and some children have avoided the need for special education services as a result of the program. There is also evidence of less criminality and less need for social services (Majnemer, 1998). It is also the case that many children with intellectual disability will have been identified through their participation in Head Start and referred to more specialized intervention services.

Model Programs

Following are descriptions of two model programs that began 35 to 40 years ago in the United States. The programs were designed to see whether it was possible to overcome the negative effects of an economically and socially deprived background through provision of a high quality preschool program. There are now many other such programs, but the two described are among the oldest and best known, and are generally regarded as having a sound research base. Both projects used a process of random assignment of children into treatment and control groups. This is a desirable experimental process, but one that would be difficult to replicate today for similar groups. There would be both legal and ethical impediments to placing a random selection of children into a "no program" group, as there is a general expectation that all children will receive the best early education program available.

Perry Preschool Project

The Perry Preschool School began in1962 as a research-based effort to see whether provision of a high-quality preschool program would have an

TABLE 4.1 Head Start Domains and Elements

Sample Domain	Elements	Sample Indicator
Language development	Listening & understanding	Understands an increasing complex and varied vocabulary
	Speaking & communicating	Uses an increasing complex and varied spoken vocabulary
Literacy	Phonological awareness	Shows growing awareness of beginning and ending sounds of words
	Book knowledge & appreciation	Shows growing interest and involvement in listening to and discussing a variety of fiction and nonfiction books and poetry
	Print awareness and concepts	Shows increasing awareness of print in classroom, home, and community settings
	Early writing	Develops understanding that writing is a way of communicating for a variety of purposes
	Alphabet knowledge	Identifies at least 10 letters of the alphabet, especially those in their own name
Mathematics	Numbers & operations	Develops increasing ability to count in sequence to 10 and beyond
	Geometry & spatial sense	Progresses in ability to put together and take apart shapes
	Patterns & measurement	Begins to make comparisons between several objects based on a single attribute
Approaches to learning	Initiative & curiosity	Develops increased ability to make independent choices
	Engagement & persistence	Grows in ability to persist in and complete a variety of tasks, activities, projects, and experience
	Reasoning and problem solving	Develops increasing abilities to classify, compare, and contrast objects, events, and experiences
Other domains: Science; Creative Arts; Social & Emotional Development; Physical Health & Development		

Adapted from: Head Start Child Outcomes Framework: Screening and Assessment in Head Start, 2001. Head Start Bulletin #70 DHHS/ACF/ACYF/HSB

impact on the educational and life outcomes of African American children from disadvantaged backgrounds. Over the years 1962 to1967, 123 children aged 3 and 4 were randomly allocated either to a preschool program based on a participatory learning approach or to a comparison group that received no preschool program. Children in the treatment group received

12.5 hours a week of preschool for 2 years, which was combined with a weekly home visit to assist parents with parenting skills.

The mean Stanford-Binet IQs of the two groups on entry were almost identical at 79.6 (treatment) and 78.5 (control). By age 5, the treatment group had a significantly higher mean IQ at 95 compared with 84 for the control group, but these differences had disappeared by age 15, with both groups testing with mean IQs in the early 80s. However, there did appear to be some enduring educational benefits for the preschool group. Only 15% of the treatment group spent a year or more in special education programs for students with mild intellectual disability, compared with 34% of the control group. The program group also had significantly higher school achievement at age 14 and significantly higher literacy scores at age 19 (Schweinhart & Weikart, 1993).

The most recent report on outcomes for the 1962–1967 group compared progress at age 40 (Nores, Belfield, Barnett, & Schweinhart, 2005). Surprisingly, some differences remained between the groups, even 35 years after they had finished in the program. In particular, the number of people with zero arrests for various crimes was significantly better for the treatment group than for the control group. In some respects, this might be expected if the treatment group had higher school achievement, as it is well known that crime rates are related to school achievement. However, for such differences to persist more than 35 years after an educational intervention suggests that if the effects are replicable, that early intervention of this type has the potential to be extraordinarily powerful. Indeed, Nores et al. (2005) calculated that the return on investment was from $6 to $13 for each dollar spent on the Perry Preschool Project.

Nevertheless, despite the apparent long-term social and educational benefits arising from being part of the preschool program, there was no evidence of long-term effects on intellectual ability or disability for the group, although such effects on individual participants are possible.

Abecedarian Project

The Abecedarian Project (ABC project) began in 1972 at the Frank Porter Graham Center, University of North Carolina. It differed from the Perry Preschool Project both in the additional intensity of the intervention provided and in the early age of commencement. Children started in the ABC project at 4 to 6 months of age (compared with 3 to 4 years for Perry) and received intervention in a full-time preschool program, 5 days per week for 50 weeks per year. Children were selected for the project on the basis of demographic variables, which placed them at very high risk of school failure. Parental income was 50% of the federal poverty line, maternal education was low, and most parents were single and unemployed. The average maternal IQ was around 80, and 98% of the group were African American. Children were not included if they had a medical or other condition known to be associated with intellectual disability.

The 111 children were randomly assigned to treatment (57) or control (54) groups. All families were provided with nutritional advice and support, social service support, and access to free or low-cost primary health care. The difference for the treatment group was that these children were enrolled in the intensive early intervention program described above. The program was provided by well-trained staff, with low student:staff ratios. The study was based on the theory that developmental outcomes result from interactions between a number of systems involving the child, the family, the school, and society (Campbell & Ramey, 1994). The intervention utilized a specially developed curriculum providing seven types of experiences designed to optimize normal brain and behavioral development and school readiness (Ramey & Ramey, p. 473, 2004), namely,

- Encourage exploration;
- Mentor in basic skills;
- Celebrate developmental advances;
- Rehearse and extend new skills;
- Protect from inappropriate disapproval, teasing, and punishment;
- Communicate richly and responsively; and
- Guide and limit behavior.

Assessment on individual intelligence tests from age 3 years to age 21 years revealed higher scores for the treatment group at all ages. At age 3 the difference was around 16 points; by age 21 around 5 points. While the IQs and the differences between groups declined over time, differences in IQ were found to be significant both in the preschool period and in the follow-up period (Campbell, Pungello, Miller-Johnson, Burchinal, & Ramey, 2001). Significant long-term positive treatment effects were also found in reading and math achievement, although both groups showed a relative decline in mathematics achievement, compared with national norms, over time (Campbell et al., 2001). There were also other long-term benefits for the treatment group. They were less likely to be placed in a special education class, less likely to repeat a grade, more likely to be enrolled in higher education, and more likely to delay the onset of parenting (Ramey, Ramey, & Lanzi, 2007).

Barnett and Masse recently completed a cost-to-benefit comparison of the Perry Preschool Program and the ABC project. The ABC project was, of course, particularly expensive to run, as it was provided on a full-time basis over several years, with high staff input and comprehensive additional services provided to both treatment and control groups. However, the full-time model of operation provided a financial benefit to families by removing the cost of childcare and providing opportunities for mothers to seek full-time employment, an opportunity not provided in the Perry Program (Barnett & Masse, 2007). Clearly if parents are employed and not drawing social security, there is an overall financial benefit to the nation. The researchers calculated a cost-benefit ratio of $1:$9 for the Perry Program and $1:$2.5 for ABC. In other words, while the ABC project was much more expensive to operate than the Perry Program, it still provided an overall benefit that was more than double the cost of the program.

An important question arising from the study of early intervention programs is whether a child's IQ is itself modifiable by such a program. The results from the Perry Program suggest that, in groups of at-risk children, IQs may be modifiable in the short term but not in the long term. ABC results with similar groups suggest that some differences may carry through into adulthood. There does appear to be clear evidence that both programs reduced the significant likelihood that "treated" children would be in special education classes.

A criticism that could be made of the ABC project is that, while successful, it achieved this success by taking over a large part of the parental educational and nurturing role from a very early age. Not only was this extremely expensive and therefore difficult to replicate on a widespread basis, it did nothing to enhance parental capacity and competence, which is now seen as an important aspect of early intervention (Dunst, 2007). The ABC and Perry programs provide strong evidence of ongoing benefits to children in the projects, but Dunst has expressed concern that other less extensive or intensive early intervention programs and programs that focus on children with disabilities use ABC and Perry results as indefensible justification for the efficacy of service-based intervention (p. 171).

FOR DISCUSSION AND REFLECTION:

- What have been the general outcomes of research on overcoming environmental disadvantage?
- To what extent is early intervention a form of interference with normal child rearing?

Intervening to Overcome the Effects of Disability

The Head Start, Perry, and Abecedarian programs were focused on overcoming the effects of disadvantage. As a result of the programs, it is likely that some children who otherwise would have been identified as having a mild intellectual disability were not so identified, and the programs could therefore be said to have prevented intellectual disability in some children. However, children in these programs were chosen because of their environmental circumstances, not because they had a syndrome or other medical condition associated with the risk of intellectual disability. The ABC program, for example, eliminated such children from their study, as their focus was on overcoming the effects of poverty. At about the same time as the programs designed to overcome the effects of poverty were starting, other researchers in intellectual disability were wondering whether early educational intervention could alter the developmental pattern of children known to be at high risk of having an intellectual disability or whose development was already delayed.

Some of the earliest programs aimed at reducing intellectual and other disability were targeted specifically at children with Down syndrome (Gunn, Berry, & Andrews, 1979; Hayden & Dmitriev, 1975). Subsequently, the majority of programs, but not all of them, have become noncategorical, catering to young children with a range of disabilities and syndromes. Some programs have targeted children with a disorder in the autism spectrum (see later in this Chapter), while others have endeavored to prevent possible adverse effects of prematurity and low birth weight (Bonnier, 2008; Brooks-Gunn, Klebanov, Fong-ruey, & Spiker, 1993). Examples of programs in various categories are given below.

Intervention Programs for Children with Down Syndrome

Children with Down syndrome (DS) were an early focus of intervention programs for young children at risk of intellectual disability. They presented as ideal candidates for intervention. For a start, they were a well-identified group with a clear diagnosis, whose intellectual characteristics were quite well understood. Most children with Down syndrome are assessed as having a moderate level of intellectual disability, with individual quotients typically in the 40 to 50 IQ range.Yet practitioners had observed that children with DS who had been raised in large, poor quality, institutions were often assessed as having a severe degree of intellectual disability, while some other children with DS, often from a stimulating home background, tested with only a mild disability. Was it possible that a stimulating early intervention program could alter the typical developmental pattern?

Pioneering work in the provision of educationally based early intervention programs for young children with Down syndrome took place at the University of Washington Model Preschool Center (Hayden & Dmitriev, 1975). The program was based on the concept of sequential development, with new skills being built on those already acquired. The evaluation process was to use each child as their own control: the number of developmental skills acquired by the child was monitored as a percentage of the number expected in a typically developing child, based on scales of normal development. However, the instrument on which the children were assessed formed the basis of their curriculum, so it could not necessarily be concluded that the developmental gains would generalize to skills other than those that had been specifically taught.

In another early study, Ludlow and Allen (1979) investigated the effects of early intervention through a research project that included most children with Down syndrome born over a 10-year period in an English county. A total of 192 children were studied in three groups: a home-reared group receiving early intervention; a home-reared group not receiving outside assistance; and a group of children institutionalized shortly after birth. It was found that children receiving early intervention showed significantly less decline in developmental quotient than children in the other two groups and were less likely to require special education than children in the two control groups (Ludlow & Allen, 1979).

Less positive outcomes were reported by Piper and Pless (1980), who found no differences on the Griffiths Developmental Scales between an experimental group of 21 young children with Down syndrome who had received early intervention over a 6-month period, and 16 children who had not received any intervention. This study was criticized by early intervention advocates because of the small sample and the brevity of the intervention (Bricker, Carlson, & Schwartz, 1981; Ludlow, 1980). Cunningham, also working in the early days of intervention research, provided evidence that appropriate teaching and parental support could accelerate the acquisition of skills in children with Down syndrome (Cunningham, 1979).

Even in the early days of intervention for young children with Down syndrome, concerns were expressed about whether parents were being given unrealistic expectations, whether infants were overstimulated, whether maturation was sufficiently considered, and whether benefits justified costs (Denhoff, 1983; Graves, 1978). There was also concern about the implication that stimulation would somehow grow new brain cells (Ferry, 1981). However, the source of most educationally based early intervention programs is in behavioral and developmental psychology and does not make assumptions about changes in neurology. Nevertheless, it is possible that some parents of babies with Down syndrome gained the impression that enough time and effort spent in early intervention would remove their child's intellectual disability, an expectation that was very likely to be disappointed.

Despite the debates and controversy, which have continued, early intervention in various forms is offered to most children in developed countries who are born with Down syndrome. Researchers have continued to investigate optimal ways for this to be presented and focused. For example, because of the language difficulties experienced by many children with Down syndrome, many studies have researched ways of stimulating early language development (Sanz Aparicio & Balana, 2002; Thomson, Cotnoir-Bichelman, McKerchar, Tate, & Dancho, 2007). Other studies have sought to assist inclusion in regular classes by focusing on academic and reading readiness skills such as phonological awareness (Buckley, 2003; van Bysterveldt, Gillon, & Moran, 2006).

A common feature of much of the recent research on early intervention in Down syndrome has been a focus on the pivotal role of parents in their child's development (Pretis, 2000; Rix & Paige-Smith, 2008; Van Hooste & Maes, 2003). Some parents of children diagnosed at birth (or before) as having a syndrome associated with significant intellectual disability are likely to face challenges in their normal parent-child interactions, and this is certainly the case when a baby is diagnosed with Down syndrome. Research has suggested that the most effective interventions will be those that promote and support the parents' relationship with their child, and increase parents' competence and confidence (Dunst, 2007; Majnemer, 1998) (see Box 4.1). This issue is discussed further later in this chapter.

BOX 4.1 ADAM'S STORY

Adam is Marnie and David's second child. Their first child, Lyndie, was 3 when Adam was born and was looking forward to having a new sister or brother. Both in their late 20s, Marnie and David were not in a risk category for Down syndrome and had no specific prenatal testing other than nuchal translucency testing in the 14th week of pregnancy. Although this placed them at slightly higher risk, they felt that more intrusive tests were unwarranted and their obstetrician supported this decision. Adam was born 8 days early after a straightforward pregnancy and labor. David was present at the birth and they both remember the anxiety they felt when the head nurse and obstetrician went into hurried conference after examining the newborn child. They still remember the obstetrician's words: "You have a beautiful little boy, but I have to tell you we are fairly certain he has Down syndrome. He also has lots of back hair like his daddy, and a very healthy cry." Adam was later confirmed as having standard Trisomy 21 (see Chapter 2), and the head nurse provided Marnie and David with a letter from the local Down Syndrome Association inviting them to make contact at any time to discuss options available to assist Adam. When Adam was 3 weeks old, Marnie decided to make an appointment to see a social worker, Alice, at the Down Syndrome Association (DSA). Alice explained that there were many support options that Marnie and David could use as they saw fit. These included a daytime playgroup, a discussion group for fathers, a home-based early intervention program, and a center-based program for children 2 to 3 years old, which could be combined with home visits. The usual goal was enrollment in a regular preschool by age 4, with continued home-based support, as requested, from the DSA. No decisions needed to be made yet, and decisions could be changed at any time. Marnie enjoyed her visit with the DSA. She was particularly happy when she observed the program for 3-year-olds to see the children playing in the sandpit, building with blocks, and playing with cars in a toy town. Lyndie joined in with three little girls at a make-believe tea party and, while their language was not as developed as Lyndie's, they communicated with each other and Lyndie joined in the conversation.

DISCUSSION QUESTIONS:

1. What do you think about the hospital's treatment of Adam's birth and diagnosis? What was positive about it? Was there anything negative about it?
2. What about the approach of the DSA? Did this take into account the need to focus on the need to foster parental competence and competence? (The second "competence" seems to want an adjective, otherwise is seems a non sequitur.)
3. Why do you think Marnie enjoyed seeing the program for 3-year-olds in operation?

Programs for Children with Autism

The term "autism spectrum disorder" (ASD) is used to describe children (and adults) who, while they differ in many ways, all demonstrate marked qualitative deficits in social and communicative behavior and have a restricted range of activities and interests (Dawson, 2008). Because the characteristics of ASD are usually identified and described in behavioral terms, it seems plausible that programs designed to change children's behavior could impact positively on the number of autistic behaviors they exhibit, and therefore reduce their autism. In most children with autism, the disorder is not identified until the children are at least 1 to 2 years of age. Perhaps if the likelihood of a particular child developing autism could be identified in very young infants, programs could be implemented that would mean that autism could be prevented or reduced (Dawson, 2008).

One of the first and most influential early intervention programs aimed at changing the behavior of young children with autism was reported by Lovaas (1987). Lovaas reported the outcomes of two programs for young children with autism, both starting before the children were aged 3.5 years. In one program, 19 children received an intensive home-based behavioral intervention program for 40 hours per week (treatment group). In the control group, 17 children received a less intensive intervention. The treatment group was reported to have shown significant gains in IQ and social functioning when compared with the control group (Lovaas, 1987). A follow-up study reported that the gains were maintained at 11.5 years, and several 11-year-old children who had received the "best outcomes" as preschoolers were not identified as having autism by assessors who were unaware of their group status (McEachin, Smith, & Lovaas, 1993).

The Lovaas program has sparked much interest and discussion, both in the United States and internationally. In the UK, for example, Remington and his colleagues have recently reported the outcome of a 2-year home-based early intervention program for children with autism using an intensive Lovaas-type applied behavioral analysis (ABA) program for approximately 25 hours per week. They found significant differences after 2 years favoring the intensive ABA group in IQ scores, language skills, daily living skills, positive social behavior and "best outcome." While mean IQs for both the treatment group and a comparison group were around 62 at commencement, there was a 13-point difference at the end of 2 years, with the mean IQ score for the ABA group at 73 and for the comparison group at 60 (Remington et al., 2007).

While Lovaas's claims of improvements in IQ and reduction or elimination of autistic behavior have not been empirically refuted, there has been criticism of both the financial and personal cost of providing an intensive, home-based program for up to 6 hours per day. Lovaas has also been criticized for claims that complete recovery from autism is possible (Tews, 2007). On the other hand, applied behavioral analysis, as practiced by Lovaas, has been widely accepted as an effective treatment for children with autism. In their study, Remington et al. (2007) did not find that the intensive behavioral programs led to problems for the parents of the children receiving them.

There have been many other more conservative approaches to early intervention for children with autism. For example, the Treatment and Education of Autistic and related Communication Handicapped Children (TEACCH) program focuses on individualized assessment and structured teaching (Mesibov, Shea, & Schopler, 2006). The goal is not to remove the child's autism but rather to assist children to understand the world around them, to communicate, to learn skills for adult life, and to become independent. Levy, Kim, and Olive (2006) reviewed interventions for young children with autism and concluded that those that had the largest effect sizes shared three characteristics:

a. They focused on a variety of areas including language, behavior management, and social skills.
b. They were intensive and lasted a long time.
c. They involved the children's parents (Levy, Kim, & Olive, 2006).

The fields of developmental neuroscience, psychopathology, neurobiology, and genetics are all contributing to our understanding of autism spectrum disorder and how it develops in individual children (Dawson, 2008). It is likely that, in the future, we will be able to identify in early infancy those children who are at high risk, genetically, of developing an ASD. This will be before the infants have displayed any behaviors suggestive of autism. Early intervention may by then be aimed specifically at making best use of early brain plasticity to prevent, rather than treat, autism.

Other Types of Early Intervention Programs

The majority of early intervention programs available nowadays are noncategorical in nature. That is to say, they cater to children with any form of disability or any syndrome that is known to be associated with a disability. Some specialized programs still exist to cater to children with specific disabilities such as blindness, deafness, autism, or cerebral palsy. These are often sponsored and/or managed by associations that support parents of children with such disabilities. However, most programs cater to children who have one or more of a wide spectrum of disabilities. Thus, a single program may, for example, enroll children with cerebral palsy, sensory impairment, spina bifida, autism, Down syndrome, and developmental delay of unknown cause.

Because of the wide range of disabilities found among children in an early intervention program, no teacher will have expertise in all areas. Ideally, a teacher will have qualifications in special education and in early childhood education and will have received supervision and training related to working with young children with disabilities. In many situations, the advice of other professionals such as occupational therapists, physical therapists, and speech therapists will assist in the preparation of teaching programs.

Early intervention programs follow many different operational models. Some are home-based, some are center-based, and some provide a mixture of both. A child may visit a center anywhere from 1 morning a week to 4 or 5 days per week. Home visits may occur several days a week, as in the Lovaas program, once a week, once or twice a month, or never. Home visits may focus on parent education and support or on working directly with the child, or both. Programs may follow an applied behavioral analysis model, a play-based model, a cognitive model, a parent support model or an eclectic mixture of these approaches. There is a diversity of views as to what is the optimal program, and all varieties have their proponents. Some further research and practice issues related to the provision of early intervention services are discussed later in this chapter.

FOR DISCUSSION AND REFLECTION:

- What impact does early intervention appear to have on the development of children with Down syndrome?
- Does the Lovaas program appear to be too intrusive? How successful would it need to be to justify the cost and the time commitment?

Legislative and Policy Basis for Early Intervention

The apparent impact of early intervention on the prevention or amelioration of disabilities has led governments in most developed countries to develop policy or legislation to help make early intervention available to all children with identified disabilities or developmental delays. When early intervention programs started around 35 years ago, they tended to be university based and were accessible to only a small portion of the children with potential to benefit from them. Parents needed to be living near a university program and to be aware of its existence. Often they needed to provide their own transport and pay a service fee.

That situation has now changed dramatically. In 1986 in the United States, Part C of the Individuals with Disabilities Education Act (IDEA) commenced funding the provision of comprehensive early intervention programs for babies and toddlers aged birth to 2 years. The goals of Part C were to enhance the development of children with disabilities, reduce the need for later special education, reduce the risk of institutionalization, enhance the capacities of families, and increase the likelihood of the child becoming able to live independently. All states now provide such services, and in 2005, 2.4% of the population of children under 3 were participating in Part C programs (Hebbeler et al., 2007). This is about the number that would be expected if the program was accurately targeting all children with significant risk of a substantial developmental disability. Part B of the Act provides for early intervention services for children from 3 to 5 years old, and currently around 5% of that age group in the United States are receiving early intervention services.

Under current legislation in the United States, early childhood intervention is expected to follow "family-centered practice" and take place in "natural environments" (U.S. Congress, 2004). Under family-centered practice, the child must be considered as part of a complex family system. Natural environments are ones that are typical of other children of a similar age. Thus placing a young baby into the full-time care of "experts" in an experimental program would meet neither criterion. Under Part C of IDEA, each child is required to have an Individual Family Service Plan (IFSP), which outlines the child's current level of development, the family's priorities, the expected outcomes for the program, and the services the child needs in order to achieve those outcomes. A service coordinator must be appointed, and there must be a transition plan to assist the child's smooth passage into preschool services.

Although most developed countries make a range of early intervention services available to young children with identified disabilities or identified risk of disability, it is not usually mandated in the way that it is in the United States. For example, in Australia there is no legislation mandating the universal availability of early childhood intervention services. All states have accepted responsibility for such services and have developed policies for how they will be funded and supported. The most common model is for state funding of services through a community group, disability association, or university-affiliated organization. States receive much of their funding through a Commonwealth-State Disability Agreement, and through this, the federal government influences the way in which disability services, including early intervention, are provided in each state. The federal government also has the capacity to introduce national initiatives such as a recent announcement of support for the funding of early intervention services for young children with autism.

FOR DISCUSSION AND REFLECTION:

- How did some of the first early intervention programs depart from "family-centered practice"?

Issues in Early Intervention Research and Practice

Early intervention for young children with disabilities has been a controversial area of research and practice, sometimes associated with extravagant claims and limited evidence. One of the earliest sources of controversy, the Milwaukee Project, began in the 1960s. The project identified 40 children from poor backgrounds whose mothers had an IQ below 75, and provided half of the children with a highly intensive center-based preschool program over several years. Mothers were also assisted in gaining vocational skills and employment. The Milwaukee Project was criticized by Page and Grandon (1981) as "more a media event than a scientific exercise" (p. 240). However, the Milwaukee researchers' claims of up to 30-points increase in IQ as a result of intervention were highly influential and were quoted frequently in support of funding for early intervention services (Page & Grandon, 1981). Page and Grandon hypothesized that the reported differences in IQ may have resulted from a narrow instructional program focusing on specific tasks from early developmental tests and from practice in the kinds of tasks contained in tests of intelligence. If that was the case, the test results would not have provided a valid estimate of cognitive functioning.

Despite the criticisms, the Milwaukee Project continues to be cited as evidence of the impact of early intervention (Ramey et al., 2007), and the project had the positive outcome of encouraging increased governmental support for early childhood programs for children from disadvantaged backgrounds. A disadvantage of the program is that it may have encouraged a "we will take your child and fix him" approach among early intervention proponents. This approach has been criticized by Dunst (2007), whose work is based on the "assumption that responsibility for child rearing rests within the family, and that professionals working with a family [should] intervene in ways that support and strengthen parent capacity to carry out child-rearing responsibilities effectively and efficiently" (p. 163).

Even when parents are involved in early intervention programs in a family-centered way, it may not always improve their confidence or competence. Dunst investigated three help-giving practices: relational (involving empathy, listening, and reassurance); participatory (involving promotion of parental decision making); and collaborative (involving parents working as partners to plan courses of action). Surprisingly, while all three approaches would generally be regarded as positive for parental involvement, it was only participatory help-giving that was found to have a mediational effect on the competence, confidence, and enjoyment of parents (Dunst, 2007).

Part C early intervention in the United States has always been intended to have a family focus. The original 1986 legislation referred to enhancing the capacity of families to meet the special needs of their infants and toddlers, and the family-centered requirement continues in current legislation (U.S. Congress, 2004). The final report of the National Early Intervention Longitudinal Study (NEILS) (Hebbeler et al., 2007) concluded that parents reported many positive outcomes of early intervention, including being able to be better carers and advocates for their children. On the other hand, Dunst (2007) concludes that Part C early intervention "bears only a faint resemblance to what we know are evidence-based practices" (p. 174). Dunst is critical of programs that passively manipulate or stimulate children or require parents only to follow professionally prescribed practices. He argues that practice-based research shows capacity-building results from programs in which children are producers of their own behavior through strengthening of existing skills and promotion of new skills. He suggests that parents need to be assisted to acquire "knowledge and skills that can be used more broadly to provide their children with development-enhancing opportunities" (p. 175).

While there will continue to be debate and discussion about the impact of early intervention and the form it should take, there is now reasonable evidence that the decline in intellectual development observed in some groups of young children with intellectual disability, or the risk of disability, can be prevented or reduced by a well-planned and implemented early intervention program (Guralnick & Conlon, 2007). Guralnick and Conlon advocate what they refer to as a Developmental Systems Model, based on an integration of the developmental science of normative development, the science of risk and disability, and intervention science. The model incorporates 10 principles, including being family-centered with a developmental framework; integration and coordination; inclusion in typical community programs; early identification; surveillance and monitoring; individualization; evaluation and feedback; sensitivity to cultural differences; use of evidence-based practices; and use of a systems perspective (Guralnick, 2005; Guralnick & Conlon, 2007).

The exaggerated expectations associated with some of the first early childhood intervention programs appear to have dissipated, and early intervention is now an accepted part of an educational program at the early childhood level. We don't expect programs for school-aged children with intellectual disability to raise their IQ levels, and we don't evaluate them in that way. However, we do expect all educational programs, including early intervention programs, to meet the individual needs of all children, to follow evidence-based practice, and to be sensitive to the needs of the child's family. Those that focus too much on teachers or therapists as experts run the risk of lessening parent competence and being counterproductive, particularly in early childhood.

This is not to say that parents who have a child with a disability do not value expert input. The current situation, in which a woman who gives birth to a child with Down syndrome or another disability is likely to be immediately put in touch with professionals who have expertise in the development of young children with disabilities, is a vast improvement on the situation of 40 years ago when the family was left to their own resources, or may have been advised to institutionalize their child. Parents report that they greatly value the opportunity to get advice on developmental issues and to have contact with other parents in a similar situation. Professional contact can reduce stress and enhance parent-child relationships (Pretis, 2000). However, professionals who work in early intervention need to be constantly aware that it is the parents' relationship with their child that is the most consistent, pervasive, and long-lasting, and will be most likely to influence the child's development. Early intervention programs that strengthen the parent-child relationship and increase the parents' confidence and competence are likely to have positive outcomes, and vice versa.

FOR DISCUSSION AND REFLECTION:

- Discuss the ten principles of Guralnick's Developmental Systems Model. How would these principles operate in practice?
- How might parents benefit from their child's participation in an early intervention program?

Transition to School

In most education systems, children will move into the main school structure at some time after their fifth birthday. Different systems will have different policies, but there is reasonable acceptance in most systems that the age of 5 is a reasonable time for children to proceed into a full-time school program. If a child does not have a disability, the transition to school will usually be an exciting milestone for the child's family, tinged as it may be with some anxiety about how well the child will cope, and sadness at the end of a particular stage of childhood. When a child has an intellectual disability, transition to school is often a much more difficult process.

The transition to school begins with a decision about which school the child will attend. In the past, this decision may have been made by officers of the school system, with little or no parental input. Current legislation and policy in most developed countries ensures that parents are active participants in the process of deciding which school their child will attend. Within certain constraints, parents will usually make the final decision.

The first aspect of the decision will be whether the child will enroll in a mainstream or special class. This decision will be influenced by the child's functional level, by the facilities available in the area, by regional or national education policy and, in particular, by the parents' views on the type of educational program they want for their child. Some parents will have the view that, regardless of their child's degree of disability, his place is at the local neighborhood school that his siblings attend. Others will have a view that their child's disability necessitates placement in a small separate class with specialized teaching. Both views are valid and both will be supported in most education systems (see Box 4.2).

BOX 4.2 THE SPECIAL SCHOOL/REGULAR SCHOOL DECISION

Alexis is 5 years old and is due to start school next year. She has been assessed as having a moderate degree of intellectual disability. Her language has been assessed at 2 to 3 years below her chronological age, and she has some speech problems. Strangers find it very hard to understand what she is saying, which she finds very frustrating. Her mother, Rebecca, is making good progress with Alexis's toilet training but she still has "accidents" if she is not regularly reminded to use the bathroom. She is a fussy eater and is likely to leave her food unless prompted to eat. There is a special school for children with intellectual disability in the large city where Rebecca and Alexis live, and Rebecca has decided to send her to the special school rather than seek her enrollment in a regular class. She says that the special school will be able to cope better with Alexis' toileting and eating, and will take the time to understand her language. It will also save Alexis from embarrassment if she does have a toileting accident and will also save Rebecca from having to explain her problems all the time. As Rebecca says, "If Alexis goes to Sunnybrook [special school] and wets her pants, they will have to apologize to me for missing out on her toilet timing. If she is in the local regular kindergarten class and has an accident, I will have to apologize for the trouble she is causing."

Thomas is also 5 and is finishing in his early childhood program this year. He attends a regular preschool but is provided with a full-time aide as he is nonverbal and nonmobile. He is in a wheelchair, but cannot operate it himself. He has been assessed as having a severe intellectual disability, although he is aware of his surroundings and is very pleased when he sees people he knows. He is not toilet trained and still uses diapers. He has two older brothers at the local elementary school and his parents, Max and Margaret, want Thomas to attend the same school as his brothers. There expectation is that the school district will provide the resources to make this happen.

DISCUSSION QUESTIONS:

1. Do you agree with Rebecca's decision and her reason for making it?
2. What impact will Rebecca's decision have on Alexis' life and future?
3. Is Max and Margaret's decision reasonable, given Thomas's high level of support needs?
4. How would you advise and support Rebecca, Max, and Margaret if you were on the transition team, assisting with the transition to formal schooling?

The child's functional level will often be a major determinant of the type of placement that is sought. For most children who have a mild disability, a group that constitutes the vast majority of children with an intellectual disability, there will be no suggestion of anything other than an inclusive placement. As the child's disability level becomes more severe, consideration of a specialized class, unit or school placement will be more likely. However, many school systems now have a policy, reinforced in some countries by legislation, that resources will go with the student as needed. If parents want a regular class placement for a child with severe, multiple disabilities, the system will provide a full-time aide and other personnel and physical resources at the neighborhood school to allow that to happen.

Another crucial factor impacting on the parents' decision will be the type of educational choices available in the local area. Issues related to the selection of an appropriate placement are discussed in more detail in the next chapter.

Surprisingly, the transition to an inclusive setting may prove to be more straightforward for a child with a severe intellectual disability than for a child with a mild disability. Children with mild disabilities are generally required to conform to the social and academic expectations of all children in the class. However, if, as a consequence of her mild intellectual disability, the child has difficulty looking after her own toileting needs, following teacher instructions, or socializing appropriately with other children, her schooling could be problematic. By contrast, a child whose disability is more severe, and therefore more obvious, is likely to have a carefully formulated transition plan that predicts any adjustment difficulties and provides processes and resources for dealing with them.

Transition Planning

Educators working with preschool-age children who have an intellectual disability will need to develop a transition plan for children moving into the formal education system. This will sometimes involve the formation of a transition team to coordinate the planning and facilitate the process (North & Carruthers, 2008). The team will include the child's parents, current teacher/s and other professionals and, once a decision has been made about the school the child will attend, her next teacher or other representative from the school to be attended. Some school systems will have a person appointed as transition-to-school coordinator, whose role is to assist in all aspects of the process and make sure that it is as positive as possible for all concerned, in particular for the child. The NSW Department of Education & Training, for example, provides a detailed planning document that outlines the roles of all parties and gives a timetable and structure for transition planning (NSW Department of Education & Training, 1997). In the United States, federal law mandates the development of a transition to kindergarten program (U.S. Congress, 2004). An outline of the functions of a transition support team as suggested by North and Carruthers (2008) is provided in Box 4.3.

BOX 4.3 FUNCTIONS OF A TRANSITION-TO-SCHOOL TEAM

Functions of a transition-to-school team include

- ensuring that the family is informed about the school options that are available in the area
- supporting the family in their interactions with the education system and/or personnel from non-government schools
- organising visits to schools and meetings with school executives and facilitating the exploration and consideration of these options
- providing the opportunity for families to examine the advantages and disadvantages of the options available for their child

- developing a plan to prepare the child and their family for school that will include orientation activities in cooperation with the school
- ensuring that relevant assessment information is compiled cooperatively into a report for school personnel
- ensuring that relevant information about the transition process is shared with parents and service providers
- assisting parents with the collection of medical and developmental history relevant to the child's enrolment and/or program, and the transfer of this information to the proposed school
- ensuring that parents are informed as soon as possible about enrolment and support decisions
- organising for a relevant expert to address the staff and/or the parent group about the disability of the child to be integrated if and when this is appropriate or required
- establishment of an integrated program with shared goals that will be implemented in a co-ordinated and cooperative manner.

From: North, J., & Carruthers, A. (2008). Inclusion in early childhood. In P. Foreman (Ed.), *Inclusion in action.* Melbourne: Thomson. (© Cengage Learning, reproduced with permission.)

Child Factors Influencing Successful Transition

There is some debate about the child factors that are most likely to facilitate successful transition and inclusion in regular classes. Are academic skills such as counting and letter recognition important? Is it communication or language skills that will make the difference, or perhaps social skills or self-care skills? Kemp and Carter have investigated these questions by following the experiences of 33 children, all of whom had an intellectual disability, who moved from a university-based preschool into a regular education class. Since on-task behavior and direction-following skills are often regarded as important skills for successful inclusion, Kemp and Carter measured these skills in the children after they had been in kindergarten (the first year of formal schooling) for one term. They also sought teachers' perceptions of these skills after a term and at the end of a year's schooling and asked teachers what skills they rated as most important for successful inclusion. The top four skills rated were following teacher directions, independent toileting, following classroom rules, and staying on task for short periods (Kemp & Carter, 2005). They found that those children rated by their teacher as being most successfully integrated tended to have better on-task behavior and to respond better to group directions. Kemp and Carter suggest that these findings could give direction to early childhood intervention service providers who are readying preschool children for the transition to formal schooling.

McIntyre and her colleagues compared the adaptation to school of children with intellectual disability and typically developing children. As might have been predicted, children with intellectual disability were found to have significantly more problem behaviors, poorer teacher-student relationships, fewer social skills, and fewer self-regulation skills than children without an intellectual disability (McIntyre, Blacher, & Baker, 2006). The researchers suggested that early childhood programs preparing children for school should concentrate on decreasing children's maladaptive behavior and increasing their social skills. Good family-school partnerships were also seen as an important part of the transition process. McIntyre et al. acknowledge the difficulties that are likely to be experienced by students with intellectual disability as they enter the formal education system, and stress the need for appropriate supports, services, and programs to be in place if successful transitions are to occur.

When children with intellectual disability arrive in formal schooling, it is likely that the receiving teacher will have been part of an extensive planning process that has prepared the child for a smooth transition to school. There will typically be a transition plan, prepared by a transition team, containing many of the elements listed in Box 4.3. Teachers need to be aware of the significance of the transition process for the child and the child's family, and should ensure that the child's education continues to be an effective partnership between home and school, as it is very likely to have been during the early intervention phase of the child's education.

FOR DISCUSSION AND REFLECTION:

- Kemp and Carter found that children rated by their teacher as being most successfully integrated had better on-task behavior and responded better to group directions. What influence could a preschool teacher have in preparing children for a successful transition to school?

Summary

Changes in views about the modifiability of intelligence were among the factors that led to the establishment of early intervention programs. Programs designed to overcome the effects of poverty have been implemented both on a national scale and as model programs. Debate about whether these programs can have a long-term impact on intelligence continues. Other programs have been designed to assist young children with diagnosed disabilities and their families, or children who are at established risk for intellectual or developmental problems. In some countries, early intervention is supported by government legislation, in others by policy. The fact that early intervention is widely available does not mean that it is always beneficial and effective, although several cost-benefit analyses have shown financial benefits if intervention can reduce the need for special education and other services. There are strong arguments for intervention to be family focused with recognition that parents are the most significant influences on their children's lives. Early intervention should conclude with a well-planned transition into a preschool program or the formal education system.

References

Barnett, W. S., & Masse, L. N. (2007). Comparative benefit-cost analysis of the Abecedarian program and its policy implications. *Economics of Education Review, 26,* 113–125.

Bierman, K. L., Nix, R. L., Greenberg, M. T., Blair, C., & Domitrovich, C. E. (2008). Executive functions and school readiness: Impact, moderation, and mediation in the Head Start REDI program. *Development and Psychopathology, 20,* 821–843.

Bonnier, C. (2008). Evaluation of early stimulation programs for enhancing brain development. *Acta Paediatrica, 97,* 853–858.

Bricker, D., Carlson, L., & Schwartz, R. (1981). A discussion of early intervention for infants with Down syndrome. *Pediatrics, 67,* 45–46.

Brooks-Gunn, J., Klebanov, P. K., Fong-ruey, L., & Spiker, D. (1993). Enhancing the development of low-birthweight, premature infants: Changes in cognition and behavior over the first three years. *Child Development, 64,* 736–753.

Buckley, S. (2003). Literacy and language. In J. A. Rondal & S. Buckley (Eds.), *Speech and language intervention in Down syndrome* (pp. 132–153). London: Whurr Publishers Ltd.

Campbell, F. A., Pungello, E. P., Miller-Johnson, S., Burchinal, M., & Ramey, C. T. (2001). The development of cognitive and academic abilities: Growth curves from an early childhood educational experiment. *Developmental Psychology, 37*(2), 231–242.

Campbell, F. A., & Ramey, C. T. (1994). Effects of early intervention on intellectual and academic achievement: A follow-up study of children from low-income families. *Child Development, 65,* 684–698.

Cunningham, C. C. (1979). *Early stimulation of the mentally handicapped child.* Manchester, UK: Hester Adrian Research Centre, University of Manchester.

Dawson, G. (2008). Early behavioral intervention, brain plasticity, and the prevention of autism spectrum disorder. *Development and Psychopathology, 20,* 775–803.

Denhoff, E. (1983). Intervention practices for developmentally disabled and high-risk infants: Rationale and management. *Exceptional Child, 30,* 67–75.

Dunst, C. J. (2007). Early intervention for infants and toddlers with developmental disabilities. In S. L. Odom, R. H. Horner, M. E. Snell, & J. Blacher (Eds.), *Handbook of developmental disabilities* (pp. 161–180). New York: The Guilford Press.

Fenichel, E., & Mann, T. L. (2001). Early Head Start for low-income families with infants and toddlers. *The Future of Children, 11*(1), 135–141.

Ferry, P. C. (1981). On growing new neurons: Are early intervention programs effective? *Pediatrics, 67,* 38–41.

Graves, P. (1978). Early intervention: A personal view. *Australasian Journal of Mental Retardation, 5,* 85–87.

Gunn, P., Berry, P., & Andrews, R. (1979). Vocalization and looking behaviour of Down's syndrome infants. *British Journal of Psychology, 70,* 259–263.

Guralnick, M. J. (Ed.). (2005). *The Developmental Systems approach to early intervention.* Baltimore: Paul H. Brookes.

Guralnick, M. J., & Conlon, C. (2007). Early intervention. In M. Batshaw, L. Pelligrino, & N. Roizen (Eds.), *Children with disabilities* (6th ed.) (pp. 511–521). Baltimore: Paul H. Brookes.

Hawken, L. S., Johnston, S. S., & McDonnell, A. P. (2005). Emerging literacy views and practices: Results from a national survey of Head Start preschool teachers. *Topics in Early Childhood Special Education, 25*(4), 232–242.

Hayden, A. H., & Dmitriev, V. (1975). Multidisciplinary preschool program for Down's syndrome children in the University of Washington Model Preschool Center. In B. Z. Friedlander, G. Kirk, & G. Sterritt (Eds.), *The exceptional infant: Volume III.* New York: Brunner Mazel.

Hebbeler, K., Spiker, D., Bailey, D., Scarborough, A., Malik, S., Simeonsson, R., et al. (2007). *Early intervention for infants and toddlers with disabilities and their families: Participants, services and outcomes. Final report of the National Early Intervention Longitudinal Study (NEILS).* Menlo Park, CA: SRI International.

Kemp, C., & Carter, M. (2005). Identifying skills for promoting successful inclusion in kindergarten. *Journal of Intellectual and Developmental Disability, 30*(1), 31–44.

Levy, S., Kim, A.-H., & Olive, M. L. (2006). Interventions for young children with autism: A synthesis of the literature. *Focus on Autism and Other Developmental Disabilities, 21*(1), 55–62.

Lovaas, O. I. (1987). Behavioral treatment and normal educational functioning in young autistic children. *Journal of Consulting and Clinical Psychology, 55*, 3–9.

Ludlow, J. R. (1980). Early intervention in Down's syndrome [Letter]. *British Medical Journal, 281*, 1143.

Ludlow, J. R., & Allen, L. M. (1979). The effect of early intervention and preschool stimulus on the development of the Down's syndrome child. *Journal of Mental Deficiency Research, 23*, 29–44.

Ludwig, J., & Phillips, D. A. (2008). Long-term effects of Head Start on low income children. *Annals of the New York Academy of Sciences, 1136*, 257–268.

Majnemer, A. (1998). Benefits of early intervention for children with developmental disabilities. *Seminars in Pediatric Neurology, 5*(1), 62–69.

McEachin, J. J., Smith, T. T., & Lovaas, O. I. (1993). Long-term outcome for children with autism who received early intensive behavioral treatment. *American Journal on Mental Retardation, 97*, 359–372.

McIntyre, L. L., Blacher, J., & Baker, B. L. (2006). The transition to school: Adaptation in young children with and without intellectual disability. *Journal of Intellectual Disability Research, 50*(5), 349–361.

Mesibov, G. B., Shea, V., & Schopler, E. (2006). *The TEACCH approach to autism spectrum disorders.* New York: Springer.

Nores, M., Belfield, C. R., Barnett, S. W., & Schweinhart, L. (2005). Updating the economic impacts of the High/Scope Perry Preschool Program. *Educational Evaluation and Policy Analysis, 27*(3), 245–261.

North, J., & Carruthers, A. (2008). Inclusion in early childhood. In P. Foreman (Ed.), *Inclusion in action.* Melbourne: Thomson.

NSW Department of Education & Training. (1997). Transition to school for young children with special learning needs: Guidelines for families, early childhood services and schools. In Department of Education and Training (Ed.): Author.

Page, E. B., & Grandon, G. M. (1981). Massive intervention and child intelligence: The Milwaukee Project in critical perspective. *Journal of Special Education, 15*(2), 239–256.

Piper, M. C., & Pless, I. B. (1980). Early intervention for infants with Down syndrome: A controlled trial. *Pediatrics, 65*, 463–468.

Pretis, M. (2000). Early intervention in children with Down syndrome: From evaluation to methodology. *Infants and Young Children, 12*(3), 23–31.

Ramey, C. T., & Ramey, S. L. (2004). Early learning and school readiness: Can early intervention make a difference? *Merrill-Palmer Quarterly, 50*(4), 471–491.

Ramey, S. L., Ramey, C. T., & Lanzi, R. G. (2007). Early intervention: Background, research findings, and future directions. In J. W. Jacobson, J. A. Mulick, & J. Rojahn (Eds.), *Handbook of intellectual and developmental disabilities* (pp. 445–463). New York: Springer.

Remington, B., Hastings, R. P., Kovshov, H., degli-Espona, F., Jahr, E., Brown, T., et al. (2007). Early intensive behavioral intervention: Outcomes for children with autism and their parents after two years. *American Journal on Mental Retardation, 112*(6), 418–438.

Rix, J., & Paige-Smith, A. (2008). A different head? Parental agency and early intervention. *Disability and Society, 23*(3), 211–221.

Sanz Aparicio, M., & Balana, J. M. (2002). Early language stimulation of Down's syndrome babies: A study of the optimum age to begin. *Early Child Development and Care, 172*, 651–656.

Schweinhart, L. J., & Weikart, D. L. (1993). *Significant benefits: The High/Scope Perry Preschool study through age 27.* Ypsilanti, MI: High/Scope Press.

Tews, L. (2007). Early intervention for children with autism: Methodologies critique. *Developmental Disabilities Bulletin, 35*(1/2), 149–168.

Thomson, R. H., Cotnoir-Bichelman, N. M., McKerchar, P. M., Tate, T. L., & Dancho, K. A. (2007). Enhancing early communication through infant sign training. *Journal of Applied Behavior Analysis, 40*(1), 15–23.

United States Congress. (2004). *Individuals With Disabilities Education Improvement Act of 2004.* Washington, DC: Author.

van Bysterveldt, A. K., Gillon, G. T., & Moran, C. (2006). Enhancing phonological awareness and letter knowledge in preschool children with Down syndrome. *International Journal of Disability, Development and Education, 53*(3), 301–329.

Van Hooste, A., & Maes, B. (2003). Family factors in the early development of children with Down syndrome. *Journal of Early Intervention, 25*(4), 296–309.

5

Educational Options

The School Years

Overview: This chapter reviews the various choices parents of children with an intellectual disability make when their child commences formal schooling. It also considers aspects of the debate on access to the general education curriculum. The chapter examines research and debate on the outcomes and impact of inclusive school placements versus segregated placements for students who have an intellectual disability.

Introduction

As outlined in the previous chapter, the transition into formal schooling is a significant milestone for all children. Parents typically give a lot of thought to which school their child will attend. In some cases, the choice is an obvious one: it may be the neighborhood public school, the school attended by one of the child's parents, or a private school that fits with the parents' wishes for their child's education. In the case of many children with an intellectual disability, the choice is likely to be much more difficult. For a start, parents will need to check what schools are available in their area and, assuming that such choices are available, parents may need to choose between a special school, a special class or unit, and a regular class.

Education of Students with an Intellectual Disability, pages 125–167

One of the principles that can be considered when deciding what school a child should attend is that of the *least restrictive environment.* It can easily be demonstrated that some environments are intrinsically more restrictive than others. For many years, large residential institutions, often structured as hospitals, were the recommended placement for people with an intellectual disability, particularly those who had severe or multiple disabilities. The way some of these institutions operated could make them as restrictive as jails, and in the 1970s this level of restriction was seen by most people as unnecessary and undesirable. It is now relatively rare for children in developed countries to be placed in full-time care, particularly from birth. Residential schools for children with intellectual disability are now uncommon. The institutions that do continue to operate in the United States, the UK, and other developed countries are usually much smaller than previously, and provide more choice for their residents, a more normal lifestyle, and fewer restrictions.

Most school systems provide a range of different educational settings for students with an intellectual disability, and the trend over the last 30 years has been to move toward less restrictive settings (Dempsey & Foreman, 1997; Dempsey, Foreman, & Jenkinson, 2002; Handler, 2003). The range of educational settings provided by most school systems, from most restrictive (1) to least restrictive (7) is as follows:

1. residential school for students with a disability
2. separate special day school
3. separate special school on regular campus
4. special unit (usually 2 or 3 classes) located in regular school
5. single special class in regular school
6. single special class in regular school, with part-time regular placement
7. regular class (Foreman, 2008)

Some students with a mild intellectual disability will attend a regular class with only minimal adjustments by the school and will access the general education curriculum. Students with a more severe disability may require the help of a teacher's aide as well as significant curriculum adaptations if they are going to attend a regular class. Another alternative for students with a higher level of educational need is a mixed placement: part-time in a special class and part-time in a regular class.

Parents often find the decision about placement to be a very complex one. They will reach their decision on the basis of the types of placements and support that are available in their region, their perception of their child's needs, and advice provided by professionals. When children have a higher level of intellectual disability, or multiple disabilities, parents will sometimes choose a specialized unit that has specific expertise in teaching children with a disability (Gilmore, Campbell, & Cuskelly, 2003). However, other parents would prefer that regardless of their child's level of disability, the child should attend the neighborhood school along with their siblings and neighbors, and that any necessary services should be provided at that school (Leyser & Kirk, 2004). The right of parents to choose a regular school placement for their child, regardless of their level of disability, is supported by legislation in the United States and in some other countries. A case study of a family making such as decision is found in Box 5.1.

BOX 5.1 DECIDING WHICH SCHOOL FOR TODD

Todd has just turned 5 and will be starting school in the next term. He was identified prenatally through amniocentesis as having Down syndrome, but his parents did not see this as a major issue and proceeded with the pregnancy. He is the youngest of four children, with brothers, Dean aged 11, and Jay aged 9, and sister Ella aged 7. He lives in a large town where his parents are active in the community. His dad, David, is a construction foreman, and his mother, Lauren, is a legal secretary, currently working part time.

When Todd was born, Lauren was visited in hospital by a teacher from the local early educational intervention program. Lauren started attending the program with Todd when he was 2 months old for two mornings per week. From 6 months she also took him to a playgroup organized by one of the local churches. When he turned 2, she sought enrollment for him at the childcare center that had been attended by her other three children, and was still attended by Ella in her final year before school. They agreed to enroll Todd for three mornings a week. This was increased to three full days a week when he was 3. Todd appeared to enjoy all these activities, and following some initial separation anxiety, began to look forward to preschool, asking, "School today?" each morning.

When he was 4, Lauren and David started thinking about his formal schooling program. They visited a school on the other side of town that had a specialized unit of two classes for students with an intellectual disability. They then visited their local school, which was attended by Todd's siblings. Todd had already visited the school on multiple occasions, when dropping off and picking up his siblings, and for sports days, concerts, and prize days. It was the place Todd referred to as "big school."

The local school principal had seen Todd grow from a baby and was very welcoming of the family. She said that if they decided to send Todd to the school he would be made as welcome as his siblings had been. She made some notes about Todd's communication and self-help skills and suggested that the family take as much time as needed to decide whether they wanted Todd to attend "big school" or the special unit.

That night there was a family discussion to see what Dean, Jay, and Ella thought of the idea of Todd going to their school. The three children were adamant that Todd would go to school with them. They mentioned three other children with special needs who were in their classes and said that Todd would be able to do as well as them. Ella said that she would look after Todd on the playground, but Lauren said that, while that would be helpful in the short term, he would need to look after himself eventually. She told them that he currently looks after himself well at preschool, and that he would learn to look after himself well at school.

The next day, Lauren called the school to advise the principal that Todd would definitely start in the following term. The principal said that she would like Lauren to visit the school again so that she could arrange for some assessments and to obtain Lauren and David's permission to request reports from his preschool and professionals who had assessed him. She would then arrange a meeting of a learning support team, including Lauren and David, to start planning his individualized education program and see what additional supports might be needed to ensure that his educational progress was maximized.

By the time Todd started school, it had been agreed that he would share the services of a teaching assistant who also worked with three other children in the school. The assistant would focus on Todd for the first weeks of his schooling to help him learn to use the school bathroom, eat his lunch with the other students, and learn the school routines, particularly those related to playground activities and movement in and out of the school. Several learning goals were set that were related to general class curriculum goals as well as some specific skills Todd needed to help him manage at school. It was agreed that a speech pathologist would see Todd on her weekly visits to the school and would advise the teacher on ways to further develop his communication skills. An occupational therapist would visit monthly to consult on ways to improve his fine and gross motor skills.

DISCUSSION QUESTIONS

1. What factors made you think that it was likely that Lauren and David would choose the local school for Todd?

2. Todd's siblings were eager for him to come to their school. What if they weren't? Is it fair to send a child to a regular school if his siblings see it as an intrusion on their lives?
3. What benefits might Todd have obtained in the specialized unit that were not available in the regular school?
4. What benefits might Todd have obtained in the regular school that were not available in the special unit?

When a child is placed in a regular class and given access to the same opportunities as other students, this is generally referred to as "inclusion" or inclusive practice, as opposed to segregation which, by its nature, is an "exclusive" practice. Inclusion is also sometimes referred to as "mainstreaming," although inclusion can be applied much more broadly than within a special education or disability context, and includes the philosophical notion that all schools should welcome and celebrate diversity, and should provide appropriate educational programs for all children in the community, without exclusion. Indeed, inclusion is seen by some as extending to the provision of appropriate educational opportunities for all children including, for example, the estimated 72 million children in the world who are not currently in primary school (Ainscow & Miles, 2008). However, the focus of this section of the chapter is on inclusion of students who have a disability, and legislation supporting inclusive practices for students with an intellectual disability is outlined below.

FOR REFLECTION OR DISCUSSION:

- What issues do parents need to consider when deciding the optimal educational placement for a child with an intellectual disability?
- What is meant by inclusive practice?

Legislation Supporting Inclusion[1]

In the United States there is specific legislation relating to schools that requires school systems to provide mainstream places as a first option, if that is what the parents wish. The Individuals with Disabilities Education Improvement Act (U.S. Congress, 2004) stipulates that there must be parental involvement in assessment of children and review of their placement and progress. Services must be provided in the regular class if the decision is for regular class placement. For example, if the child needs daily speech therapy or occupational therapy, the answer is not to send her to a special school where those services are available, but to provide the therapy services at her regular school. During the 1990s, the number of students in the United States with intellectual disability who were enrolled in regular education classrooms for some or most of the school day increased from 27% to 45% (Williamson, McLeskey, Hoppey, & Rentz, 2006).

Another piece of U.S. legislation with potential to impact on the education of students with an intellectual disability is the No Child Left Behind Act (Public Law 107-110), which focused on accountability through the establishment of standards in basic skills (U.S. Congress, 2002). This has been a controversial act that some educators see as providing negative outcomes for some less able students. It is discussed in more detail under "Access to the General Education Curriculum," later in this chapter.

In the UK, the Special Educational Needs and Disability Act stipulates that

> A student with a disability... must be educated in a mainstream school unless that is incompatible with the wishes of his parent or the provision of efficient education for other children. (UK Parlaiment, 2001)

However, in this case, "the provision of efficient education for other children" is a significant loophole that lessens the ability of parents to insist on a particular placement. This clause could allow schools to refuse entry to a student with a disability if the school considers that the student would disrupt the class and interfere with "efficient education for other children." However, UK policy is generally supportive of inclusion. In Removing Barriers to Achievement, the UK Department for Education and Skills (2004) stated that

> All teachers should expect to teach children with special educational needs (SEN) and all schools should play their part in educating children from their local community, whatever their background or ability. (Department for Education and Skills, 2004)

In Australia inclusive schooling is educational policy rather than law, and the policy has been adopted in some form by all of the state and territory authorities who have responsibility for education (Jenkinson, 2001). Although there is no specific legislation applying to schools, there is legislative support for inclusion through the Disability Discrimination Act (DDA)

(Commonwealth Government of Australia, 1992) and its state counterparts. The DDA makes it illegal to discriminate against a person in education on the basis of their disability. The Act applies to disabilities that individuals may presently experience, have had in the past, or may have in the future, and it undoubtedly applies to people who have been diagnosed as having an intellectual disability.

The DDA's relevance to schooling and education was strengthened in 2005 by the enacting of Education Standards, which provide more detail about the expectations of the Act on educational providers. The Act applies to all levels of education: schools in the public sector, schools registered through school registration authorities in the private sector, to postcompulsory education and training providers, and to higher education providers.

The areas covered by the standards are

- Enrollment and admission: a person with a disability must be able to seek admission and receive advice and support on the same basis as a person without a disability, and without discrimination.
- Participation: students with a disability must be able to participate in courses or programs without discrimination.
- Curriculum development, delivery, and accreditation: all students must be able to participate appropriately in learning experiences.
- Provision of student support services: a student with a disability must be able to use services that other students use or, if necessary, specialized services.
- Harassment and victimization: processes must be developed to prevent harassment or victimization of students with a disability.

To meet the Education Standards, education providers are expected to make "reasonable adjustments" to meet the needs of students with a disability. In doing so they must consider the views of students and the family, and the effects of the adjustment on the students and on others in the school. The provider is entitled to maintain the academic integrity of the course and its inherent components. This is particularly relevant for vocational education providers and universities. The Standards have provided clear guidance for providers, but are yet to be tested at law.

FOR REFLECTION OR DISCUSSION:

- Discuss the impact of legislation and policy as drivers of inclusion.

Social Justice Principles Supporting Inclusion

Many of the relatively recent changes to the way education is provided to students with intellectual disability and other special educational needs can be traced to the 1960s and 1970s, when various researchers and commentators evaluated and analyzed the nature of the provision of services to people with a disability from a social justice perspective. In most cases they did not argue from a research or evidence base, but rather from a rights or philosophical base. Three of the leading names at this time were Bengt Nirje, Niels Erik Bank-Mikkelsen, and Wolf Wolfensberger. Nirje developed perhaps the most significant and influential social justice principle of the time, that of "normalization," which was further developed by Bank-Mikkelsen and introduced to the English-speaking world by Wolfensberger (Bank-Mikkelsen, 1969; Nirje, 1970, 1985; Wolfensberger, 1972, 1980). The general thesis of the normalization principle is that all people are entitled to live a lifestyle that other people who live in their community would describe as "normal." Normal can be defined as what most others in that culture usually do or would prefer to do. In terms of education, the normal or most common thing to do is to attend a regular school chosen by the child's parents, either in the public or independent system. A normalization philosophy applied to school choice means that all children should have the opportunity to attend a regular school, if that is what they or their parents see as the best thing for them. The implementation of principles such as normalization has led to changes in legislation and policy and, in turn, has led to changes in practice (Dempsey, 2008).

The normalization principle has been influential in the way services are provided to persons with a disability and has been useful in the evaluation of both policy and practice. For example, policymakers can evaluate whether a policy leads to an approach or practice that is culturally normative. The principle has provided a basis for development of policy and practice by organizations concerned with people with disabilities, and has had a major influence on the development of government disability policy. Another advantage is that the principle is applicable in a variety of settings. Policymakers in the area of education, housing, social welfare, and community living have all been able to use the concept of normalization to guide and assess policy and practice. For example, an organization establishing a group home for people with an intellectual disability would wish to ensure that the home looked like others in the neighborhood, and that the lives lived and the choices made by the residents were as similar as possible to those of other people in the community—that they were culturally normative.

The concept of normalization has not been without its controversies. One of the problems has been with interpretation of the concept of normality. Some have interpreted the concept as meaning that people with disabilities have to change to be more normal to be accepted. This led to debate between the interpretations of Wolfensberger and Nirje about whether we should, on the one hand, be seeking to "normalize" people or, by contrast, should be celebrating difference and diversity (Nirje, 1985). One side of the argument would say that by helping people with an intellectual disability to act and dress as much as possible like other people in the community, we are improving their lives and making it more possible for them to "fit in" to and participate in society, which is an important life goal for most people and their families. The opposite view is that society should welcome and celebrate diversity, and that all people should be able to take their place in the community regardless of how they talk, act, or look.

FOR REFLECTION OR DISCUSSION:

- Maria, aged 15, who has a moderate intellectual disability, tells her teacher she is going to wear her confirmation dress to the school social. The teacher, Mrs. James, knows the other children will be dressed casually. Should Mrs. James encourage Maria to fit in by wearing something more suitable, or encourage the other students to accept Maria's unconventional style?

Conventions and Statements on Human Rights

In 1948 the United Nation's Universal Declaration of Human Rights included explicit statements about rights and freedoms of parents in relation to their children's education. These statements have subsequently been used to support arguments for inclusive practices. For example

> *Article 26* (3) Parents have a prior right to choose the kind of education that shall be given to their children.

This declaration did not have a direct impact on the way students with a disability were treated or educated, but it provided a basis for parent groups and educators to argue for equal accessibility to schooling, and for parental choice. However, even in the latter part of the 20th century, 40 or 50 years after Article 26 (3) had been declared, there were still many parents who believed that they had little or no "prior right to choose" the type of education that their child would be given. In some parts of the world, this remains the case today.

Some more recent statements have been much more specific about equal access to education as a right for persons with a disability. The World Declaration on Education for All (UNESCO, 1990) stated in Article III (5):

> Steps need to be taken to provide equal access to education to every category of disabled persons as an integral part of the education system.

Another important statement arose from the World Conference on Special Needs Education, held at Salamanca, Spain, in 1994. As a result of the Conference, 90 countries agreed on a statement that specifically supported inclusion as the standard form of education for students with a disability. Article 2 of the Salamanca Statement came to the following conclusion:

> Regular schools with [an] inclusive orientation are the most effective means of combating discriminatory attitudes, creating welcoming communities, building an inclusive society and achieving education for all. (UNESCO, 1994)

Ainscow and Miles (2008) have suggested that the Salamanca Statement is "arguably the most significant international document that has ever appeared in the field of special education" (p. 16).

On December 13, 2006, the United Nations passed the Convention on the Rights of Persons with Disabilities. This Convention provides unambiguous support for inclusive schooling:

> *Article 24–Education*
>
> 1. States Parties recognize the right of persons with disabilities to education. With a view to realizing this right without discrimination and on the basis of equal opportunity. States Parties shall ensure an inclusive education system at all levels. (United Nations General Assembly, 2006)

As of February 2009 there were 137 signatories to the Convention and 81 signatories to the Optional Protocol that allows the Committee on the Rights of Persons with a Disability to receive communications from persons who believe that they have been a victim of a violation of the Convention. The Optional Protocol strengthens the impact of Article 24 on students with a disability. The 137 signatories to the Convention include, for example, Algeria, Australia, Brazil, Chile, China, Germany, India, the Russian Federation, and the United Kingdom. However, the United States, while supporting the concept of the Convention, had not signed (as of February 2009) because of previously expressed concerns about a paragraph in the preamble that referred to the protection of persons with disabilities during armed conflicts and foreign occupation (Miller, 2006). However, signing the Convention was part of Barack Obama's election platform, so it is likely that it will have been signed by the United States by the time this book is published.

In Australia there have been recent statements on educational inclusion at a national level. The Melbourne Declaration on Educational Goals for Young Australians made the following commitments:

> Australian governments, in collaboration with all school sectors, commit to promoting equity and excellence in Australian schooling. This means that all Australian governments and all school sectors must provide all students with access to high-quality schooling that is free from discrimination based on gender, language, sexual orientation, pregnancy, culture, ethnicity, religion, health or disability, socioeconomic background, or geographic location. (Ministerial Council on Education Employment Training and Youth Affairs, 2008)

FOR REFLECTION OR DISCUSSION:

- Discuss the following statement: "Regardless of the outcomes, it is a basic human right for all children to be able to attend a regular school." Do you agree or disagree? Defend your position.

Decisions about Curriculum

Whether a student is enrolled in an inclusive school setting, a special school, or a combination of these, decisions will need to be made about the curriculum that will be followed. Over the last 30 to 40 years there have been several changes to curriculum approaches for children with an intellectual disability. Browder et al. (2003) have summarized the changes over time as follows:

1. Developmental model—1975: curriculum is based on child's "mental age." In this model, school age students will tend to follow a preschool curriculum (e.g. puzzles, finger-painting, nursery rhymes).

2. Functional curriculum—1975 to late 1980s: curriculum is based on life needs in major domains: vocational, home, community, leisure.
3. Social inclusion—Mid 1980s–1990s: focus on social participation and learning social skills through interaction.
4. Self-determination—1990s: focus on person's ability to make choices and participate in decision-making for and about themselves.
5. General curriculum access—1990s to present: general curriculum content (reading, math science etc.) is the starting point for planning for all students. (Browder et al., 2003)

Curriculum decisions will inevitably be related to the child's level of ability or disability. In the case of students with more serious intellectual disability, the debate is often between a *functional* curriculum and the *general education* curriculum, although the answer will often be a combination of the two. These approaches to curriculum will now be discussed in more detail.

Functional Curricula

Functional curricula are based on the current and future skill needs of the student rather than on their general developmental level. The significant curriculum question is, "What skills does the child need to be able to function well within her current and future environments?" The areas or components of the curriculum are the areas that relate to everyday functioning. These include vocational skills, independent living skills, work skills, leisure skills, academic skills, and social skills. Unlike a developmental curriculum that focuses on developmental (or "mental" age), the basis for a functional curriculum is a student's *chronological* age. As far as possible, the student participates in activities and develops skills for activities that are appropriate to a student of her age. However, there have been arguments for the continued use of a developmental approach for students who have very severe intellectual and multiple disabilities (Carnaby, 2007).

Parents and teachers have often found functional curricula to have a high level of relevance to the lives of their children and students. Prior to the development of functional curricula, educational programs for students with moderate or severe intellectual disability had limited relevance to their lives. In some cases, teachers who conducted preschool-type activities with older students worried that they were undertaking child-minding rather than teaching. In other cases, teachers worried about the relevance of trying to follow a modified regular curriculum that seemed to be unrelated to their students' current and future lives. For example, a modified or "remedial" mathematics curriculum for secondary students might have included very simplified algebra or geometry. Such topics would not be part of a functional curriculum unless they were seen as having relevance to the students' current and future lives. Wagner (2001), writing primarily about middle school students with autism, has suggested that decisions about the balance between a functional and general curriculum will depend on parents' answers to questions such as

- Will the student go on to post-secondary education?
- Where would they live?
- Would they be able to look after their home, cook and shop?
- How much independence will they have?
- Will they have a job, travel independently, look after their own finances?
- Will they drive a car?
- Will they access the local community independently?

The answers to these questions, combined with the teacher's analysis of the student's current functional level, will help to determine the extent to which a functional curriculum needs to be incorporated within the student's educational program (Wagner, 2001).

Among the leaders in the development of functional curricula were Peter Valletutti and Michael Bender (Bender, Valletutti, & Baglin, 2008; Valletutti & Bender, 1982). Their series of manuals on functional assessment and teaching has been both popular and influential. Box 5.2 summarizes the contents of the manuals, the latest editions of which appeared in 2008. In doing so, it provides an overview of the content of a functional curriculum.

The components outlined in Box 5.2 make it very clear that a functional curriculum is very different from either a developmental curriculum or the general education curriculum. For example "responding to facial expressions" and "refraining from disturbing, distracting and destructive behavior" would not be found in either of those curricula. There is greater potential for overlap between the general education curriculum and the academics component of the functional curriculum. For example, "carrying out written directions" could be found in either of them. However, in all cases, the functional curriculum would emphasize the relevance of the skill to the student's current and future needs. This would not normally be the primary focus of the general education curriculum.

BOX 5.2 COMPONENTS OF A FUNCTIONAL CURRICULUM

A Functional Assessment & Curriculum for Teaching Students with Disabilities (Vols I–IV) by Peter J. Valletutti, Michael Bender, Carol Baglin, Audrey Smith Hoffnung

Volume I

Self-Care, Motor Skills, Household Management, and Living Skills

Unit 1: Self-Care Skills

- Toileting
- Eating and drinking
- Dressing and undressing
- Personal cleanliness and grooming

Unit 2: Gross Motor Skills

- Basic gross motor skills
- Function with assistive devices
- Function in diverse settings
- Recreation and leisure

Unit 3: Fine Motor Skills

- Initial manipulative skills
- Dress and undressing using fine motor skills
- Leisure activities
- Vocational/work activities

Unit 4: Household Management and Living Skills

- Planning and preparing meals
- Purchasing and maintaining clothes
- Caring for living quarters
- Operating simple appliances

Volume II

Nonverbal Communication, Oral Communications, and Literacy Preparation

Unit 1: Nonverbal Communication

- Responding to gestures
- Using gestures

- Responding to tone
- Using tone
- Responding to facial expressions
- Using facial expressions
- Using augmentative or alternate communication

Unit 2: Oral Communication

- Progressing through the one-word stage (0–12 months)
- Progressing through stages 1–IV (0–12 months)
- Acquiring skills for various learning situations
- Acquiring skills for work situations
- Acquiring skills for leisure pursuits
- Acquiring skills for household participation
- Acquiring skills to be a friend and family member
- Acquiring skills to be a community member
- Acquiring skills to be a consumer and participant in financial transactions
- Acquiring skills to be a traveler within the community

Unit 3: Literacy Preparation

- Acquiring phonological and other oral language skills that facilitate literacy
- Acquiring skills for narrative activities
- Comprehending and using idioms

Volume III

Functional Academics

Unit 1: Functional Reading

- Developing oral language skills
- Identifying personal data
- Identifying time
- Operating tools using instructions
- Responding to written information
- Carrying out written instructions
- Locating and utilizing information from simple charts, diagrams, maps, and menus
- Locating and utilizing information from directories, schedules, and bulletin boards
- Carrying out written directions

- Identifying key words on simple forms and providing information
- Locating and utilizing information on bills, timecards, check stubs, and receipts
- Locating and utilizing information on classified ads, brochures, and pamphlets
- Acquiring requested information
- Reading for pleasure
- Seeking assistance

Unit 2: Functional Writing

- Acquiring perceptual motor skills for writing
- Writing to readily communicate to readers
- Communicating to be understood
- Creating narratives to explain, persuade, and influence others

Unit 3: Functional Mathematics

- Acquiring basic arithmetic skills for functional independence
- Participating independently in monetary transactions
- Gaining competency in measuring instruments and utilizing units of measurement
- Acquiring functional skills for time management
- Solving mathematical problems needed for independence

Volume IV

Interpersonal, Competitive Job-Finding, and Leisure-Time Skills

Unit 1: Interpersonal Skills

- Functioning in diverse interpersonal and social situations
- Functioning in situations that depend on oral communication skills
- Refraining from disturbing, distracting, and destructive behavior

Unit 2: Competitive Job-Finding Skills

- Acquiring skills to competitively apply for work
- Acquiring skills to get ready for work
- Acquiring skills to go to work

- Following work rules and policies
- Demonstrating appropriate interpersonal skills in the workplace
- Understanding compensation for work and developing a bill paying and savings plan

Unit 3: Leisure-Time Skills

- Participating in play activities and games of leisure
- Engaging in sports and physical fitness
- Participating in camping and outdoor activities
- Studying nature to engage in leisure activities
- Engaging in hobbies
- Engaging in crafts
- Engaging in performing and visual arts
- Seeking a variety of entertainment and cultural opportunities

Note:

From *A Functional Assessment and Curriculum for Teaching Students with Disabilities, Vol. I: Self-Care, Motor Skills, Household Management, and Living Skills, 4th Ed.*, by M.Bender, P. J. Valletutti, and C. Baglin; *Vol. II: Nonverbal Communication, Oral Communication, and Literacy Preparation, 4th Ed*, by P. J. Valletutti, M. Bender, A. S. Hoffnung, and C. A. Baglin; *Vol. III: Functional Academics, 3rd Ed.*, by P. J. Valletutti, M. Bender, and C. A. Baglin; *Vol. IV: Interpersonal, Competitive Job-Finding, and Leisure-Time Skills, 2nd Ed.*, by M. Bender, P. J. Valletutti, and C. A. Baglin, 2008, Austin, TX: PRO-ED. Copyright 2008 by PRO-ED, Inc. Reprinted with permission.

Access to the General Education Curriculum

The Individuals With Disabilities Education Act (IDEA) (U.S. Congress, 1997) required that reference be made in a child's Individualized Education Program (IEP) to the extent to which the child would be involved in the general education curriculum; that is, the regular curriculum that applies to students in regular schools. This requirement became much stronger with IDEA's 2004 amendments, which reinforced the No Child Left Behind Act (U.S. Congress, 2002) in endeavoring to ensure that all students, regardless of their level of disability, should achieve high standards related to the general education curriculum. Students were to participate in the mandated educational accountability processes, and IEPs were to specify what accommodations would be made in general curriculum and assessment processes. The rationale was that involvement in the regular curriculum would lead to increased teacher expectations and, consequently, to improved student outcomes.

There are similar views encouraging access to the general curriculum in other developed countries. For example, in New South Wales, Australia, the Board of Studies stipulates that for the elementary section of the curriculum (ages 5 to12), there is one syllabus for all students, although students with special educational needs would require additional support or adjustments to be able to achieve syllabus outcomes. Outcomes are described as part of a continuum of learning statements in a particular content area and, most importantly, these learnings are the shared focus for all students. For secondary students (ages 12 to 18), a life-skills curriculum can be provided for students with a moderate or severe intellectual disability. This brings a functional dimension to the skills, knowledge, and values offered to students.

There is considerable debate about what is meant by the concept of "access to the general curriculum." Dymond et al. (2007) point out that while access to the general curriculum is frequently interpreted as meaning access to an academic curriculum, there are also many other interpretations. According to Dymond et al (2007), diverse definitions of access to the general curriculum can include

- Access to information, materials and the classroom where instruction is delivered
- Access to learning
- Access to a curriculum aligned with the state learning standards
- Access to the core curriculum
- Access to all experiences included in general curriculum
- Access to a curriculum that extends beyond academic skills into life skills. (Dymond, Renzaglia, Gilson, & Slagor, 2007)

With such variation in definition, there are many different school practices that may be interpreted by teachers as providing access to the general curriculum. For example, Dymond et al. (2007) interviewed 25 teachers in a large urban high school in the midwestern United States, seeking their interpretation of issues related to access to the general curriculum for students with significant cognitive disabilities. Responses of general educators and regular educators were compared. General educators tended to define curriculum access in terms of access to similar content and materials, whereas the special educators focused on individualization and access to academics and life skills. Agran and colleagues found that while special education teachers agreed that access to the general curriculum would increase expectations for students with disabilities, they also believed that such students should not have to meet the same state-based curriculum performance standards as other students (Agran, Alper, & Wehmeyer, 2002).

In the United States the establishment of state-based standards has been part of a reform process designed to increase student performance by increasing school accountability for student outcomes. All states have provided alternative assessments for students whose disability prevents them from participating in standard assessments. This has led to considerable debate about whether some students should be "excused" from meeting the alternative assessment standards, and whether the results of alternative assessments should be in the school's annual yearly progress reports.

On the positive side, alternative assessments are seen as a way of involving students who have an intellectual disability in state accountability systems, thereby increasing expectations and consequently outcomes. Critics view the inclusion of students with disabilities in accountability systems as counterproductive, leading to a narrowing of the curriculum and teaching of irrelevant, test-based skills. At worst, they may lead to exclusion or discouragement of low-achieving students. Flowers and her colleagues have reported on a large-scale study of teachers' perceptions of alternative assessments (AA) (Flowers, Ahlgrim-Delzell, Browder, & Spooner, 2005). As a result, they made the following recommendations:

- Ways need to be developed to make AA more efficient with more efficient data-collection procedures.
- Technical evidence needs to be provided on the validity and reliability of AAs. Once they are shown to be valid and reliable, this evidence needs to be provided to parents and educators.
- Teachers should be given professional development regarding the strategies they need to be able to increase access of students with disabilities to the general curriculum.

Most significantly, they recommended that all students should be included in school accountability processes. This suggestion was based on their research finding that teachers see more benefits in AA procedures when their students' scores are part of the accountability system.

Wehmeyer and colleagues conducted an observational study of the way in which middle school students with an intellectual disability accessed the general curriculum (Wehmeyer, Lattin, Lapp-Prinker, & Agran, 2003). Observations took place in both segregated and inclusive classrooms. They found that students who had more intense support needs spent less time on tasks linked to a standard. They also found that students in inclusive settings were more likely to be working on standards-linked tasks, and that IEP objectives were most likely to be worked on in segregated settings. Importantly, they pointed out the difference between *access* to the general curriculum and *progress* in the general curriculum, and note that the federal law requires not just access, but progress. They made the following suggestions to improve both access and progress:

- Standards should be written as open-ended, based on principles of universal design for learning (see below);
- An individualized planning process should ensure that the program is based on the general curriculum, but take into account the unique learning needs of the student;
- Universally designed curricular materials and quality instructional strategies should be used throughout the school;
- Students who need more intensive instruction should be targeted for group instruction to ensure they progress in the curriculum;
- Additional strategies should be used to ensure progress for students whose learning needs are not met by school-wide or group efforts. (Wehmeyer et al., 2003; Wehmeyer, Sands, Knowlton, & Kozleski, 2002)

The findings of Wehmeyer et al. (2003) were generally confirmed in a follow-up study by Soukup and colleagues, which also observed the extent to which students with intellectual disabilities accessed the general education curriculum in a variety of settings (Soukup, Wehmeyer, Bashinski, & Bovaird, 2007). Soukup et al. found, among other things, that students in highly inclusive classrooms were more likely to be working on grade-level standards, and students in special education classrooms were more likely to be working on IEP-based goals. These differences were not explained by the support-needs ratings of the groups, as the support needs for low inclusion and high inclusion groups were similar. Agran et al. (2006) have demonstrated that when a specific self-determined instructional model is employed and the appropriate supports are available, it is possible to achieve mastery levels of progress in students with moderate or severe disability who are provided with access to the general education curriculum in regular classrooms (Agran, Cavin, Wehmeyer, & Palmer, 2006).

Debate, discussion, and research on the concept of access to the general curriculum will continue. Some will argue that while such access is appropriate for students with a mild intellectual disability, it is more useful for students with moderate or severe disabilities to have an individualized educational plan that is based on an assessment of their current and future life-skill needs. The contrary argument is that by considering how every student can access the regular curriculum and, as importantly, progress in the regular curriculum, higher expectations will be both set and achieved.

FOR REFLECTION OR DISCUSSION:

- Discuss the different curriculum models. Are you aware of what curriculum models are being used in classes you have observed? How well have those models served the needs of students who have an intellectual disability?

Universal Design for Learning

The principle of universal design for learning is one that has arisen from the disability movement. It recognizes that many of the handicaps experienced by people with a disability result from their interaction with the environment (Hitchcock, Meyer, Rose, & Jackson, 2002). If the environment changes, the handicap is lessened or may disappear. The major impetus for universal design has come from architecture. It is very easy to see that making all buildings wheelchair accessible removes huge impediments to the ability of people who use wheelchairs to shop, work, and socialize in the community. An unplanned positive consequence is that the buildings also become more accessible to people with delivery carts and baby strollers. Other architectural changes that improve access for all include audible walk signs, talking elevators, and clear signage.

The work of the Center for Universal Design at North Carolina State University has been highly influential as a national research, information, and technical assistance center, promoting accessible and universal design in housing, buildings, outdoor, and urban environments. The Center works to promote the view that all new environments and products should be usable by everyone regardless of their ability, or other circumstances. In 1997 the Center published seven principles of universal design that had been developed by architects, product designers, engineers, and environmental design researchers. The principles are summarized below.

1. *Equitable use*: The design should be useful and marketable to people with diverse abilities. The means of use should be identical for all users, or equivalent, and should avoid segregating or stigmatizing any users.

2. *Flexibility in use*: The design should accommodate a wide range of individual preferences and abilities by providing choice in methods of use, facilitating user accuracy and providing adaptability to the user's pace.
3. *Simple and intuitive use*: Use of the design should be easy to understand, regardless of the user's experience, knowledge, language skills, or concentration level. The design should eliminate unnecessary complexity and accommodate a range of literacy and language skills.
4. *Perceptible information*: The design should communicate necessary information effectively to the user, regardless of ambient conditions or the user's abilities. Pictorial, verbal and tactile modes should be used and the legibility of essential information should ne maximized. The design should be compatible with techniques used by people with sensory limitations.
5. *Tolerance for error*: The design should minimize hazards and avoid the adverse consequences of accidental or unintended actions. Fail-safe features should be provided where possible, and there should be warnings about hazards or errors.
6. *Low physical effort*: The design should be able to be used efficiently and comfortably with a minimum of fatigue. The need for sustained physical effort should be minimized.
7. *Size and space for approach and use*: Appropriate size and space should be provided for approach, reach, manipulation, and use, regardless of the user's body size or mobility (Center for Universal Design, 1997).

When the universal design principles are applied to learning, it is easy to see that failure can frequently be conceptualized as problems in the interaction between the child and the curriculum. For example, if a person who used a wheelchair was unable to attend work because of the steps at the entrance to the building, we would nowadays regard that as a failure of the building design, rather than as a failure of the person. If a student with a disability fails to achieve at school, we must ask the question, is that a failure of the student or does it raise questions related to curriculum, materials, and teaching?

Proponents of UDL would argue that inflexible curricula create barriers to learning, particularly for students who have a disability. They would argue that schools need to recognize that a characteristic of all schools is the diversity of their student population. Just as buildings are designed, from the outset, to be as accessible as possible to as many people as possible, a universally designed curriculum would be designed so that it was sufficiently flexible to meet the needs of the greatest variety of learners.

UDL Guidelines

Much of the work in developing and encouraging UDL in education has been done by researchers at the Center for Applied Special Technology (CAST). The organization began in 1984 with a focus on improving the accessibility of computer technology to students with a disability. They have recently published a set of UDL guidelines, which they refer to as Version 1.0, with the expectation that they will be further developed and refined (CAST, 2008). The guiding principles are provided under three headings: (a) representation, (b) expression, and (c) engagement, as it is argued that these are the aspects of curriculum where universal design is essential. The CAST guidelines are summarized below.

Principle 1: Provide Multiple Means of Representation

Provide options for perception. Representation refers to the way in which material is presented, and the material needs to be accessible to students. A textbook can be presented as standard printed text, in large print, as Braille, or digitally. If it is available in digital form it can be transformed into a variety of other forms, depending on what is most perceptible to the student. A novel available also as a film becomes immediately perceptible to many more students.

Provide options for language and symbols. Many students have difficulty comprehending language and symbols. Options should be provided that define the vocabulary to be used, clarify any complex syntax and structure, and ensure that the material is accessible to children with language difficulties or whose first language is not English. We can probably all recall situations in which a concept we were finding difficult to understand was made suddenly clearer by presentation of a flow-chart or diagram.

Provide options for comprehension. UDL proponents argue that properly designed curricula will include “cognitive ramps” to ensure that all students have access to knowledge. The curriculum needs to include options that provide or activate background knowledge, highlight critical features, emphasize major ideas and relationships, guide information processing, and support memory and transfer. Examples of these are advance organizers, multiple examples, explicit prompts, graduated scaffolds, and concept maps.

Principle 2: Provide Multiple Means of Action and Expression

The first principle referred to the ways in which students receive knowledge and information. The second principle suggests that there should also be flexibility in the way students are expected to act on and express information. The options that could be presented are outlined below.

Provide options for physical actions. This guideline refers primarily to ways in which common assistive technologies are used. In order to provide a clear link between technology and the curriculum, there need to be options in the type of physical response expected of the student, the mechanism for navigation, and the ways in which various technologies are accessed. This could be done through technologies such as switch options, adapted keyboards, touch screens, or voice-activated commands.

Provide options for expressive skills and fluency. Students with problems in writing may nevertheless be able to produce a good oral story. Alternative media should be made available for students who have difficulty with the written form, and there should be a variety of supports to guide students who are at different levels of expressive competence. There should be variety in the media provided for communication, for composition and problem solving, and for supporting practice and performance.

Provide options for executive functions. Executive functions are the highest levels of the capacity to act skillfully, to set goals, plan strategies and monitor outcomes. The UDL approach suggests that there should be options that guide effective goal-setting, support planning and development, facilitate managing information and resources, and enhance capacity for monitoring process. These can include embedded prompts, checklists, self-monitoring questions, and graphs of progress.

Principle 3: Provide Multiple Means of Engagement

An essential requirement for learning is engagement or motivation. Different means of representation need to be used to ensure that all students are engaged and motivated to learn. Options that might increase engagement are outlined below.

Provide options for recruiting interest. Students differ from each other in what engages them, and their interests will vary over time and even from day to day. Engagement can be increased if teachers provide options that increase individual choice and autonomy, enhance relevance to the student interests, and reduce threats and distractions. For example, activities can be related to students' lives, and should be appropriate to their age and ability. There should be variations in the number of features or items presented at a time and the perceived level of support.

Provide options for sustaining effort and persistence. Learning usually requires sustained attention and effort. While many students can regulate their attention and effort as required, students with an intellectual disability are likely to find this difficult. In order to sustain effort and persistence, options should be provided that heighten the relevance and attractiveness of goals and objectives, vary levels of challenge and support, foster collaboration and communication, and increase mastery-oriented feedback. This could involve division of goals into short-term objectives, use of prompts or scaffolds, providing opportunities for collaboration, and use of peer tutoring and support.

Provide options for self-regulation. Students need to develop their intrinsic ability to regulate their emotions and motivations. This can be assisted through options that guide personal goal-setting and expectations, scaffold coping skills and strategies, and develop self-assessment and reflection. Strategies might include provision of coaches or mentors to model goal-setting, using charts to monitor changes in behaviors and providing a variety of sources of feedback.

Readers who are interested in obtaining more detail about the application of the above principles should consult the original CAST (2008) document, where more information is presented than could be included in this summary (see Reference list).

UDL in Action in Schools

The UDL movement has had a significant impact on educational practice for students with disabilities. For example, Lieberman, Lytle, and Clarcq (2008) provide case studies of universal design in action. Their paper includes a checklist that outlines strategies which can be used to ensure that universal design principles are used to provide an inclusive classroom. The strategies are listed under the headings of inclusiveness, physical access, delivery modes, interaction, feedback, and multiple ways to develop knowledge or skills. Meo outlines a PAL (planning for all learners) process, based on UDL principles and provides a case study of how the process was implemented in a secondary reading-comprehension program in a regular class including five students with disabilities (Meo, 2008). Van Kraayenoord provides an example of the use of UDL principles to improve the inclusiveness of a primary classroom (van Kraayenoord, 2007). Box 5.3 provides an example of how one teacher attempted to include UDL principles in designing a unit of work for her sixth grade class.

Computer technology is an area where universal design principles have a particular application. Wehmeyer et al. (2004) have highlighted the UDL principles that have direct relevance in ensuring that students with an intellectual disability are able to access classroom technology. These include

- Flexibility in use
- Simplicity and intuitiveness of use
- Perceptible information
- Tolerance for error (Wehmeyer, Smith, Palmer, & Davies, 2004).

The issue of use of classroom technology for students with an intellectual disability is treated in more detail in the next chapter.

FOR REFLECTION OR DISCUSSION:

- See Box 5.3

BOX 5.3 APPLYING UDL PRINCIPLES IN THE CLASSROOM

Mrs. McGill is planning a unit of work on the water cycle for her Grade 6 science class. She is very aware that it is a mixed ability class, and she is keen to use UDL principles in preparing the unit. She has one student in her class with a moderate intellectual disability and one with a mild disability. She also had four students who have reading difficulties and one who has been diagnosed with ADHD.

In her first lesson, the class works in four table groups of 5 to 6 students. Each group is given four plastic glasses; one is full of water and three are empty:

- The full glass is labeled ALL THE WATER IN THE WORLD
- One glass is labeled SALT WATER
- One is labeled FRESH WATER WE CAN'T GET TO DRINK (e.g., ICEBERGS)
- The third glass is labeled FRESH WATER WE CAN DRINK

Each group is asked to guess how much water goes into each empty glass. This is then discussed by the class as a whole, and each group's glasses are displayed to the class and then converted to column graphs that are as close as possible to the appearance of the three glasses. Mrs. McGill uses an Excel program on the class electronic whiteboard to create the graphs. Each student is given a copy of their group's graph and they are asked to investigate the correct answer before the next lesson. Mrs. McGill suggests the following ways they could find out:

- Research the Internet in the school library or at home
- Consult an encyclopedia or textbook in the library
- Ask their local librarian for help
- See if a parent or sibling can help.

Mrs. McGill says the students can research in pairs if they wish, and she encourages more able students to act as peer models for the students in the class with learning difficulties. Supporting other students is a highly praised activity, and Mrs. McGill encourages cooperation rather than competition in the classroom.

At the next lesson, groups meet to discuss their findings and try to agree on what is the correct answer to the problem that has been set. This is then reported to the class. Mrs. McGill hears the group reports and gives feedback on who is the closest to correct. She asks how each group came to their conclusions and praises the process as much as the outcome. In fact, the answer is that one teaspoon represents the water available for drinking, two teaspoons the nonavailable fresh water, and the rest (97%) is salt water.

The next part of the unit concerns how water gets to the tap. Mrs. McGill has located a short video showing people gathering water from a river, from a well, and from a town pump. This leads to a discussion of where town water comes from and Mrs. McGill uses a Flash presentation she had downloaded from the Internet that provides a clear and simple explanation of the water cycle. Students are then asked to do their own research in their groups on how water gets to the tap, and report back. This is the major activity for the unit and can be done over 3 weeks. Lessons in between will hear reports on progress and will provide additional activities related to the water cycle, including investigating what happens to the water when it rains at school.

For the major project, Mrs. McGill provides a variety of resources the groups can use. These include simple and more complex books, some easily read handouts and diagrams, and several computer-based resources. Groups are asked to report back on their findings and can do so in a format negotiated with Mrs. McGill. The report could be a written and illustrated report, an oral presentation with PowerPoint slides, a video, or a mixture of these. Each student in the group must contribute in some way to the group report. For example, it is agreed that Larry, who has a moderate intellectual disability, will operate the PowerPont demonstration and explain one of the diagrams for his group's report.

DISCUSSION QUESTIONS:

1. Mrs. McGill hoped to follow UDL principles in designing the unit. Do you think she was successful? Specifically, how did she provide
   a. multiple means of representation;
   b. multiple means of expression;
   c. multiple means of engagement?
2. Can you think of any other ways that UDL principles could have been used to make this unit accessible to all students in the classroom?

Research Base for Inclusive Educational Practice

The type of classroom curriculum that is followed by a student has been shown sometimes to be related to the type of educational placement (inclusive or segregated). It has been stated earlier in this chapter that the trend since the 1970s has been toward more inclusive placements for students with an intellectual disability, although a range of separate specialized provisions remains. Most of the policy and legislative decisions that have led to placement of students with an intellectual disability into regular schools have arisen from a social justice and equity perspective (Jenkinson, 2001). The policy and legislative decisions related to education have not necessarily been supported by or instigated as a result of research evidence demonstrating that students with disabilities achieve more academically or are happier or more socially integrated in mainstream settings. However, there is a long history of research on the impacts of segregation of children with a disability. For example, around 70 years ago, Skeels and Dye reported on the impact of institutionalization on young children, suggesting that being in a nonstimulating environment could lead to lowering of IQ (Skeels & Dye, 1939). An influential study by Lloyd Dunn questioned the efficacy of segregated classes for students with a mild disability (Dunn, 1968). Dunn found that there was limited evidence of better outcomes for students in segregated classes; that there was an overrepresentation of minority and disadvantaged groups; and that the growth of special classes hindered development of instructional options in regular classes. Dunn's work was much cited by opponents of segregated classes and gave support to social-justice-based views opposing separation on the grounds of disability, although his work was not without its critics. For example, there was criticism of the methodology of studies used to demonstrate that withdrawal into special education classes was ineffective (Tindal, 1985). On the other hand, a report published by the National Academy of Sciences in the United States concluded that classification and placement of children in separate special education classes is ineffective and discriminatory (Heller, Holtzman, & Messick, 1982).The passing of Public Law 94/142, the Education of All Handicapped Children's Act, in the United States in 1975 was the culmination of strong antidiscrimination activity supported by research such as that of Dunn.

During the 1970s the focus of many researchers in special education was on the impact and outcomes of behaviorally based instructional approaches for learners with various disabilities. There was limited investigation at the time of the effects of location, and most research was conducted in segregated settings. After that time, research in integrated and inclusive settings moved toward a focus on interaction and on attitudinal surveys rather than on the efficacy of instructional strategies and their outcomes. There was a movement from discussion on *what and how* to teach to a discussion of *where* teaching should take place (Baker & Zigmond, 1995).

There are major methodological difficulties in researching the effects of inclusion on students with an intellectual disability. First there is the problem of comparability of included and segregated samples. For ethical and practical reasons, it is very difficult to assign students to inclusive or segregated settings on a random basis for research purposes (Cole, 1999). Educational placement decisions are complex and are not subject to simple research manipulation. There is always the possibility that there will be systematic differences between the two groups that have led to their placement in one or other of the settings and are not, therefore, outcomes of the placement. Parents of students who are more alert, more interactive, and more socially capable may be more likely to seek their placement in a regular class than parents of students with a similar level of disability, but with poorer social functioning. Further, schools may be more likely to accept requests for regular placements if the students are more capable and seem more likely to be able to "fit in."

A second problem in evaluating the effects of particular types of placement is deciding on the outcome measures. Decisions need to be made about how the success or otherwise of inclusion is to be measured and how it can be determined if inclusion has been successful. Possible measurements of success include academic outcomes, social outcomes, parental satisfaction, student satisfaction, and teacher satisfaction. As a result there have been critics of the research that has suggested positive outcomes of inclusive educational practices (Kavale, 2002; Kavale & Mostert, 2003). From his analysis of research on inclusion, Kavale concluded that "although the ideological and political support for inclusion are steadfast, the empirical evidence is less convincing" (2002, p. 210). Kavale and Mostert argued that "full inclusionists" have begun "parroting leftist political thought as a substitute for empiricism" (2003, p. 193).

However, if there are benefits arising from the education in mainstream classes of students who have an intellectual disability, it should be possible to demonstrate some differences between included and nonincluded groups in terms of academic outcomes, degree of social interaction, and/or the attitudes of others toward them and their inclusion. The research evidence for these outcomes is now considered.

Academic Outcomes

Perhaps for some of the methodological reasons outlined above, there has not been a huge amount of research on the academic benefits of enrolling children with an intellectual disability in mainstream classes. Several of the studies that are available have been done with children who have Down syndrome. This helps to overcome some of the methodological problems. While there are differences among children with Down syndrome, the fact that they have been diagnosed with DS is usually the reason why some form of special placement is being considered. In addition, the achievements of students with DS in special education settings are quite well understood. As a result, study of the achievements of students with DS in mainstream settings can be seen as a reasonable measure of the outcomes of inclusive educational practices.

In an early study, Casey, Jones, Kugler, and Watkins (1988) compared two groups of 18 children with Down syndrome aged 3 to10 years over a period of 2 years. One group was in a special school and one group was in a regular class. They found that the children in regular classes performed better on all cognitive and academic variables measured. These variables included comprehension, expressive language, verbal, fluency, numeracy, and drawing. Surprisingly, they also showed a significantly greater gain in mental age than their special school counterparts (Casey, Jones, Kugler, & Watkins, 1988).

Studies by Sloper and colleagues have given an indication of the complexity involved when comparisons such as these are being made. While they found mainstream schooling to be a predictor of academic success, other predictors included female gender, mental age, excitability scores, and mother's coping style (Sloper, Cunningham, Turner, & Knussen, 1990; Sloper & Turner, 1994). In a recent report, one of the research team (Turner) and colleagues followed up the remaining members of the cohort at age 21 (Turner, Alborz, & Gayle, 2008). They found that while the level of intellectual impairment was a significant predictor of academic outcomes at age 9 and 14, it was less influential by age 21. By that age, those who had attended mainstream schools showed better academic outcomes than students who had been in special schools. One reason for this could be that that mainstream schools, regardless of the child's ability level, will tend to have a greater focus on academic and literacy skills and will be more likely to be providing access to the general education curriculum than special schools.

In a detailed small-scale study, Rietveld (2005) used a case study methodology to investigate the mathematical learning experiences of three young boys with Down syndrome enrolled in mainstream or special classes in New Zealand. Rietveld was critical of the pedagogy used in all of the classes. She found that no one helped the children to develop error awareness or self-checking. She observed that children were regularly praised for being busy and keeping on task, but that the children frequently did not know what they were being praised for. Professional development for teachers tended to be focused on behavior management rather than on teaching and learning (Rietveld, 2005).

Baker, Wang, and Walberg (1995) summarized the results of three meta-analyses of research on the impact of inclusion on academic and social skills. All the effect sizes were positive for inclusion, both for academic and social skills, although the effects were "not huge." Baker and colleagues concluded that the results of 15 years of research suggest "that segregation of special students in separate classrooms is actually deleterious to their academic performance and social adjustment." However, the studies included in the various meta-analyses would tend not to have included studies of students with moderate or severe intellectual disability (Baker, Wang, & Walberg, 1995).

Freeman and Alkin (2000) reviewed a large number of studies of effectiveness of special class placement for students with intellectual disability. They found that children with milder levels of intellectual disability achieved better academically in inclusive classrooms than in special classrooms. They also found that the social skills and competence of students with mild intellectual disability improved in regular classrooms compared with special classrooms. Outcomes of research related to students with more severe disability were more mixed. They found that inclusive classroom placements led to improved social skill attainments for students with severe disability, but results for academic skills showed a benefit for inclusive placement in only some of the studies examined. The researchers concluded that the greater the degree of inclusion (i.e., full time rather than part time), the better the academic outcomes (Freeman & Alkin, 2000).

A large study conducted in the Netherlands was reported by Peetsma and colleagues (Peetsma, Vergeer, Roeleveld, & Karsten, 2001). The study compared matched pairs of students with mild intellectual disability or learning and behavioral difficulties over a 2-year and 4-year period. Initially there were 252 matched pairs. The researchers found only a few differences after the 2-year period. At this time, pupils with learning or behavioral difficulties in regular education made more progress in mathematics than matched pupils in special education, while school motivation was better in special education for students with intellectual disability. After 4 years, students with both types of disability performed better in cognitive skills if they were in regular classes, but no differences were observed in school motivation. Teachers were also interviewed to assess the extent to which internal differentiation was used in the classroom and whether specialist provisions were available in the classroom for students with additional needs. Surprisingly, they found that more internal differentiation in the classroom could, under some circumstances, produce negative outcomes, including poorer outcomes in mathematics, school motivation, and self-confidence. More research is obviously needed to see whether this finding can be confirmed, as differentiation is usually regarded as an essential aspect of good teaching in heterogeneous classrooms (Tomlinson, 2004).

The question of whether inclusive classrooms lead to improved academic outcomes for students with an intellectual disability is clearly a complex one, without a simple answer. Research suggests that it can lead to better academic progress than special classes for comparable students, particularly if it leads to a greater focus on teaching academic skills. However, the fact that a student is in an inclusive classroom does not, by itself, produce better outcomes. Decisions about placement are individual ones, usually made by parents, with advice from a learning support team. Once the decision has been made it becomes the school's responsibility to ensure that each child obtains maximum benefit from their educational program, regardless of location.

Attitudinal Studies

Many of the early studies of the outcomes of inclusion focused on the attitudes of teachers, principals, parents, and students to the mainstreaming of students with a disability. One of the reasons for this was the belief, at the time, that the main impediment to successful inclusion was the negative attitude of some teachers, principals, and peers. It was believed that if attitudes were positive, inclusion would be successful. The most common finding on attitudes was summarized in a meta-analysis by Scruggs and Mastropieri (1996), based on nearly 40 years of research studies. Their finding was that while regular education teachers were supportive of the principle of inclusion, they were not keen to have students with disabilities in their own classes. Teachers' concerns included their lack of knowledge of special education strategies and the likelihood that they would not receive the resources and support required to assist mainstreamed students (Scruggs & Mastropieri, 1996). Teachers express even greater concern about lack of support and resources if the students who are mainstreamed have a severe disability (McNally, Cole, & Waugh, 2001).

There is some evidence that professionals who are more remote from the classroom such as principals and counselors are more likely to have positive attitudes than regular class teachers or special class teachers (Center & Ward, 1989; Center, Ward, Parmenter, & Nash, 1985). Several studies have shown that student teachers, teachers, and some principals worry that they will not have the teaching competencies or physical resources needed to include children with a disability in their classes (Bailey & du Plessis, 1988; Lambe & Bones, 2006).

A feature of attitudes is that they are dynamic and can be changed. For example, Campbell and colleagues found that student teachers are likely to improve their attitudes to children with Down syndrome following formal instruction and structured fieldwork (Campbell, Gilmore, & Cuskelly, 2003). A study of early childhood care providers in the United States found that training and experience leads to better attitudes and fewer perceptions of barriers to inclusion (Mulvihill, Shearer, & Van Horn, 2002). Another study found that, although teachers and the general public regard inclusion as socially beneficial for students with Down syndrome, a majority of teachers and the general public believe that such children will "do better" in a setting other than a regular class with children of their own age (Gilmore et al., 2003).

Studies of the attitudes of peers suggest that while they lack specific knowledge of disability, they tend to have generally positive attitudes to students with disabilities (Kyle & Davies, 1991). However, in a relatively large study in Canada, McDougall and colleagues found that while the majority of high school students had positive to very positive attitudes toward their mainstreamed peers with disabilities, 20% of students held negative to very negative attitudes. They also found that attitudes were related to specific aspects of the school culture (McDougall, DeWit, King, Miller, & Killip, 2006). If even a small minority of students display negative attitudes, the school experiences of students with a disability could be made very unpleasant.

Another study suggesting that attitudes are amenable to change was conducted by Rillotta and Nettlebeck (2007). They found that training programs for secondary school students could lead to improved attitudes to students with an intellectual disability, and that these improvements may be sustained over time. Longer training produced more positive attitudes (Rillotta & Nettlebeck, 2007). As is typical for such studies, attitude was measured by responses to an attitude survey rather than by a more direct measure. This can lead to results that are artificially positive. Respondents will sometimes say the "right thing" in a questionnaire; for example, agreeing with a statement such as, "I would be happy to invite a child with a disability to my birthday party." However, this does not always mean that the statement would be reflected in practice. The party invitations may not go out!

The complexity of investigating children's attitudes was observed by Nowicki and Sandieson (2002) who conducted a meta-analysis of studies of children's attitudes to people with intellectual or physical disabilities over the period 1990–2000. They found that while children's attitudes to people with a disability were not as positive as they might have been, there are many difficulties in investigating such attitudes that make it problematic to try to reach firm conclusions from the research that has been done. The researchers concluded that further careful research is needed if appropriate strategies to promote positive attitudes to inclusion are to be implemented (Nowicki & Sandieson, 2002).

While many of the attitudinal studies have been of the attitudes of "others" to the enrollment of students with a disability, it is also important to know what the students themselves think. Research with students with disabilities suggests that they have mixed views, and tend to report the location they are in as their preferred option, whether it is segregation or inclusion (Curtin & Clarke, 2005). Parents also have varying views about the type of placement that is best for their child, with some very much in favor of inclusion, while others express a strong preference for specialized placements (Palmer, Fuller, Arora, & Nelson, 2001). Sometimes parents who have positive attitudes toward inclusion are nevertheless worried about issues such as a lack of resources, the need for specialized teaching, or potential social isolation for their children if placed in a mainstream setting (Elkins, van Kraayenoord, & Jobling, 2003; Leyser & Kirk, 2004).

The attitudes of all participants are undoubtedly significant variables when students with an intellectual disability are enrolled in mainstream schools. It is likely that they are both dependent and independent variables. In other words, the attitudes of parents, students with disabilities, peers, and professionals will affect the outcomes of inclusive placements.

Conversely, the outcomes of inclusive placements will affect the attitudes of all participants.

Social Interaction Outcomes

A common argument in favor of inclusive schooling is that placing people together will lead them to interact positively with each other. A moment's thought will make it clear that this does not always happen. We are all aware that schools are places where social interaction can be difficult and children can be excluded for a variety of reasons. Many different cliques form and friendship patterns are often problematic, even for children without any disability and with relatively good social skills. It is therefore naïve to think that students with a disability will achieve instant acceptance if they are placed in a regular class. Some students report isolation, stigmatization, and exclusion in mainstreamed settings (Cooney, Jahoda, Gumley, & Knott, 2006; Curtin & Clarke, 2005).

Some developmental problems associated with intellectual disability make interaction difficult for the people who have them. Children with poor language skills, social skills, or mobility skills will have their interactions necessarily restricted. For example, Macintosh and Dissanayake, in an Australian study, found that children with high functioning autism and children with Asperger syndrome observed in playground settings were significantly less likely than their typically developing peers to be in ongoing social exchanges or in interactions with three or more peers (Macintosh & Dissanayake, 2006). Whether these interaction difficulties are able to be modified through teaching or other forms of intervention is an important continuing research question. In a useful discussion, Meyer points out that adult mediation can have a significant impact on friendship interactions, both positively and negatively (Meyer, 2001). Another recent study has suggested that students with intellectual disability can demonstrate social competence in both segregated and inclusive settings (Hardiman, Guerin, & Fitzsimons, 2009).

Friendship interactions among typically developing children is a subject that has been extensively investigated by researchers in child psychology and development. The study of relationships between children with developmental disabilities and their peers without disabilities is much less developed. Webster and Carter (2007) recently reviewed 36 studies of social relationships between children with and without developmental disabilities and criticized such research as "patchy at best, limited in scope, and nonlinear in its development." Another research review found that while inclusion appears to improve social skills, students with intellectual disability in regular classrooms tended to receive lower social acceptance scores than students without a disability (Freeman & Alkin, 2000).

The question arises of whether students need a particular level of social competence for a regular class placement to lead to positive social interactions. On an intuitive level, it seems likely that positive interactions will occur when students who are included have good social competence and are sufficiently able to interact on a normal social level with their peers. However, Cutts and Sigafoos (2001) studied a group of adolescents with intellectual disability in a regular high school in Australia and found that their level of social interaction with peers was not significantly correlated with their level of social competence. It should be noted, nevertheless, that the social interactions of the students with intellectual disability were largely, although not exclusively, with other students who also had an intellectual disability (Cutts & Sigafoos, 2001). This is not entirely unexpected as school groupings often involve friendships among groups of students of similar age and with similar interests and abilities. The important question is whether the student with a disability has the opportunity for positive interactions in the school, regardless of whom that interaction is with.

It is sometimes argued that inclusion is appropriate for students with a mild intellectual disability who can access the general curriculum, but does not benefit students with more severe or multiple disabilities (Fox & Ysseldyke, 1997). However, recent Australian research has suggested that students with the most severe disabilities can benefit from regular class placements. Such students are likely to experience more communicative interactions in regular classes than in special classes (Foreman, Arthur-Kelly, Pascoe, & Smyth-King, 2004). A probable reason for this is that there is more opportunity for social and communicative interaction in regular classes. If a student with severe intellectual disability attends a regular class, the rest of the class will be verbal, so there is often a special teacher's aide assigned to the student. This greatly increases the opportunities for communication partners to attempt to interact with the child. This does not necessarily mean that all students with multiple and severe disabilities should be in regular classes. However it does suggest that if they are in special classes, particularly when the other students also have multiple and severe disabilities, communicative interactions may need to be encouraged through specific interventions. These interventions are likely to involve teachers and other communication partners becoming more aware of the communicative intent of their students and using specific strategies to foster communicative interactions (Foreman, Arthur-Kelly, Pascoe, & Bennett, 2008).

Parents have varying views about inclusion, which are generally respected by school systems. Some parents will have strong views that they want specialized services and are not concerned about whether their child has contact with students without a disability. Others hold similarly strong views that they want their child to attend a neighborhood school and to have the opportunity to mix with a diversity of students. Both views are defensible, and research does not come down exclusively or unequivocally on the side of either viewpoint. However, parents' rights to choose an inclusive placement, if that is their preference, have been strongly supported by legislation and policy.

FOR REFLECTION OR DISCUSSION:

- Draw up a list of the advantages and disadvantages of placement in a regular class for a student with an intellectual disability
- How would you adapt your classroom to provide for the needs of a student with spina bifida and mild intellectual disability?
- On balance, does research appear to support inclusion or special class placement?

Summary

The start of formal schooling is an important step for children with an intellectual disability, many of whom will have already been involved with an early educational program in a mainstream or specialized setting. As a result of legislation supporting the inclusion of people with disabilities in society, and the impact of this on educational policy, many parents will choose to send their child to the neighborhood school or other regular school of their preference. Whether the student is in a regular class or a special class, decisions will need to be made about the type of curriculum that will be followed. In many school systems, the expectation will be that all students will access the general curriculum, although some will require considerable adaptation and support. Access to the general curriculum will be increased if Universal Design for Learning principles are applied in curriculum design. Whether inclusive education leads to measurable improved academic and social outcomes is a question that has been extensively researched, without a definitive answer. Like many questions in education, an absolute response is difficult because of variability among students. However, all teachers in regular classes should anticipate that they will have students with an intellectual disability included in their class at some stage and should use all the resources available to make this a positive experience for all concerned.

References

Agran, M., Alper, S., & Wehmeyer, M. (2002). Access to the general curriculum for students with significant disabilities: What it means to teachers. *Education and Training in Mental Retardation and Developmental Disabilities, 37*(2), 123–133.

Agran, M., Cavin, M., Wehmeyer, M., & Palmer, S. (2006). Participation of students with moderate to severe disabilities in the general curriculum: The effects of the Self-Determined Model of Instruction. *Research and Practice for Persons with Severe Disabilities, 31*(3), 230–241.

Ainscow, M., & Miles, S. (2008). Making education for all inclusive: Where next? *Prospects, 38,* 15–34.

Bailey, J., & du Plessis, D. (1988). An investigation of school principals' attitudes towards inclusion. *Australasian Journal of Special Education, 22,* 12–29.

Baker, E. T., Wang, M. C., & Walberg, H. J. (1995). The effects of inclusion on learning. *Educational Leadership, 52*(4), 33–35.

Baker, J. M., & Zigmond, N. (1995). The meaning and practice of inclusion for students with learning disabilities: Themes and implications from the five cases. *Journal of Special Education, 29,* 163–180.

Bank-Mikkelsen, N. E. (1969). *Normalization: Letting the mentally retarded obtain an existence as close to normal as possible.* Washington, DC: President's Committee on Mental Retardation.

Bender, M., Valletutti, P. J., & Baglin, C. (2008). *A functional assessment & curriculum for teaching students with disabilities: Volume 1, Self-care skills.* Austin, TX: ProEd.

Browder, D., Spooner, F., Ahlgrim-Delzell, L., Flowers, C., Algozzine, B., & Karvonen, M. (2003). A content analysis of the curricular philosophies reflected in states' alternate assessment performance indicators. *Research and Practice for Persons with Severe Disabilities, 28*(4), 165–181.

Campbell, J., Gilmore, L., & Cuskelly, M. (2003). Changing students' attitudes towards disability and inclusion. *Journal of Intellectual and Developmental Disability, 28,* 369–379.

Carnaby, S. (2007). Developing good practices in the clinical assessment of people with profound intellectual disabilities and multiple impairment. *Journal of Policy and Practice in Intellectual Disabilities, 4*(2), 88–96.

Casey, W., Jones, D., Kugler, B., & Watkins, B. (1988). Integration of Down's syndrome children in the primary school: A longitudinal study of cognitive development and academic attainments. *British Journal of Educational Psychology, 58,* 279–286.

CAST. (2008). *Universal Design for Learning guidelines: Version 1.0.* Wakefield, MA: Author.

Center for Universal Design. (1997). *The principles of universal Design.* Raleigh: North Carolina State University.

Center, Y., & Ward, J. (1989). Attitudes of school psychologists towards the integration of children with disabilities. *International Journal of Disability, Development and Education, 36,* 117–131.

Center, Y., Ward, J., Parmenter, T., & Nash, R. (1985). Principals' attitudes towards the integration of disabled children into regular schools. *The Exceptional Child, 32,* 149–161.

Cole, P. G. (1999). The structure of arguments used to support or oppose policies for students with disabilities. *Journal of Intellectual and Developmental Disability, 24,* 215–225.

Commonwealth Government of Australia. (1992). *Disability Discrimination Act (Cth).* Canberra, Australian Capital Territory: Author.

Cooney, G., Jahoda, A., Gumley, A., & Knott, F. (2006). Young people with intellectual disabilities attending mainstream and segregated schooling: Perceived stigma, social comparison and future aspirations. *Journal of Intellectual Disability Research, 50,* 432–444.

Curtin, M., & Clarke, G. (2005). Listening to young people with physical disabilities experiences of education. *International Journal of Disability, Development and Education, 52,* 195–214.

Cutts, S., & Sigafoos, J. (2001). Social competence and peer interactions of students with intellectual disability in an inclusive high school. *Journal of Intellectual and Developmental Disability, 26,* 127–141.

Dempsey, I. (2008). Legislation, policies and inclusive practices. In P. Foreman (Ed.), *Inclusion in action* (2nd ed., pp. 37–62). Melbourne: Thomson.

Dempsey, I., & Foreman, P. (1997). Trends in the educational placement of students with a disability in New South Wales. *International Journal of Disability, Development and Education, 44,* 207–216.

Dempsey, I., Foreman, P., & Jenkinson, J. (2002). Educational placement of students with a disability in New South Wales and Victoria. *International Journal of Disability, Development and Education, 49,* 31–36.

Department for Education and Skills. (2004). *Removing barriers to achievement: Department for Education and Skills.* London: Author.

Dunn, L. M. (1968). Special education for the mentally retarded: Is much of it justifiable? *Exceptional Children, 35,* 5–22.

Dymond, S. K., Renzaglia, A., Gilson, C., & Slagor, M. (2007). Defining access to the general curriculum for high school students with significant cognitive disabilities. *Research and Practice for Persons with Severe Disabilities, 32*(1), 1–15.

Elkins, J., van Kraayenoord, C. E., & Jobling, A. (2003). Parents' attitudes to inclusion of their children with special needs. *Journal of Research in Special Educational Needs, 3,* 122–129.

Flowers, C., Ahlgrim-Delzell, L., Browder, D., & Spooner, F. (2005). Teachers' perceptions of alternate assessments. *Research and Practice for Persons with Severe Disabilities, 30*(2), 81–92.

Foreman, P. (2008). Setting the scene: Teachers and inclusion. In P. Foreman (Ed.), *Inclusion in action* (2nd ed., pp. 1–36). Melbourne: Thomson.

Foreman, P., Arthur-Kelly, M., Pascoe, D., & Bennett, D. (2008, August). Improving communication of students with PMID through training of communication partners [Abstract]. IASSID World Congress on Intellectual Disability, Capetown, South Africa. *Journal of Intellectual Disability Research, 52*(8/9), 772.

Foreman, P., Arthur-Kelly, M., Pascoe, D., & Smyth-King, N. (2004). Evaluating the educational experiences of students with profound and multiple disabilities in inclusive and segregated classroom settings: An Australian perspective. *Research and Practice for Persons with Severe Disabilities, 29*(3), 183–193.

Fox, N. E., & Ysseldyke, J. E. (1997). Implementing inclusion at the middle school level: Lessons from a negative example. *Exceptional Children, 64*, 81–98.

Freeman, S. F., & Alkin, M. C. (2000). Academic and social attainments of children with mental retardation in general education and special education settings. *Remedial and Special Education, 21*, 3–18.

Gilmore, L., Campbell, J., & Cuskelly, M. (2003). Developmental expectations, personality stereotypes, and attitudes towards inclusive education: Community and teacher views of Down syndrome. *International Journal of Disability, Development and Education, 50*, 65–76.

Handler, B. R. (2003). *Special education practices: An evaluation of educational environmental placement trends since the Regular Education Initiative.* Paper presented at the annual meeting of the American Educational Research Association, Chicago.

Hardiman, S., Guerin, G., & Fitzsimons, E. (2009). A comparison of the social competence of children with moderate intellectual disability in inclusive versus segregated school settings. *Research in Developmental Disabilities, 30*(2), 397–407.

Heller, K., Holtzman, W., & Messick, S. (1982). *Placing children in special education: A strategy for equity.* Washington, DC: National Academy of Science Press.

Hitchcock, C., Meyer, A., Rose, D., & Jackson, R. (2002). Providing new access to the general curriculum. *Teaching Exceptional Children, 35*(2), 8–17.

Jenkinson, J. (2001). *Special education: A matter of choice.* Melbourne: ACER Press.

Kavale, K. A. (2002). Mainstreaming to full inclusion: From orthogenesis to pathogenesis of an idea. *International Journal of Disability, Development and Education, 49*, 201–214.

Kavale, K. A., & Mostert, M. P. (2003). Rivers of ideology, islands of evidence. *Exceptionality, 11*, 191–208.

Kyle, C., & Davies, D. (1991). Attitudes of mainstreamed pupils towards mental retardation: Pilot study at a Leeds secondary school. *British Journal of Special Education, 18*, 103–106.

Lambe, J., & Bones, R. (2006). Student teachers' perceptions about inclusive classroom teaching in Northern Ireland prior to teaching practice experience. *European Journal of Special Needs Education, 21,* 167–186.

Leyser, Y., & Kirk, R. (2004). Evaluating inclusion: An examination of parent views and factors influencing their perspective. *International Journal of Disability, Development and Education, 51,* 271–285.

Lieberman, L. J., Lytle, R. K., & Clarcq, J. A. (2008). Getting it right from the start: Employing the universal design for learning approach to your curriculum. *Journal of Physical Education, Recreation & Dance, 79*(2), 32–39.

Macintosh, K., & Dissanayake, C. (2006). A comparative study of the spontaneous social interactions of children with high-functioning autism and children with Asperger's syndrome. *Autism, 10,* 199–220.

McDougall, J., DeWit, D. J., King, G., Miller, L. T., & Killip, S. (2006). High school aged youths' attitudes towards their peers with disabilities: The role of school and student interpersonal factors. *International Journal of Disability, Development and Education, 51,* 287–313.

McNally, R., Cole, P., & Waugh, R. (2001). Regular teachers' attitudes to the need for additional classroom support for the inclusion of students with intellectual disability. *Journal of Intellectual and Developmental Disability, 26,* 257–273.

Meo, G. (2008). Curriculum planning for all learners: Applying universal design for learning (UDL) to a high school reading comprehension program. *Preventing School Failure, 52*(2), 21–30.

Meyer, L. (2001). The impact of inclusion on children's lives: Multiple outcomes, and friendship in particular. *International Journal of Disability, Development and Education, 48,* 9–31.

Miller, R. T. (2006). Explanation of position on the Convention on the Rights of Persons with Disabilities, Agenda Item 67(b), in the General Assembly, *USUN Press Release #396(06).*

Ministerial Council on Education Employment Training and Youth Affairs. (2008). Melbourne Declaration on Educational Goals for Young Australians. In E. Ministerial Council on Education, Training and Youth Affairs (Ed.).: Author.

Mulvihill, B., Shearer, D., & Van Horn, M. L. (2002). Training, experience and child care providers' perceptions of inclusion. *Early Childhood Research Quarterly, 17,* 197–215.

Nirje, B. (1970). The normalization principle: Implications and comments. *British Journal of Mental Subnormality, 16,* 62–70.

Nirje, B. (1985). The basis and logic of the normalization principle. *Australia and New Zealand Journal of Developmental Disabilities, 11,* 65–68.

Nowicki, E., & Sandieson, R. (2002). A meta-analysis of school-age children's attitudes towards persons with physical or intellectual disabilities. *International Journal of Disability, Development and Education, 49,* 243–265.

Palmer, D., Fuller, K., Arora, T., & Nelson, M. (2001). Taking sides: Parent views on inclusion for their children with severe disabilities. *Exceptional Children, 67*, 467–484.

Peetsma, T., Vergeer, M., Roeleveld, J., & Karsten, S. (2001). Inclusion in education: Comparing pupils' development in special and regular education. *Educational Review, 53*(2), 125–135.

Rietveld, C. (2005). Classroom learning experiences of mathematics by new entrant children with Down syndrome. *Journal of Intellectual and Developmental Disability, 30*(3), 127–138.

Rillotta, F., & Nettlebeck, T. (2007). Effects of an awareness program on attitudes of students without an intellectual disability towards persons with an intellectual disability. *Journal of Intellectual and Developmental Disability, 32*, 19–27.

Scruggs, T. E., & Mastropieri, M. A. (1996). Teacher perceptions of mainstreaming / inclusion 1958–1995: A research synthesis. *Exceptional Children, 63*, 59–74.

Skeels, H., & Dye, H. (1939). A study of the effects of differential stimulation on mentally retarded children. *Proceedings of the American Association on Mental Deficiency, 44*, 114–136.

Sloper, P., Cunningham, C., Turner, C., & Knussen, C. (1990). Factors related to the academic attainments of children with Down's syndrome. *British Journal of Educational Psychology, 60*, 284–298.

Sloper, P., & Turner, C. (1994). *Families of teenagers with Down's syndrome: Parent, child and sibling adaptation.* Manchester: Hester Adrian Research Centre, University of Manchester.

Soukup, J. H., Wehmeyer, M., Bashinski, S. M., & Bovaird, J. (2007). Classroom variables and access to the general curriculum for students with disabilities. *Exceptional Children, 74*(1), 101–120.

Tindal, G. (1985). Investigating the effectiveness of special education: An analysis of methodology. *Journal of Learning Disabilities, 18*, 101–112.

Tomlinson, C. A. (2004). Sharing responsibility for differentiating instruction. *Roeper Review, 26*(4), 188–189.

Turner, C., Alborz, A., & Gayle, V. (2008). Predictors of academic attainments of young people with Down's syndrome. *Journal of Intellectual Disability Research, 52*(5), 380–392.

UK Parlaiment. (2001). *Special Educational Needs and Disability Act.* Her Majesty's Stationery Office. Author.

UNESCO. (1990). *World Declaration on Education for All (Jomtien, Thailand).* Paris: United Nations.

UNESCO. (1994). *Salamanca statement and framework for action on special educational needs. Paris:* Paris: United Nations.

United Nations General Assembly. (2006). Convention on the rights of persons with disabilities. New York: Author.

United States Congress. (1997). *Individuals with Disabilities Education Act, 1997 Amendments.* Washington, DC: Author.

United States Congress. (2002). *No Child Left Behind Act of 2001*. Washington, DC: Author.

United States Congress. (2004). *Individuals With Disabilities Education Improvement Act of 2004*. Washington, DC: Author.

Valletutti, P., & Bender, M. (1982). *Teaching interpersonal and community living skills: A curriculum model for handicapped adolescents and adults*. Baltimore: University Park.

van Kraayenoord, C. (2007). School and classroom practices in inclusive education in Australia. *Childhood Education, 83*(6), 390–394.

Wagner, S. (2001). *Inclusive programming for middle school students with autism: Topics and issues for consideration by teachers and parents*. Arlington, TX: Future Horizons.

Webster, A., & Carter, M. (2007). Social relationships and friendships of children with developmental disabilities: Implications for inclusive settings. A systematic review. *Journal of Intellectual and Developmental Disability, 32*, 200–213.

Wehmeyer, M., Lattin, D. L., Lapp-Prinker, G., & Agran, M. (2003). Access to the general curriculum for middle school students with mental retardation. *Remedial and Special Education, 34*(5), 262–272.

Wehmeyer, M., Sands, D. J., Knowlton, H. E., & Kozleski, E. B. (2002). *Teaching students with mental retardation: Providing access to the general curriculum*. Baltimore: Paul H. Brookes.

Wehmeyer, M., Smith, S. J., Palmer, S. B., & Davies, D. K. (2004). Technology use by students with intellectual disabilities: An overview. *Journal of Special Education Technology, 19*(4), 7–21.

Williamson, P., McLeskey, J., Hoppey, D., & Rentz, T. (2006). Educating children with mental retardation in general education classrooms. *Exceptional Children, 72*(3), 347–361.

Wolfensberger, W. (1972). *The principle of normalization in human services*. Toronto: National Institute on Mental Retardation.

Wolfensberger, W. (1980). A brief overview of the principle of normalization. In R. J. Flynn & K. E. Nitsch (Eds.), *Normalization, social integration, and community services* (pp. 7–30). Baltimore: University Park Press.

Note

1. Some sections of this chapter related to inclusion are based on P. Foreman & M. Arthur-Kelly (2008). Social justice principles, the law, and research, as bases for inclusion. *Australasian Journal of Special Education, 30*, 109–124.

6

Teaching and Intervening with Students with an Intellectual Disability

Overview: This chapter provides an overview of research on best practice in teaching children with an intellectual disability. It deals with teaching approaches and their outcomes, and how teaching approaches reflect legislative requirements. The chapter also examines research related to the use of computer-assisted instruction and other forms of assistive technology in teaching students with an intellectual disability. Functional behavior analysis is described as an approach to dealing with behavioral problems in students with an intellectual disability.

Introduction

As has been demonstrated in earlier chapters, there is a huge amount of variability among people with an intellectual disability. In some instances, there will be more similarities between people with and without an intellectual disability than there are between two people with a disability. For this reason there are no teaching practices that can be "prescribed" specifically for students with an intellectual disability. A student with a severe intellectual disability, perhaps combined with physical and sensory disabilities, will

Education of Students with an Intellectual Disability, pages 169–200

require a very different teaching approach from that of a student with mild intellectual disability who may be able to access the general curriculum with minor adaptations.

Despite this, there are some principles and practices that have been proven to be effective with students who have a variety of disabilities, and many of these practices should be considered by teachers of students with an intellectual disability. In addition, there has been a great deal of research on specific approaches to teaching students with an intellectual disability, and this will be reported later in the chapter. In many cases, what is needed is what can generally be regarded as good teaching practice in any school setting: careful assessment, planning of teaching strategies, thoughtful consideration of curriculum, encouraging positive interactions between students, considering the interests and needs of individuals, making the best use of resources and technology, and working collaboratively with colleagues and families.

Approaches to Teaching Students with Intellectual Disability

Educational Assessment

By the time a child with intellectual disability is placed in a mainstream or special class, a great deal of assessment will already have taken place. At the very least the child will have been assessed on an individual intelligence test such as the Stanford-Binet or WISC and on an adaptive behavior scale such as the Vineland or the Scales of Independent Behavior (see Chapter 3). It is likely that the child will also have been assessed by other medical and allied health professionals. Parents may have a file of reports that they are willing to share with their child's teacher. Many parents keep thorough dossiers of the many assessments of their child that have been done, which can become the starting point of the educational assessment process and provide a guide to instructional planning. If the child has been in an educational setting previously, her last teacher will also be an important potential source of information.

The fact that there is such a wide diversity of students with an intellectual disability means that educational assessment will vary greatly depending on the child's current functional level. For some students, educational assessment will require an evaluation of their skills in literacy, numeracy, and other academic areas. For others, it will involve an assessment of the stage they have reached in feeding themselves or communicating their needs to others. In undertaking such assessments, teachers may utilize one of the many commercially available assessment devices appropriate to the child's level of functioning, such as the Developmental Assessment for Students with Severe Disabilities (DASH-2) (Dykes & Erin, 1999). Many teachers devise their own assessment instruments and are very skilled observers of children's educational needs.

Planning for Instruction

Whether the child is in a mainstream or special class, careful planning is an important early step in teaching students with an intellectual disability. The type of planning required will depend on the needs of each student. Some students will have no difficulty progressing in some parts of the regular curriculum, and planning may need to focus only on the areas of difficulty. For others, all aspects of the curriculum will require careful planning.

Following assessment, the first aspect of planning for most students with an intellectual disability is the individualization of goals. This means that goals are set individually for each student, leading to an Individualized Educational Program (IEP). In the United States, this process is considered to be so important that the details of it have been included in legislation since 1975 when PL 94-142, the Education of All Handicapped Children Act, required the establishment of an IEP planning team for all students with a disability (U.S. Congress, 1975). This requirement has been further developed in subsequent amendments and in replacement acts. The 2004 amendments to the Individuals with Disabilities Education Act (IDEA) require that each student with a disability will have an IEP, which includes

> a statement of the special education and related services and supplementary aids and services, based on peer-reviewed research to the extent practicable, to be provided to the child, or on behalf of the child, and a statement of the program modifications or supports for school personnel that will be provided for the child:
>
> 1. to advance appropriately toward attaining the annual goals;
> 2. to be involved in and make progress in the general education curriculum... and to participate in extracurricular and other nonacademic activities; and
> 3. to be educated and participate with other children with disabilities and nondisabled children. (U.S. Congress, 2004)

The 2004 Amendments and associated regulations provide further clear directions to educators about the way in which IEPs should be planned and what needs to be included in them. Among the requirements of IDEA 2004 are the following:

- The IEP team should include the student (where appropriate), her parents, a regular educator (if the program has a mainstream component), a special educator, an appropriately qualified representative of the Local Education Authority, and other expertise as needed.
- Each IEP must include
  - A statement of the child's present levels of academic and functional performance and how this affects participation in the general curriculum;
  - A statement of measurable annual academic and functional goals;
  - For children with disabilities who undertake alternative assessments, a statement of short-term objectives or benchmarks;
  - A statement of the special education and other specialized services to be provided, including program modifications, involvement in the general curriculum, extent of inclusion in regular education, and an explanation of the reason for any segregated teaching;
  - Statement of modifications for any statewide assessments;
  - Statement of how progress in meeting goals will be measured and reported;
  - Dates for implementation of all aspects of the program; and
  - For students aged 16+, a transition plan (see Chapter 7).

A feature of the requirements for the development of IEPs in the United States is the need for meaningful participation of parents. Parents must have the opportunity for a great deal of involvement in any educational decisions made on behalf of their child, and must have access to all documentation and testing results that are the basis of decision making. They have to give their written consent before their child is assessed and can ask for an independent evaluation if they disagree with the school's evaluation. They can see the child's records at any time and can challenge information if they believe it to be inaccurate. Schools are expected to provide parents with regular reports on their child's progress in relation to objectives.

The requirements give parents much more power than they might have had in the past. As such, there is potential for conflicts in relationships between schools and parents. For this reason, it is very important that teachers develop positive relationships with parents. The relationship needs to be a person-centered approach of collaborative consultation where parents, the student, and educators see themselves as members of a team leading, ideally, to consensus (O'Reilly et al., 2007).

Not all countries mandate individualized planning in as detailed a manner as the United States. In Australia there is no specific legislation about the components of a school education program for students with a disability. However, the Commonwealth Disability Discrimination Act and, in particular, the Act's Education Standards, introduced in 2005, are quite specific about expectations of educational programs (Commonwealth Government of Australia, 2005). The standards deal with enrollment, participation, curriculum, student support services, and elimination of harassment and victimization. Extracts from the standards that impact on curriculum planning are shown in italics below.

> *The education provider must take reasonable steps to ensure that the course or program is designed in such a way that the student is, or any student with a disability is, able to participate in the learning experiences (including the assessment and certification requirements) of the course or program, and any relevant supplementary course or program, on the same basis as a student without a disability, and without experiencing discrimination.*

This requirement relates to the provision of supported access to the general curriculum and all components of it. The concept of "reasonable steps" suggests that unreasonable steps do not need to be taken if the child's disability is so severe that access to the general curriculum is impracticable.

> *If a student is enrolled in the course or program, the provider must:*
>
> (a) *consult the student, or an associate of the student, about whether the disability affects the student's ability to participate in learning experiences of the course or program, or any relevant supplementary course or program; and*
> (b) *in the light of that consultation, decide whether an adjustment is necessary to ensure that the student is able to participate in those learning experiences on the same basis as a student without a disability who is enrolled in the course or program; and*
> (c) *The provider must repeat the process . . . as necessary to allow for the changing needs of the student over time.*

This paragraph relates to the need to involve the student and/or her family in the planning process, to provide necessary support, and to repeat the planning process as regularly as needed.

> *Measures that the education provider may implement to enable the student to participate in the learning experiences (including the assessment and certification requirements) of the course or program, and any relevant supplementary course or program, on the same basis as a student without a disability, include measures ensuring that:*
>
> (a) *the curriculum, teaching materials, and the assessment and certification requirements for the course or program are appropriate to the needs of the student and accessible to him or her; and*

(b) *the course or program delivery modes and learning activities take account of intended educational outcomes and the learning capacities and needs of the student; and*

(c) *the course or program study materials are made available in a format that is appropriate for the student and, where conversion of materials into alternative accessible formats is required, the student is not disadvantaged by the time taken for conversion; and*

(d) *the teaching and delivery strategies for the course or program are adjusted to meet the learning needs of the student and address any disadvantage in the student's learning resulting from his or her disability, including through the provision of additional support, such as bridging or enabling courses, or the development of disability-specific skills; and*

(e) *any activities that are not conducted in a classroom, such as field trips, industry site visits and work placements, or activities that are part of the broader course or educational program of which the course or program is a part, are designed to include the student; and*

(f) *the assessment procedures and methodologies for the course or program are adapted to enable the student to demonstrate the knowledge, skills or competencies being assessed.*

These components of the Education Standards make it mandatory for education providers to provide appropriate and accessible curriculum, relate goals to student needs, adapt curriculum and materials as needed, make sure that that all aspects of the program are accessible, and adapt assessment procedures so that all students can participate in them.

Curriculum Adaptations

An important aspect of planning for instruction is adaptation of the curriculum. Chapter 5 introduced some of the debate about access to the general education curriculum for students with an intellectual disability. In most, but not all, cases the starting point will be the regular curriculum. The role of the teacher will be to find ways in which the regular curriculum can be made accessible to the student. Conway (2008) provides a useful overview of how curriculum and teaching strategies can be adapted to provide for students with a disability. He gives examples of how curriculum materials can be adapted so that they become accessible to students with a disability, particularly if that disability is relatively mild. He points out that in facilitating access to the general curriculum, teachers can consider what students "must know," "should know," and "could know." It may be that students with a mild or moderate degree of intellectual disability will be able to participate in the "must know" components of the curriculum, and perhaps some of the "should know" components. More able students will proceed to all of the "should know" and much of the "could know" (Conway, 2008).

However, while access to the general education program is regarded as desirable for all students, there is no school system that insists every student must follow the same curriculum and achieve the same outcomes as all other students. While the first preference would be for a student with intellectual disability to follow the same curriculum as all other students, this may not be possible, and it may be necessary to adapt the curriculum to make it more relevant and to the student's current life and future needs. If the principles of Universal Design for Learning, outlined in Chapter 5, have been followed, the student's access to the general curriculum will be facilitated.

Provided that a student is progressing in an appropriately planned curriculum, it is not always helpful to focus on how the student's progress compares with that of others in the same grade. If the student has an IEP, his progress in relation to the goals that have been set for him in his IEP is what is important. He may never achieve the same outcomes as those of his classmates. The goals that have been agreed upon by his parents and teachers should form the focus of any assessment of whether his program is being successfully achieved. Some issues relating to the use of state standards in the United States were discussed in Chapter 5.

Partial or Supported Participation

Although students may not be able to participate fully in a given activity, it may be possible for ways to be found for them to participate partially, rather than for them to be totally excluded from the activity. This is particularly important if the student is in a mainstream class, but also applies in special classes. Some educators don't like the term "partial participation" because of the implication that the student is only partially included in the class's activities. The term "supported participation" will be used interchangeably with "partial participation" in this chapter.

The concept of partial participation was developed primarily by Baumgart et al. (1982). They pointed out that, particularly for students with severe disabilities, access to appropriate educational programs was often restricted or prevented by *false* hypotheses such as the following:

a. that students need to progress to an appropriate developmental age before a task could be attempted;

b. that teaching should not be initiated until students have all the skills necessary to complete the task;

c. that all components of the task must be able to be performed independently; and

d. that prerequisite skills must be acquired before teaching of the task is commenced. (Baumgart et al., 1982)

Baumgart and colleagues argued that through partial participation, all students, regardless of their level of disability, can be included in instructional programs that are appropriate to their age and relevant to their lives. However, they pointed out that partial participation would be misused if the participation was merely symbolic. For example, if a student had no literacy skills and was unlikely ever to gain them, it would not be appropriate to teach her to open a word processing program on a computer and to sit at the keyboard pretending to write. On the other hand, it would be appropriate to give her access to relevant programs on the computer, even if considerable support was needed for the student to access the programs. An analysis of the components of the task would show which components the student could perform independently and which components required support.

Supported participation can contribute to the student's feeling of self-worth and can allow the other students to see that the student has something to contribute to the group. For example, a student with problems in speaking and communicating may be able to participate if provided with an augmentative and alternative communication (AAC) system. These systems range from light unaided technology, such as sign language, through light aided technology, such as symbol boards, to high technology, such as synthesized speech (Balandin, Sweep, & Hand, 2008). This topic is discussed further in the next section of this chapter.

While supported participation is not the same as full participation, it still allows the person to participate in an activity that is appropriate to the student's age and is enjoyable. Some examples of how partial or supported participation can be used include the following:

a. Students who have difficulty with the complexity of a full deck of cards may still be able to play cards with a deck from which some of the cards have been removed. For older students, this is preferable to playing with a children's deck.

b. Audio-visual equipment and computers can have the switching simplified or adapted so that they are easier to operate. As outlined in the technology section below, there are many commercially available switches and adaptors that allow students to operate a variety of electronic equipment.

c. In group work, a student may be given a useful role that is appropriate to his ability level, even if he can't participate in all group tasks.

d. In a science classroom, a student may be able to participate with support in aspects of a practical lesson.

In a follow-up article to the influential Baumgart et al. (1982) publication, Ferguson and Baumgart (1991) were critical of the way in which partial participation had been implemented by some teachers. They argued that there were four major errors made by teachers that needed to be avoided when partial participation was being planned. These errors occurred when participation was "passive," "myopic," "piecemeal," or "missed." They suggested how these errors should be avoided as follows:

a. Participation needs to be active rather than passive. Students need to be actively engaged in practicing behaviors as part of real activities, not passively observing others in action.

b. Participation should involve multiple perspectives and should not be "myopic." Planning should focus on the student's abilities and should include family and community perspectives, as relevant, and be responsive to change. If teaching is isolated from the rest of the student's activities, skills learned will be less likely to transfer into their everyday lives.

c. Curricular planning should use information from multiple sources to avoid piecemeal participation. Ferguson and Baumgart suggest that activity-based, developmental, behavioral, adaptive, communicative, and biobehavioral perspectives can be merged, rather than seen as competing with each other.

d. In order to avoid "missed participation," planning needs to consider whether the student will have another person present to assist; what abilities can be practiced in each component and how it can be maximized; what skills can be developed to expand participation; how image can be maximized; and how the student's relationships with others can be maximized in this and similar settings (Ferguson & Baumgart, 1991)?

The teaching approaches and strategies referred to so far (educational assessment, individualized instruction, curriculum adaptations, and partial/supported participation) are all related to each other. They all imply that students with an intellectual disability, whether they are in a regular class or a special class, should have an educational program that is (1) designed individually for them; (2) has a curriculum that is adapted to their needs and related to their lives; and (3) allows them to participate as fully as possible in all activities of the classroom and school. Many teaching strategies that will assist students with an intellectual disability can be supported by appropriate use of technology, as outlined below.

FOR DISCUSSION OR REFLECTION:

- Discuss the role of parents in planning a student's program. What benefits will derive from this, and what difficulties might it cause?
- Think of some typical school activities and brainstorm ways in which students with an intellectual disability could be involved through supported participation

Use of Technology to Support Teaching

Technology has become an important part of all of our lives. Most students in developed countries have regular access to computers and the Internet, often at home as well as at school. If students with an intellectual disability are denied access to technology, the gap between students with and without a disability will only widen. The use of technology with students who have an intellectual disability is discussed under four headings: communication, teaching programs, assisted access, and teaching social skills.

Communication

The ability to communicate with family, friends, and the community is an essential aspect of humanity. Parents of children with an intellectual disability who are unable to speak are often aware that their child understands much of what is said to them, but their child's attempts at oral communication are often difficult to understand and frustrating for the children and those around them. Such children can be assisted by an augmentative and alternative communication (AAC) system.

An important role of AAC systems for children whose communication problems are associated with intellectual disability is to assist the child in expressing choices and making requests. At the simplest level, an AAC system may be a picture board that allows a child to choose between two or more objects. For example, at snack time a student may be shown a board containing pictures of three or four pieces of fruit, and asked what he would like for a snack. Communication boards can range from those that allow choice between two real objects to boards that contain multiple symbols or words, and allow the student to communicate in a relatively complex way.

At a more sophisticated level, there are speech-generating devices with a synthesized voice output. This allows the student to "talk" to the people around them. At the less complex end of the range, this might be a device with several symbols from which the student can select in order to be able to communicate via a number of preselected phrases, such as "My name's Toby," "What's your name?" "I'm fine thanks, how are you?" "I'm hungry," "I'm tired," and so on. At a more sophisticated level, there are keyboard activated devices that can be used for unlimited communication. Such a device is used by noted physicist Professor Stephen Hawking to give speeches, write papers, and communicate with fellow scientists around the world. The devices can be adapted for input from head or finger operated switches, or for infrared input. Students with an intellectual disability are more likely to use devices on the simpler end of the continuum, sometimes referred to as "mid-tech" devices, or "light-tech" devices such as symbol boards. An overview of mid-tech devices, written by autism consultant Susan Stokes, is provided in Box 6.1.

BOX 6.1 EXAMPLES OF "MID-TECH" STRATEGIES TO ASSIST STUDENTS WITH COMMUNICATION DIFFICULTIES

This box contains material written by Susan Stokes under a contract with CESA 7 and funded by a discretionary grant from the Wisconsin Department of Public Instruction. It has been made available by the copyright owners for the public benefit. Although the material has a focus on students with autism, it is equally relevant to students with an intellectual disability and associated communication problems. Additional information about low-tech and high-tech strategies may be found at http://www.specialed.us/autism/assist/asst10.htm

Listed below are descriptions of several "mid" tech devices that can be used by children with autism to enhance specific skill areas. Most of these devices are very appealing to these children and provide them with motivation to participate and focus on various skills and classroom activities successfully. These devices are called Voice Output Communication Aids (VOCAs). Any type of visual representation system can be placed on simple voice output devices for children to access by a simple push of a "button." Most of these devices are battery operated and are easy to operate for recording messages. It is important to note that these devices were created for use as an augmentative means to expressively communicate. However, for many children with autism, as noted above, these devices are very appealing and motivating, and can be used in numerous ways to focus attention on various skill areas, as well as increase classroom participation, focus and communication. The following list identifies a number of such VOCAs mid tech devices.

- **"Big Mack":** A single switch/button device available from

AbleNet (1) which allows for 20 seconds of record time. Approximate cost is $89.00.

- **Talk Pad:** A 4-message/button battery operated device, which allows for 15 seconds of record time per button. Available from **Frame Technologies** (6) for approximately $99.00.
- **"Voice in the Box":** Multi-message battery operated communication devices available in 16, 24 or 40 messages/buttons from **FrameTechnologies** (6) for approximately $195.00.

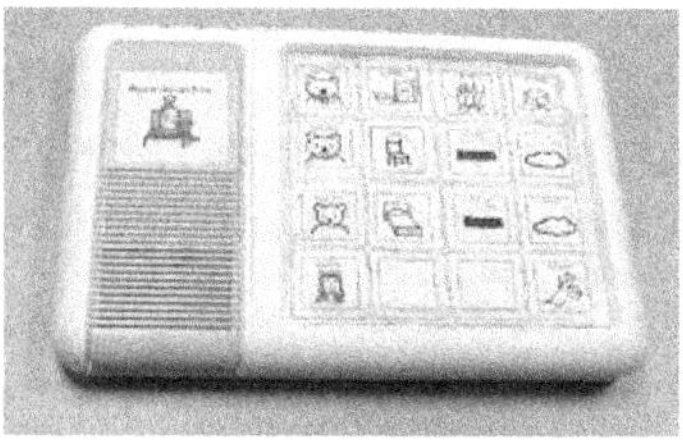

Voice in the Box

- **"Cheap Talk 4":** A 4-message/button device which allows for 5 seconds of record time per button available from **Enabling Devices** (5) for approximately $69.00.
- **"Step-by-Step Communicator":** A battery operated device which allows for prerecording a series of unlimited sequenced messages up to a total of 75 seconds of record time. Available from **AbleNet** (1) for $129.00.
- **Language Master:** The Language Master is a "mid" tech piece of equipment that has been used for more than 20 years (25). The Language Master is an electronic device about the size of an old tape recorder. The cards, which are

Language Master

approximately 3" by 8" with a "recordable strip" across the bottom, are played "through" the Language Master. A short verbal message can be recorded on each card. The cards are also big enough to include corresponding visual cues (e.g., words, PCS, photos) of the recorded message.

- **Tape recorder:** Any easily operated tape recorder can be effective in addressing various skill areas in children with autism spectrum disorder.

Voice Output Communication Aids (VOCAs) can be used to develop the following groups of skills for children with autism: Language Comprehension Skills, Expressive Communication Skills, Social Skills, Attending Skills, Organization Skills and Academic Skills. The following is a discussion of these skill areas and the possible use of specific VOCAs to help children with autism function more independently.

LANGUAGE COMPREHENSION SKILLS:

- **Talk Pad:** This device can be programmed with simple 1–4 step directions. The child is motivated to hit the buttons and thus complete the sequence of steps.

  Example: A child with autism experiences great difficulty following the 3-step sequence to complete his "job," which is to prepare for snack time. The child requires continual verbal and physical prompting from an adult to attend to the task—as the child typically runs around the room—and then to complete each step of the task. The 3 steps of the task are recorded on the Talk Pad, with the 4th message telling the child to "Sit in chair." Visual cues, corresponding with each verbal message, are placed on top of each "button" on the Talk Pad with Velcro. The child is extremely motivated to "push the buttons" on this device and, following the initial teaching, is now able to independently do his "job" for snack time.

- **Language Master:** The teacher may record multi-step directions on the cards, one step per card. If a student cannot remember the auditory directions that were given, he can run the cards through the Language Master to hear some or all of the directions (16).

EXPRESSIVE COMMUNICATION SKILLS:

Big Mack

- **Voice Output Communication Aid (VOCA):** Children can express themselves with the assistance of any visual representation mode, or visual cues placed on a "simple" voice output communication aid/device. Many children with autism are motivated to communicate by use of these devices, particularly by the auditory feedback immediately given as they use the device. Use of VOCAs has proven effective in teaching a child the cause/effect of language through activities which are stimulating to him.

  Example: Use of the Big Mack for a child to request highly desired sensory activities, such as "chase me"; "tickle me"; "hug me"; "listen to music."

The use of **VOCAs** as **communication devices** is not always effective for all children with autism. Some children find the VOCAs so overly motivating and stimulating that they do not become effective communication devices. The child may repeatedly push down the button(s) on the device for the self-motivation that he receives from the auditory feedback, rather than for the cause/effect of the **communicative** message. In this case, the VOCAs can still be used with the child, since they are clearly motivating, but in a different manner. For example, they may be used to focus attention on various skill areas, as well as increase classroom participation. In this case, the child's communication needs may be more effectively addressed through the use of "low" tech expressive communication strategies.

A research study evaluating the use of VOCAs by children with autism revealed the following (22):

- Young children with autism can learn to use VOCAs to effectively communicate various language functions (i.e., request, answer yes/no questions, make social comments);
- VOCA use generalized across settings;
- Use of VOCAs increased the child's use of gestures, words and vocalizations.
- Communication partner interactions increased when VOCAs were used.
- **Audio taping:** Audio taping can be used to focus on communication skills to draw the child's attention to an inappropriate communicative behavior. (e.g., interrupting, perseverative speech, incessant question asking, topic maintenance, etc.) as well as to develop self-awareness and self-regulation of appropriate communicative interactions.
- **Language Master:** For a child, who is able to imitate, the Language Master could be used as a model for imitation, as well as an opportunity to engage in social interactions (16).

Example: At the end of a child's activity-schedule-book is a Language Master card with a picture of bubbles glued on and the written words, "I want bubbles." The child places the card in the Language Master and then takes the card and gives it to someone while repeating the utterance.

Reference: Stokes, S. *Assistive technology for children with autism.* Retrieved March 9, 2009, from http://www.specialed.us/autism/assist10.htm

There has been a large amount of research on the effect of using AAC systems with students who have a disability. In 2006 Martha Snell and colleagues published a review of intervention research using AAC systems over a 7-year period (Snell, Chen, & Hoover, 2006). In half of the 40 studies examined, problem behavior was an issue, and in 85% of these studies, a reduction in problem behavior was reported after the AAC system was introduced. This suggests that some problem behaviors may result from frustration arising from an inability to communicate. Snell et al. found that generalization and maintenance of treatment effects were measured in only half of the studies, although when measured they were generally found to be satisfactory. From their meta-analysis of 20 years of effectiveness research in AAC, Schlosser and Lee (2000) concluded that generalization and maintenance strategies need to be planned from the start of the intervention. Clearly, if an AAC system is going to be helpful, it needs to be able to be used in a variety of settings and with a variety of people (generalization), not just in the classroom and with teachers, and the positive outcomes need to be retained over time (maintenance). The researchers were able to conclude that 65% of the AAC interventions in the 50 studies they examined were "highly effective" (Schlosser & Lee, 2000).

Schlosser, Koul, and Costello (2007) propose a set of "well-built" questions that should be asked about whether AAC should be used, and if so, what form it should take. These are

- The PERSON who is being considered and the PROBLEM that is being solved
- The ENVIRONMENTS of the person and their communication partners
- The STAKEHOLDERS who may be affected by the decision
- The INTERVENTION that is proposed
- A COMPARISON with alternative approaches, including no intervention
- The OUTCOMES that are desired.

Schlosser et al. argue that using the proposed template would assist practitioners to make evidence-based decisions that are most likely to help their clients (Schlosser, Koul, & Costello, 2007). Regardless of what type of AAC system is used, it should be planned to meet the needs of the individual child and requires a careful assessment of the child's current communication processes as well as her current and future communication needs. A collaborative approach should be used with input from, as a minimum, teachers, parents, and the child's speech pathologist (Balandin et al., 2008).

Use of Technology in Teaching Programs

Computer assisted instruction (CAI) has been used extensively and successfully in education, particularly in teaching the basic skills of literacy and numeracy. CAI has the capacity to repeat practice until mastery is achieved, to sequence teaching based on skills acquired, and to keep records of progress for students with a disability in ways that would be difficult or impossible for classroom teachers (Parette, Hourcade, & VanBiervliet, 1993). In theory, this should provide an ideal teaching and learning environment for some students with an intellectual disability. There is also capacity for CAI to be used to help children with an intellectual disability to acquire social skills and skills of independent living. Many of these are skills that do not need to be taught when children do not have a disability.

Early studies of CAI and numeracy suggested that computers can assist in the automatization of mathematics skills in students with an intellectual disability. Agnes Lin and her colleagues showed that CAI produced better outcomes than pencil and paper tasks in some aspects of teaching mathematical skills, although as might be expected, students with an intellectual disability required much more practice than students without an intellectual disability (Lin, Podell, & Tournaki-Rein, 1994; Podell, Tournaki-Rein, & Lin, 1992). In particular, CAI appears to increase response rate, but does not always increase accuracy. In a more recent study, Fuchs and her colleagues found that CAI led to a significant improvement in addition combination skills in at-risk first grade students, but not in subtraction skills (Fuchs et al., 2006). This was a different finding to that of Lin et al. (1994), who found improvements in subtraction rather than addition. Irish (2002) found improved basic multiplication performance in six students with learning difficulties or mild intellectual disability, using a computer-assisted teaching program. She found that skills continued to improve during maintenance and follow-up periods (Irish, 2002).

Several studies have also examined whether CAI can improve literacy skills in students with an intellectual disability. For example, Lin, Podell, and Rein (1991) examined the effects of CAI on the word recognition skills of 45 students with a mild intellectual disability and a similar group without a disability. Students were found to increase their response times, but not their accuracy. Kinney and colleagues used computer-generated video models to teach generative spelling skills to a young girl with autism. Importantly, the skills appeared to be generalized and maintained in home and school settings (Kinney, Vedora, & Stromer, 2003). In another study, computer-assisted instruction led to improvements in spelling skills in two teenage students with developmental disabilities (Vedora & Stromer, 2007).

The sample studies that have been outlined above were with a variety of groups and participants in relation to age and ability level, and used a variety of software and hardware. The outcomes emphasize the need to select software carefully and to monitor the outcomes for individual students. There have been many developments in computer software and hardware since some of these studies were conducted, and teachers should check current Web sites for up-to-date programs and should seek evaluations of these from researchers and practitioners.

Assisted Access

Various forms of technology can be used to improve the access to schooling of students with an intellectual disability. This can refer both to physical access and to access to the curriculum. Details of the principle of universal design for learning (UDL) were provided in Chapter 5. Under this principle, all aspects of the curriculum, including methods and materials, are planned from the outset in such a way as to include all learners. Technology has a significant role to play in improving access to the curriculum.

The most obvious way in which this can be done is through the materials of the curriculum. A curriculum following UDL principles provides material in multiple representations (Hitchcock, Meyer, Rose, & Jackson, 2002). As Hitchcock et al. point out,

> Text can be displayed at any size on a screen or in print, as speech, in the context map, or as Braille.... An image can be presented in print or on-screen at any size and with colors modified to increase visibility, as a text or spoken description.... Further, this same content can potentially be displayed on various electronic devices such as hand-held computers or even telephones. (p. 12)

The Kurzweil 3000 is an example of software that allows written material, including complete textbooks, to be scanned into a computer. The material can then be read aloud by the computer to a user with limited reading skills. Sophisticated voice-recognition software is available that will write for a person who has limited writing skills or lacks the physical ability to operate a keyboard. Such software is more likely to assist students with a mild intellectual disability than with more serious intellectual disabilities. However, the general principle of improved access is likely to assist all students at some time.

There are many other ways in which computers and other technology can be adapted to assist students with an intellectual disability to access the classroom and the curriculum. These include color-coded keyboards, simplified keyboards, large-print keyboards, talking clocks, touch screens, specialized mouses, and touch tablets (Casimir & Alchin, 2001; Horejsi, 2003). These devices can be used to simplify the operation of the equipment, thereby rendering it more accessible. There is also a variety of switches that can be used for students who have a physical disability. Examples are infrared switches, light-activated switches, movement-activated switches, puff or sip switches, push switches, and voice-activated switches (Casimir & Alchin, 2001). Such sophisticated equipment would not be expected to be available in every classroom, even one that followed UDL principles, and the services of specialists such as occupational or physical therapists or a speech pathologist would be needed to promote the access of students whose intellectual disability was associated with a severe physical disability.

Using Technology to Improve Social and Living Skills

An important part of the curriculum for many students with an intellectual disability is the teaching of skills to assist them to live and interact in the community. For students without a disability, such skills are usually acquired as part of general living, but for some students with an intellectual disability, these skills need to be specifically taught. There have been a number of studies of the use of technology to improve skills of living and social interaction.

Ayres and Langone (2002) attempted to improve the purchasing skills of three children aged 6 to 10 years who had been diagnosed with mild to moderate intellectual disabilities. The procedure was designed to teach the children to use the "dollar more" process to tender the amount of money needed to make a purchase. The procedure was taught through a video-enhanced computer simulation, and generalization was tested in a community supermarket setting. The authors found that improvements through the computer simulation did not generalize to real settings, warning that classroom simulation is not sufficient to promote generalization (Ayres & Langone, 2002). Lee, McGee, and Ungar (2001) described the use of a computer-based program to teach personal safety ("stranger danger") to students with an intellectual disability. The generalization of such skills is very hard to assess, and was not assessed in the reported project (Lee, McGee, & Ungar, 2001).

Generalization to real life settings was demonstrated in a study by Mechling and her colleagues in which they taught shopping skills to four students aged 9 to17 years with moderate intellectual disability (Mechling, Gast, & Langone, 2002). The students' ability to read shopping aisle signs and to locate goods in an unfamiliar store was improved though exposure to a computer-based video program. In another study, computer-based multimedia instruction was successful in teaching three students aged 16 to 18 years to use a debit card in an automatic payment machine (Mechling, Gast, & Barthold, 2003). While the skills did generalize to a real-life setting, the authors pointed out that some components of the skills were difficult to generalize (e.g., the method of card insertion for a particular machine); these skills might need to be taught in the actual setting. Langone and colleagues suggest that video models can be used to teach functional community skills to students with moderate to severe disabilities. However, they point out that simulated practice is generally insufficient to promote generalization to real-life situations (Langone, Clees, Rieber, & Matzko, 2003).

Further Issues in the Use of Technology

Wehmeyer and his colleagues suggest that while there is a need for further research, there is evidence that students with an intellectual disability can benefit from technology in a variety of areas (Wehmeyer, Smith, Palmer, & Davies, 2004). They report that students with an intellectual disability utilize technology less than other students, and they outline the characteristics of such learners that need to be taken into account in order to provide them with appropriate classroom technology. These characteristics include the students' language ability, their reasoning ability, their response time, their memory and learning skills, their auditory and visual perception abilities, and their current level of achievement.

One of the impediments to the use of computer technologies for people with disabilities is the speed with which the technologies become obsolete. Braddock and colleagues argue that there needs to be better integration of software and hardware systems so that they can "operate seamlessly across multiple real-world environments in the home, school, community, and workplace" (Braddock, Rizzolo, Thompson, & Bell, 2004, p. 53). Parette et al. have emphasized the need to consider family and cultural issues when planning to use assistive technology. They point out that without such consideration, the effect of the technology is likely to be lessened, and they suggest ways in which parents can be involved in the planning process (Parette, VanBiervliet, & Hourcade, 2000).

In the 21st century all teachers need to be sophisticated users of educational technology if they are to provide maximum opportunities for the students in their classroom. This is particularly so if the students have an intellectual disability, as these students will be more likely to be dependent on technology for classroom and curriculum access and less likely to access the technology independently. This does not mean that teachers need to be expert in all aspects of technology; however, they must be prepared to seek out appropriate technology and resources as needed and be proactive in seeking and taking expert advice.

FOR DISCUSSION OR REFLECTION:

- Discuss ways in which technology can be used to improve access to the curriculum
- Discuss the use of technology to teach independent living skills. How can the generalization of these skills be promoted?

Other Aspects of Teaching

This chapter has focused on aspects of teaching that relate particularly to students with an intellectual disability. Kauffman and Landrum summarized what they referred to as the dimensions of instruction for "statistical outliers," meaning students who are atypical in development (Kauffman & Landrum, 2007). They suggest the following as the areas, not usually found in regular education classrooms, in which students with developmental disabilities require specialized teaching:

- Pacing or rate—students with disabilities require the pace within specific lessons and the pace at which the curriculum is treated to be slower than for typical students.
- Intensity—students with disabilities require greater concentration of treatment of classroom topics. This may include breaking down of skills, more intensive practice, and specific teaching of additional skills which may not need to be taught to other children.
- Relentlessness—additional persistence and tenacity is required by special education teachers if they are to keep teaching until a particular skill is acquired. Many skills will need to be practiced over and over if mastery is to be achieved.
- Structure—special education requires additional structure which may come from clearly explained expectations, routines, teacher direction, tolerance for misbehavior, and explicitly stated consequences.
- Reinforcement—expert use of positive reinforcement is required to maximize learning.
- Pupil–teacher ratio—because of the above requirements, students with a disability require a better teacher:pupil ratio than students without a disability.
- Curriculum—students with disabilities will require precise teaching if they are able to access the general curriculum, or explicit instruction in self-help or living skills if they are unable to access the general education curriculum.
- Monitoring or assessment—special education teaching may require an intense level of monitoring and evaluation so that instruction can be changed if progress is not being made (Kauffman & Landrum, 2007).

There would be reasonable agreement that the characteristics outlined above are exemplary of good teaching generally. However, Kauffman and Landrum argue that this type of teaching can take place only in a special education classroom, and that students who have intellectual or developmental disabilities will achieve better if placed in separate classrooms.

Houston and Thomas reported a study that identified 20 practices used in teaching children with disabilities and examined research into their effectiveness. While they expressed concern over the lack of multiple large-scale studies, they found through research that 17 of the practices had been demonstrated to be effective. These practices are summarized in Table 6.1. The three practices not listed as effective were computer-assisted instruction, naturalistic time delay, and self-monitoring. This was not because they were found to be ineffective, but because more information was needed in order to reach a conclusion (Houston & Thomas, 2003).

The teaching practices described by Houston and Thomas in Table 6.1 and the characteristics outlined above by Kauffman and Landrum are more likely to be found in special education classrooms, but there is no reason why this has to be so. The debate over segregated versus inclusive schooling was dealt with in some detail in Chapter 5, and won't be redebated here. However, there are many educators who would agree that the characteristics outlined by Houston and Thomas (2003) and by Kauffman and Landrum (2007) are important aspects of teaching students with an intellectual disability, but would nevertheless argue that it is quite possible for this type of teaching to take place in a regular classroom. For this to happen, additional resources would need to be provided to those classes so that teachers are able to provide the type of teaching that will maximize student learning.

FOR DISCUSSION OR REFLECTION:

- Discuss the dimensions of teaching from Kauffman and Landrum, outlined above. What examples have you seen of these dimensions in operation?
- What do you think of the view that these practices and those outlined in Table 6.1 are difficult to implement in regular classrooms?

Dealing with Behavior Problems in Students with an Intellectual Disability

Children who have an intellectual disability will sometimes have associated behavioral problems. Bierbaum and her colleagues have suggested that some of these problems arise from frustration when the students are presented with tasks that are beyond their ability level (Bierbaum, Henrich, & Zigler, 2005). To test this hypothesis, Bierbaum et al. gave easy and difficult block-stacking tasks to students with intellectual disability and to other

TABLE 6.1 Effective Teaching Practices for Students with Moderate Disabilities

Instructional Category	Instructional Practice
Response prompting	*Auditory prompts*—auditory input given to shape behavior to elicit a target response *Constant time delay*—specified time interval between a question and a verbal model of the correct answer *Progressive time delay*—specified increasing time interval between a question and a verbal model of the correct answer *Simultaneous prompting*—teacher asks question and immediately gives a model response (e.g., What's your name? Toby.) *Least prompts*—teacher gives progressively more assistance until student provides a correct response
Stimulus modification	*Behavior chaining*—linking of component behaviors into a more complex behavior *Stimulus shaping*—materials are gradually changed so that discrimination becomes gradually more difficult *Stimulus fading*—gradual reduction of stimulus as target response becomes more consistent
Naturalistic teaching	*Incidental teaching*—using natural opportunities to teach predetermined objectives *Observational learning*—learning by observing the behavior and responses of others *Mand model*—naturalistic language approach where teacher models answer to question if student doesn't respond
Organization of instruction	*Peer-mediated instruction1*—peers take on instructional role in dyads or small groups *Group instruction*—teaching to a number of participants at a time *Direct instruction*—explicit teaching with use of correction procedures requiring master if each step in a sequence of instruction
Learning processes	*Cognitive process strategy*—technique through which students set goals for themselves and evaluate their own progress *Multiple exemplars*—use of numerous examples of the concept or skill to be taught *Discrimination learning theory*—teaching involving match-to-sample, mastery of each step, errorless learning, sequencing and feedback

Adapted from: Houston, D., & Thomas, J. (2003). Translating research into practice for instruction of students with moderate disabilities. Paper presented at *American Educational Research Association Meeting*. Chicago, Illinois. Material used with permission of the authors.

students matched by mental age and chronological age. They found that the students with intellectual disability showed more disobedient behaviors than other groups when faced with tasks that were too difficult for them, but not when undertaking tasks within their ability level. This may have implications for curriculum planning and classroom management.

In some circumstances, behavior problems will be part of the behavioral phenotype (observable characteristics of behavior) of a particular syndrome or disability. For example, self-injurious behavior is typical for children with Lesch-Nyhan syndrome (Nyhan, 1995). This suggests that the metabolic anomaly that produces intellectual disability and other characteristics of the syndrome also leads somehow to self-injurious behavior. Harris has reported that behavioral phenotypes associated with various neurogenetic syndromes can include attention problems, hyperactivity, self-injurious behavior, autistic behavior, and perseverative behavior (Harris, 2006).

The fact that behaviors are typically associated with a particular syndrome or disability does not mean that they are not amenable to change or must be accepted as inevitable. For example, people with Prader-Willi syndrome commonly steal food as part of the overeating that is associated with the syndrome. However, there is some evidence that such behavior may be modifiable through a systematic behavioral program (Maglieri, DeLeon, Rodriguez-Catter, & Sevin, 2000). A more obvious example is that of autism, a disorder often associated with intellectual disability. While the specific causes of autism are not yet known, it is clear that they include genetic factors, although these factors may be complex and may include other influences (Dawson, 2008; Ozonoff, Goodlin-Jones, & Solomon, 2007; Rutter, 2005). Students with disorders on the autism spectrum will often demonstrate behaviors such as repetitive mannerisms and excessive preoccupation with particular activities. Although these behaviors are seen as being a result of their diagnosed disability, this does not mean that the students cannot be taught alternative behaviors that will allow them to function better with their families and their peers. There are many educational programs and interventions that have demonstrated positive changes in behavior and learning in students with autism (Tutt, Powell, & Thornton, 2006).

It is important that children with an intellectual disability have comprehensive medical assessment and monitoring to ensure that they do not have any treatable organic problems that are contributing to their problem behaviors. For example, if a child's persistent screaming is caused by some form of pain or discomfort, then the priority is to remove that discomfort. Einfeld (2005) points out that some behaviors related to the genetic basis of intellectual disability may not be under the child's control. However, once treatable medical causes have been eliminated and if the behavior is interfering with the child's social interaction and learning, the next priority becomes to find a way of reducing the interfering behavior.

The remainder of this chapter will examine some of the approaches to teaching and intervening with children who have an intellectual disability and associated behavioral problems.

Functional Behavior Assessment

The detailed observation and analysis of inappropriate behavior, followed by programs to change that behavior, has been part of special education for more than 30 years. However, recent legislative changes in the United States have become more specific about the ways in which such observations and programs should be conducted. The Individuals with Disabilities Education Act (U.S. Congress, 1997) stipulated that, where necessary, the IEP team would conduct a *functional behavior assessment* to be followed by a change strategy known as *positive behavior support.* This requirement was reinforced in the 2004 amendments (U.S. Congress, 2004).

Functional behavior assessment (FBA) is a procedure for collecting information that will help to explain why the unwanted and interfering behaviors are occurring. There are certain important assumptions that can be made about behavior. These are evidence-based assumptions; that is, they have resulted from peer-reviewed research investigations. These assumptions include that

a. Behaviors are related to their context. Problem behaviors do not occur in a vacuum; they are usually related to the very complex environments in which students operate.

b. Behaviors are affected by their consequences. What follows a particular behavior (positive reinforcement, punishment, negative reinforcement) will impact on the likelihood of that behavior recurring.

c. Behavior usually serves a function for the child, although that function may not always be simple or obvious. For example, a behavior that leads to the child being removed into a quiet space may serve the function of gaining teacher attention or being removed from teacher attention.

While there is not a single prescribed way of conducting an FBA, there are certain components that are normally considered to be necessary if a comprehensive assessment is to occur. The objective of the assessment is to form hypotheses about why the behavior is occurring. The usual components of an FBA are as follows:

Structured interviews: Interviews take place with the people who are most likely to be able to describe the behavior and provide insights into its causes. The people include the child's parents, teachers and other school personnel and, where possible and appropriate, the child. Interviews usually follow a structure that will identify the problem behavior, the things that tend to precede it (antecedents), and the things that follow it (consequences). Hearing about the behavior from a number of different perspectives may corroborate the view that is presented, or it may lead to alternative hypotheses. As a result of the interviews, it is likely that tentative hypotheses will have been generated about why the behavior is occurring. These are a starting point for the next step in the FBA.

Structured observations: The second important step in the process is structured observation of the student in her normal setting so that the observer can carefully record all aspects of the behavior, including its apparent antecedents and consequences. The simplest form of observation sheet is an ABC sheet, as shown in Figure 6.1. Some teachers may prefer to do an anec-

Student:		Observer:	
Date/Time		Class:	
Lesson:		Target behavior:	
Antecedent	**Behavior**	**Consequence/s**	**Comment**

Figure 6.1 Antecedents–Behavior–Consequences (ABC) observation form.

dotal recording or running record, where they either write down or record in detail for later analysis everything that is happening with the target child.

Sometimes, rather than waiting for the antecedents to occur in a naturalistic setting, the observation may include some contrived stimuli. For example, if a tentative hypothesis has emerged from the interviews that the child demonstrates a certain behavior only when a particular activity is happening in the classroom, the observer may contrive a situation where that activity is initiated so that the student's response can be observed.

Hypothesis formulation: The tentative hypotheses obtained from the structured interviews are considered further in the light of the data gained from naturalistic and contrived observations. This should lead to some hypotheses that can be held with more confidence and used as the basis for the development of a positive behavior support plan.

Positive behavior support plan: The next vital step after forming hypotheses is for the learning support team to redevelop the student's behavior support plan in their IEP. The Center for Effective Collaboration and Practice, a federally funded part of the American Institutes for Research, has suggested the following strategies that might be included in the behavior support plan:

> *Addressing skill deficits:* The observation may lead to a hypothesis that the child's behavior is a response to deficits in certain skills. For example, he may behave aggressively in response to any negative comments from other students because he does not have the skills to respond in any other way. He may need to be taught other ways of responding to perceived negativity. A useful strategy is to replace problem behaviors with other behaviors that perform the same function for the child.
>
> *Addressing performance deficits:* The student may have the skills, but for a variety of reasons doesn't use them. This is a performance problem rather than a skill problem. It may be that the student lacks intrinsic motivation and therefore needs some sort of planned reinforcement program to encourage him to perform the skill. Because this is seen as a positive behavior support program, the use of aversives (punishment) is usually regarded as both unethical and ineffective except in extreme circumstances where the safety of the student or others is endangered.
>
> *Modifying the environment:* The learning environment may have been found through the observation process to be one of the factors that is contributing to the student's problem behaviors. For example, it may have been observed that the student acts out whenever she is left unoccupied for more than 3 minutes. An obvious solution is to increase her activity level so that she is not left unoccupied.

Providing supports: A variety of people can be enlisted to provide additional support as part of the support plan. These might include counselors, physiotherapists, teachers, paraprofessionals, or speech pathologists. For example, a child might be hypothesized to be demonstrating problem behavior as a result of frustration caused by inability to communicate verbally. The speech pathologist may be able to develop an AAC device that will allow the child to communicate their wishes.

Evaluating the support plan: Plans need to be evaluated on a regular basis, particularly if the student's behaviors are seen as problematic. The evaluation needs to check whether the child has reached her goals and objectives, in which case new goals will need to be developed. If the general situation has changed or positive changes are not occurring, a new plan will need to be developed (Center for Effective Collaboration & Practice, 1998).

Dealing with behavior problems will be among the most difficult challenges faced by some teachers of students with an intellectual disability. Many students will present with no behavior problems, but others will display behavioral challenges that arise from their syndrome, from their life experiences, or from a combination of these. Teachers should not hesitate to seek assistance in dealing with these problems. This could be from medical personnel, from specialists in behavior support, or from other colleagues and professionals. Teachers are also in a position to have a significant influence on their students' behavior, if necessary, through development of a positive behavior support plan.

FOR DISCUSSION OR REFLECTION:

- How do you avoid behavior problems that may arise when students are faced with tasks that are beyond their ability level?
- How would you go about conducting a functional behavior assessment in a regular or special classroom for a student who was occasionally aggressive toward other children?

Summary

There is no single, simple approach to teaching students who have an intellectual disability. An individualized approach is required, and attention needs to be given to educational assessment, planning for instruction, curriculum adaptations, using partial or supported participation, and using appropriate technology to enhance learning. Many different forms of technology are available, ranging from simple choice boards to speech synthesizers and other computer-based technology. Students with intellectual disability sometimes display behavior problems that may or may not be associated with the syndrome that has caused the disability. A useful process is to conduct a functional behavior assessment involving interviews, observations, and development of a hypothesis about the child's behavior. This will be followed by the development, implementation, and evaluation of a positive behavior support plan.

References

Ayres, K. M., & Langone, J. (2002). Acquisition and generalization of purchasing skills using a video enhanced computer-based instructional program. *Journal of Special Education Technology, 17*(4), 15–28.

Balandin, S., Sweep, A., & Hand, L. (2008). Communicating together: Functional communication in the classroom. In P. Foreman (Ed.), *Inclusion in action* (2nd ed., pp. 344–387). Melbourne: Thomson.

Baumgart, D., Brown, L., Pumpian, I., Nisbet, J., Ford, A., Sweet, M., et al. (1982). Principle of partial participation and individualized adaptations in educational programs for severely handicapped students. *Journal of the Association for the Severely Handicapped, 7*(Summer), 17–27.

Bierbaum, L. J., Henrich, C. C., & Zigler, E. F. (2005). Disobedient behaviours in children with intellectual disability. *Journal of Intellectual and Developmental Disability, 30*(2), 115–119.

Braddock, D., Rizzolo, M. C., Thompson, M., & Bell, R. (2004). Emerging technologies and cognitive disability. *Journal of Special Education Technology, 19*(4), 49–56.

Casimir, G., & Alchin, G. (2001). Enhancing learning with assistive technology. In P. Foreman (Ed.), *Integration and Inclusion in Action* (2nd ed., pp. 360–388). Sydney: Harcourt.

Center for Effective Collaboration & Practice. (1998). Addressing student problem behavior. http://cecp.air.org/fba/problembehavior/text.htm. Retrieved September 23, 2008.

Commonwealth Government of Australia. (2005).*Disability Discrimination Act (Education Standards Amendment).* Canberra, Australian Capital Territory: Author.

Conway, R. (2008). Adapting curriculum, teaching and learning strategies. In P. Foreman (Ed.), *Inclusion in action* (2nd ed., pp. 95–163). Melbourne: Thomson.

Dawson, G. (2008). Early behavioral intervention, brain plasticity, and the prevention of autism spectrum disorder. *Development and Psychopathology, 20,* 775–803.

Dykes, M. K., & Erin, J. (1999). DASH-2: An assessment and programming instrument for individuals with severe disabilities (2nd ed.). Austin, TX: ProEd.

Einfeld, S. (2005). Behaviour problems in children with genetic disorders causing intellectual disability. *Educational Psychology, 25*(2–3), 341–346.

Ferguson, D. L., & Baumgart, D. (1991). Partial participation revisited. *Journal of the Association for Persons with Severe Handicapped, 16*(4), 218–227.

Fuchs, L. S., Fuchs, D., Hamlet, C. L., Powell, S., R, Capizzi, A. M., & Seethaler, P. M. (2006). The effects of computer-assisted instruction on number combination skills in at-risk first graders. *Journal of Learning Disabilities, 39*(5), 467–475.

Harris, J. C. (2006). *Intellectual disability.* New York: Oxford University Press.

Hitchcock, C., Meyer, A., Rose, D., & Jackson, R. (2002). Providing new access to the general curriculum. *Teaching Exceptional Children, 35*(2), 8–17.

Horejsi, M. (2003). Making technology inclusive. *Science and Children, 41*(3), 20–24.

Houston, D., & Thomas, J. (2003, April 21–25). *Translating research into practice for instruction of students with moderate disabilities.* Paper presented at the annual meeting of the American Educational Research Association, Chicago.

Irish, C. (2002). Using peg- and keyword mnemonics and computer-assisted instruction to enhance basic multiplication performance in elementary students with learning and cognitive disabilities. *Journal of Special Education Technology, 17*(4), 29–40.

Kauffman, J. M., & Landrum, T. J. (2007). Educational service interventions and reforms. In J. W. Jacobson, J. A. Mulick, & J. Rojahn (Eds.), *Handbook of intellectual and developmental disabilities* (pp. 173–188). New York: Springer.

Kinney, E., Vedora, J., & Stromer, R. (2003). Computer-presented video models to teach generative spelling to a child with an autism spectrum disorder. *Journal of Positive Behavior Interventions, 5,* 22–29.

Langone, J., Clees, T. J., Rieber, L., & Matzko, M. (2003). The future of computer-based interactive technology for teaching individuals with moderate to severe disabilities: Issues relating to research and practice. *Journal of Special Education Technology, 18*(1), 5–16.

Lee, D., McGee, A., & Ungar, S. (2001). Using multimedia to teach personal safety to children with severe learning difficulties. *British Journal of Special Education, 28*(2), 70.

Lin, A., Podell, D. M., & Rein, N. (1991). The effects of CAI on word recognition in mildly mentally handicapped and nonhandicapped learners. *Journal of Special Education Technology, 11*(1), 16–25.

Lin, A., Podell, D. M., & Tournaki-Rein, N. (1994). CAI and the development of automaticity in mathematics skills in students with and without mild mental handicaps. *Computers in the Schools, 11*(1), 43–58.

Maglieri, K. A., DeLeon, I. G., Rodriguez-Catter, V., & Sevin, B. M. (2000). Treatment of covert food stealing in an individual with Prader-Willi syndrome. *Journal of Applied Behavior Analysis, 33*(4), 615–618.

Mechling, L., Gast, D., & Barthold, S. (2003). Multimedia computer-based instruction to teach students with moderate intellectual disabilities to use a debit card to make purchases. *Exceptionality, 11*(4), 239–254.

Mechling, L., Gast, D., & Langone, J. (2002). Computer-based video instruction to teach persons with moderate intellectual disabilities to read grocery aisle signs and locate items. *The Journal of Special Education, 35*(4), 224–240.

Nyhan, W. (1995). Lesch-Nyhan syndrome. In G. O'Brien & W. Yule (Eds.), *Behavioural phenotypes.* Cambridge, UK: Cambridge University Press.

O'Reilly, M., O'Reilly, B., Sigafoos, J., Green, V., Lancioni, G., & Machalicek, W. (2007). Educational assessment. In J. L. Matson (Ed.), *Handbook of assessment in persons with intellectual disability* (pp. 141–162). London: Academic Press.

Ozonoff, S., Goodlin-Jones, B. L., & Solomon, M. (2007). Autism spectrum disorders. In E. J. Mash & R. A. Barkley (Eds.), *Assessment of childhood disorders* (4th ed., pp. 487–525). New York: The Guilford Press.

Parette, H., Hourcade, J., & VanBiervliet, A. (1993). Selection of appropriate technology for children with disabilities. *Teaching Exceptional Children, 25*(3), 18–22.

Parette, H., VanBiervliet, A., & Hourcade, J. (2000). Family-centered decision making in assistive technology. *Journal of Special Education Technology, 15*(1), 45–55.

Podell, D. M., Tournaki-Rein, N., & Lin, A. (1992). Automatization of mathematics skills via computer-assisted instruction among students with mild mental handicaps. *Education and Training in Mental Retardation, 27*(3), 200–206.

Rutter, M. (2005). Aetiology of autism: Findings and questions. *Journal of Intellectual Disability Research, 49*(4), 231–238.

Schlosser, R. W., Koul, R., & Costello, J. (2007). Asking well-built questions for evidence-based practice in augmentative and alternative communication. *Journal of Communication Disorders, 40,* 225–238.

Schlosser, R. W., & Lee, D. L. (2000). Promoting generalization and maintenance in augmentative and alternative communication: A meta-analysis of 20 years of effectiveness research. *Augmentative and Alternative Communication, 16,* 212–226.

Snell, M., Chen, L.-Y., & Hoover, K. (2006). Teaching augmentative and alternative communication to students with severe disabilities: A review of intervention research 1997–2003. *Research and Practice for Persons with Severe Disabilities, 31*(3), 203–214.

Tutt, R., Powell, S., R, & Thornton, M. (2006). Educational approaches in autism: What we know about what we do. *Educational Psychology in Practice, 22*(1), 69–81.

United States Congress. (1975). *Education of All Handicapped Children Act.* Washington, DC: Author.

United States Congress. (1997). *Individuals with Disabilities Education Act, 1997 Amendments.* Washington, DC: Author.

United States Congress. (2004). *Individuals With Disabilities Education Improvement Act of 2004.* Washington, DC: Author.

Vedora, J., & Stromer, R. (2007). Computer-based spelling instruction for students with developmental disabilities. *Research in Developmental Disabilities: A Multidisciplinary Journal, 28*(5), 489–505.

Wehmeyer, M., Smith, S. J., Palmer, S. B., & Davies, D. K. (2004). Technology use by students with intellectual disabilities: an overview. *Journal of Special Education Technology, 19*(4), 7–21.

7

Postschool Options

Overview: This chapter deals with the options available to teachers and parents when a student with an intellectual disability is ready to finish with formal schooling. The chapter examines transition planning, and discusses processes and programs designed to prepare students for life after formal schooling. Factors affecting employability are also considered. The chapter also examines other postschool options when employment is not a realistic or likely alternative.

Introduction

Schooling can be seen both as an end in itself and as a preparation for the future. Most families would hope that formal schooling will provide a range of benefits for their children. Formal education provides a clear structure, focus, and occupation for 10 or more years of children's lives. Hopefully it is a place of fun and enjoyment where, in addition to the development of academic skills, the norms of social interaction are learned, both formally and informally, and life-long friendships are made. For many students and their families, the success of their schooling will be judged in part by whether or not it leads to their planned postschool vocational or educational outcome. Do they manage to gain an apprenticeship as a hairdresser? Can they

Education of Students with an Intellectual Disability, pages 201–221

study to be a lawyer? Do they make it into the design course that was their ambition? For most students, the end of schooling will be an exciting time of transition into a new phase of their lives, with increased independence and the prospect of new and stimulating experiences.

For many students with an intellectual disability and their families, the end of formal schooling is a time of great anxiety. The years of the formal schooling process tend to be highly systematized and ordered. Staffing is closely regulated and monitored and accountability is an important aspect of the system. Travel is carefully organized and is provided by the government in some countries. Term dates and attendance times are established well in advance, often through legislation. Rights and expectation are widely known. By contrast, the postschool offerings for students with an intellectual disability do not generally constitute a system. They are diverse and diffuse, even though in some countries they have legislation to support them. It is often very hard for parents to gain a clear picture of what is likely to happen to their child when she leaves school, to know who they have to approach for assistance, and what paperwork or advocacy is needed (Neubert & Moon, 2006).

Despite these difficulties, the postschool situation has improved greatly for students with an intellectual disability over the last 20 or so years. Whereas in the past some students finished formal schooling and spent the rest of their lives at home, it is now much more likely in most developed countries that students will move into an appropriate postschool activity. This could range from a regular job through supported employment to voluntary work or day programs that are not focused on employment. Some students with intellectual disability now attend college. In the United States there is a growing expectation that all students, including those with a disability, will move into some form of postsecondary education (deFur & Korinek, 2008). Even parents of students with severe disabilities see integrated employment as the ideal outcome for their children, although they do not necessarily believe that their ideal is realistic (Kraemer & Blacher, 2001). Perhaps this can change. Preparation to help students access their optimal postschool option begins when they are at school.

FOR DISCUSSION OR REFLECTION:

- Why is the end of formal schooling often a time of high anxiety for students with an intellectual disability and their families?

School-Based Preparation and Transition Planning

Much of the responsibility for preparing a student for the transition to postschool life needs to be accepted by the school that the student currently attends. Schools are uniquely placed to coordinate this preparation (Dempsey, 2008). They are staffed by classroom teachers, special educators, psychologists, and career counselors. Schools have easy access to outside expertise and information. Once students have left formal schooling, parents find it much more difficult to know what their child is entitled to and from whom they should ask for help.

In the United States the Individuals with Disabilities Education Act (U.S. Congress, 2004) requires states to report on the percentage of youth aged 16+ who have an Individualized Educational Program (IEP), which includes transition planning designed to assist students in meeting their postsecondary goals. The IEP must contain "measurable postsecondary goals based upon age-appropriate transition assessments related to training, education, employment, and, where appropriate, independent living skills . . . and the transition services . . . needed to assist the child in reaching these goals" (Section 1414[d][1][A]). The 1997 IDEA required a statement of transition services to be provided from the age of 14+, but the age requirement for transition services was changed to 16+ in 2004. Many practitioners and administrators saw this as a downgrading of the focus on transition. However, others have argued that IDEA 2004, through its requirements, actually increased the expectation that schools would be preparing students for the transition to postsecondary education (deFur, 2008).

The pivotal concept in any IEP is that of *individualization.* For a student who is hoping to gain regular employment as a builder's laborer, a supermarket assistant, or a hairdresser, the goals and therefore the transition plan will be very different from those of a student who will be seeking supported employment or who will be fully supported in a day program, or from a student who hopes to go on to further study at college.

Developing an IEP/ITP

The development of an IEP, including transition planning and possibly including a separate Individual Transition Plan (ITP), for a student leaving secondary education is an important and complex process. The plan may decide to focus on the regular curriculum, on academic skills of literacy or numeracy, on social skills such as asking and turn-taking, on self-care skills, on skills of independence such as travel training, or on simple communication and choice-making skills. In some systems, the student will have access to part-time vocational education through the local technical or community college. Here students could study introductory courses related to their planned vocational area, or more general courses as preparation for postsecondary education. The ITP is also likely to include supervised work experience, if this is relevant to the student's goals.

According to IDEA (2004), the ITP is developed as a component of the IEP that focuses specifically on transition goals for the student and the services needed to ensure that those goals are met. In the United States, where the minimum school leaving age varies from 16 to 18, it can be extended to 21 for some special education students. For a transition plan to be useful, it needs to commence at least 1 year and preferably 2 years or more before the student is likely to finish secondary education, and to be evaluated regularly and updated at least annually.

Participants in ITP Planning

ITP planning meetings will generally involve the student, his parents, teachers, the school and district transition coordinators, and others as relevant. Others involved could include representatives of outside support agencies and medical personnel, if there are medical issues that may impact on the plan. Parents are usually experts on their child's abilities and difficulties and will often have a clear perception of what their postschool expectations are for their child (Cooney, 2002). For example, it may transpire at the ITP meeting that the student's uncle owns a factory where he is prepared to employ the student as a warehouseman's assistant when he leaves school. The ITP would then focus on the skills likely to be needed in that role and might include supervised work experience in the factory or a similar setting. Without the parental input, the ITP could have been seriously off-track.

Under IDEA 2004, parents have certain rights regarding IEP/ITP meetings. As well as the right of attendance, they can request additional planning meetings if they believe the current ITP is no longer relevant and can invite appropriate representatives of outside agencies to the planning meeting. They can expect their child's progress to be planned in ways that are able to be measured and can request reports of progress.

The student can also be a very important contributor to ITP planning, particularly if she has a good understanding of what the process is about. The student may have a clear perception of what she would like to do after she leaves school. If the student's goals are realistic and achievable, the ITP can focus on making them happen. If the goals are unrealistic, the ITP could include activities to help the student achieve realistic goals for her future. These might include career counseling, voluntary work, and visits to outside agencies and training organizations. If the student is part of her own ITP planning program, she is much more likely to perceive the activities that arise out of the meeting as relevant to her future.

Outside expertise is often crucial to developing a realistic ITP. If there is a regional transition coordinator, that person will be familiar with the options available in that community and how readily they can be accessed. The range of options in any well-resourced region could include

- Vocational education and training
- Postsecondary education
- Regular employment
- Integrated employment
- Supported employment
- Work teams and work centers
- Continuing community education
- Community access services
- Adult day services

Some of these options are discussed in more detail later in this chapter.

Components of an ITP

While the components and structure of an ITP are not mandated, there is reasonable agreement that a well-developed plan should provide a clear picture of the student, his hopes for the future, and an agreed-upon plan to help him achieve those hopes. Dempsey (2008) conceptualizes the elements of an ITP as:

> *Creating a positive description of the student*: This involves asking questions such as "What are the students gifts, interests, and talents? What is his story?"
> *Developing a vision*: Questions here include "What is the student's desired lifestyle? What is his dream? What are desirable images for his future?"
> *Making a plan*: Questions include "What are the student's options? What people and supports are needed to achieve these options? What timeline and steps are required?"

While different schools will have different models for the structure of a transition plan, Drew and Hardman (2004) suggest the following six components of an ITP:

Employment training and placement: If the student is likely to move into an open or supported employment situation, plans should be made for a work experience placement which will assist in the development of skills required for the work. There is no point in providing unrealistic work experience placements. For example, there is little point in providing work experience in a TV studio if there is no prospect of work in that area.

Residential placement: Sometimes the end of formal schooling will be associated with a move out of the family home into some form of residential placement. The ITP needs to consider whether the student will be at home or in another placement and what supports are needed in either situation.

Leisure activities: The plan should identify leisure activities the student will wish to engage in after leaving school and see how these can be supported.

Income and medical support: This is an area of great complexity in many countries and may require expert input from a social worker or similar professional.

Transportation: Consideration needs to be given to how the student will travel to any work placement and whether her program needs to include travel training.

Long-term support and care: In some cases the transition from school will be a time when parents will seek assistance in making sure that their child's future is covered by guardianship arrangements or other legal provisions, such as wills or trusts (Drew & Hardman, 2004).

By the end of the planning process there should be a clear picture of the student's strengths, interests, and postschool goals; the strategies that will be used to help her reach those goals; and the services that will need to be accessed, both in the school and in the community, to assist in ensuring that she achieves those goals. The plan should be student centered and should drive all subsequent aspects of the student's secondary education (Bambara, Wilson, & McKenzie, 2007). There are many inventive ways of dealing with the transition process. For example, Neubert and Redd (2008) describe an innovative program in which students with an intellectual disability spent the final 3 years of their public school program on a community college campus. The students in this case were aged 19 to 21. While students and parents reported positively on the program, the authors stressed the need for planned evaluation of student outcomes so that any expansion of the model could be evidence based.

It is important that the planned postsecondary program and service delivery model is designed to meet the needs and wishes of the student, rather than simply to slot the student into what is currently being offered (Neubert & Moon, 2006). Teaching important life skills such as assisting the student to develop self-advocacy skills could be part of the transition plan (Bambara et al., 2007). There are innovative ways of ensuring that students and their families influence the type of program they will receive. In New South Wales, for example, a government program provides a funding allocation to individual students who can then select the program that most suits their needs from among endorsed providers. All transition processes should have the student's needs and preferences at their center. An example of an individual transition plan is provided in Table 7.1.

TABLE 7.1 Sample Individual Transition Plan (ITP)—Part of an IEP

Maintown Secondary School
Individual Transition Plan

Student: Bradley Brown
Date of Birth: October 7, 1993
Date of ITP meeting: September 21, 2009
Current class: 60% integration to year 10
School leaving date: June 2014 (21 years)
Responsible teacher: Mrs. Harley, School Transition Coordinator
Transition Team Members Present
Mrs. Harley (Convenor)
Bradley
Mr. & Mrs. Brown
Donald Brown (Bradley's older brother)
Mrs. Thomas (Special Classroom Teacher)
Mr. Lucio (Community Work Experience Coordinator)
Ms. Clay (Regional Transition Coordinator)
Date for review meeting: September 2010

Educational Goals

1. To develop his literacy and numeracy skills so that he will be able to live as independently as possible
2. To develop any specialized literacy and numeracy skills that will assist him to gain his vocational goals
3. To stay at school until age 21 with possible part-time enrollment in a vocational education program

Vocational Goals

1. To move into integrated employment as a packer at the local supermarket, as part of a work crew
2. To have work experience related to Goal 1

(continued)

TABLE 7.1 Sample Individual Transition Plan (ITP)—Part of an IEP

Independent Living Goals

1. To continue living at home for the foreseeable future
2. To explore options in supported or semi-independent accommodation
3. To develop travel skills related to work at the supermarket
4. To further develop money-handling skills

Leisure Goals

1. To develop skills at bowling
2. To join a social group to bowl
3. To participate in sailing at the local yacht club

Action Plan

Goal	Action	Person Responsible	Date
E-1	Arrange intensive program of functional literacy and numeracy	Mrs. Thomas (Special Education Classroom Teacher)	February 2010
E-2	Consult supermarket work crew coordinator about specialized literacy and numeracy skills	Mrs. Harley (School Transition Coordinator)	January 2010
E-3	Explore relevant part-time vocational courses	Mrs. Harley	May 2010
V-1	Arrange visit to see supermarket work crew in action and meet coordinator	Mr. Lucio (Community Work Experience Coordinator)	March 2010
V-2	Arrange supermarket work experience	Mr. Lucio	July 2010
I-1	No action needed at this stage		
I-2	Obtain information about future accommodation options	Ms Clay (Regional Transition Coordinator)	June 2012
I-3	Travel skills to be introduced as part of special education program	Mrs. Thomas	February 2010
I-4	Program to include shopping and banking, and community-based practice of these skills	Mrs. Thomas	February 2010
L-1	Bradley to join in school bowling	Mr. Davies (Physical Education Teacher)	Semester II, 2010
L-2	Explore opportunities to join social bowling group	Mr. Davies	Semester II, 2010
L-3	Obtain information about local sailing activities and link Bradley to them	Donald Brown (Bradley's older brother)	December 2010

FOR DISCUSSION OR REFLECTION:

- Why is transition planning important for students with a disability?
- What would you regard as essential components of a transition plan?

Factors Impacting on Employability

If schools are focusing on optimizing the employment prospects of students with an intellectual disability preparing to leave school, it is important for them to be aware of personal and other factors that are likely to affect the employability of individual students. Some of these factors will be modifiable and could become part of the student's transition plan if that is agreed to by the student, his family, and other relevant parties to the plan. There will also be other systemic factors outside the control of the individual or the school.

McDermott and her colleagues investigated the individual, provider, and community characteristics that predicted the employability of people with intellectual disability. They found that the individual characteristics that increased the likelihood of employment were good adaptive skills, higher IQ level (within the intellectual disability range), being male, and being African American (McDermott, Martin, & Butkus, 1999). The final characteristic may seem surprising, as being African American would be expected by many people to be more likely to lead to disadvantage rather than advantage. However, in this case it may have been that African Americans were inappropriately overrepresented in special education classes for students with mild intellectual disability, and that their real abilities were revealed only when it became time for them to move into employment. McDermott et al. concluded from their research and a review of the literature that adaptive skill building and the maintenance and promotion of good physical and mental health are important aspects of programs preparing students for employment.

There are other studies that have found adaptive behavior to be strongly related to employment in people with an intellectual disability (Su, Lin, Wu, & Chen, 2008). However, research into the impact of adaptive skills on employability is made more complex by the reciprocal nature of these skills. The question needs to be asked, does having good adaptive skills make a person more employable, or is it that being employed improves a person's adaptive behavior? The answer is probably "yes" to both. Stephens and her colleagues conducted a longitudinal study of data held on 2,760 people receiving services through a state Developmental Disabilities Division in the United States, examining the effects of different types of employment on adaptive skills and other behaviors (Stephens, Collins, & Dodder, 2005). They studied four employment situations: none, sheltered, supported, and competitive. They found that as people moved into employment, their adaptive skills increased. As they moved out of employment, their adaptive skills decreased. In addition, as they moved further along the spectrum toward competitive employment, their adaptive skills increased, and vice versa. Stephens et al. concluded that employment, particularly competitive employment, could act as a means of improving the adaptive skills of people with developmental disabilities. In another study, Garcia-Villamisar and Hughes (2007) found that involvement in competitive employment over a period of 2 to 3 years led to improvements in the cognitive skills of a group of 44 adults with autism. A comparison group undertaking noncompetitive vocational activities showed no changes in cognitive performance over a similar period (Garcia-Villamisar & Hughes, 2007).

In contrast to the findings of McDermott et al., Martorell and colleagues did not find IQ differences between adults within a large organization who were in a sheltered workshop and others who were in a more open supported employment situation. However, they did find significant differences between the groups in behavior problems, adaptive function, psychiatric symptoms and self-determination (Martorell, Gutierrez-Recacha, Perada, & Ayuso-Mateos, 2008). Differences favored those in more open employment situations. The authors concluded that the factors showing significant differences explained the employment outcomes of the two groups, that is, better adaptive function led to more open employment. The findings of Stephens et al. (2005) suggest another possible interpretation, which is that, at least in some cases, more open employment could have been a cause of better adaptive functioning rather than a result of it.

From a teacher's perspective, research on employability emphasizes the importance of helping students to develop various adaptive behavior skills as contributors to successful employment. These could include money skills, functional literacy and numeracy, understanding signs, health and safety skills, time-telling, self-regulation, and related skills. The research also suggests that these skills will improve and develop as they are needed when the student enters employment, so there is a strong argument for aiming for the highest possible employment level, consistent with the student's goals and interests.

FOR DISCUSSION OR REFLECTION:

- Reflect on students with disabilities you have seen working in the local community. What characteristics appear to make them good employees?
- What characteristics are regarded as desirable in any employee?

Employment Options

In most societies, employment is a crucial determinant of status and self-identity. To be unemployed or to lose your job would be seen by many as a devastating situation to be in—a major life crisis. In addition to status and identity, employment brings financial benefits, perhaps the main benefit to most people. Employment also provides a structure to life, often an enjoyable daily occupation, and usually the opportunity to socialize and to meet people.

For all students, with or without a disability, one of the aims of education is to move into the best possible employment situation. For some jobs, there is fierce competition for entry into training programs and/or later employment. Some jobs depend on particular talents that need to be recognized, or on gaining a specific entry grade. As a result, many people have to settle for training or employment other than in their first choice of occupation. Not everyone can become a doctor, an astronaut, a TV star, or a writer, or even a waiter or a bricklayer's assistant. At all levels, choices and compromises will need to be made, and hopefully most people will end up in an occupation of their choosing, even if it is not necessarily their first choice.

The situation for people with an intellectual disability is no different. They and their families will hope that they can get a job that is to their liking and will produce a financial benefit. As for most people, the higher their ability, the higher will be their ambition. The top choice for those with sufficient ability will be some form of regular open employment. This does not mean that people seeking regular employment are left totally to their own resources. In most countries there are now employment agencies whose role is to assist people with disabilities to find employment. Services might include helping people choose the type of employment they are looking for, linking them with training and vocational education providers, matching them with an appropriate employer, providing specialized equipment if needed, providing direct training, and helping to arrange wage subsidies if available. For example, many governments provide initial financial support to assist people with disabilities to enter the workforce.

There does not appear to be clear agreement in the literature, among researchers, or among government agencies in various countries as to where open employment ends and supported employment begins. What some would describe as "open employment," others describe as "supported employment," and vice versa. For example, in the United States, the use of the term "supported employment" often includes provision of training activities to achieve work integration, searching the labor market for work, and monitoring the workplace to assist workers who have a disability achieve their work goals (Vila, Pallisera, & Fullana, 2007), and is contrasted with sheltered employment. In Australia, supported employment describes a sheltered employment or business-services model, as opposed to open employment, where the person is in a regular job in the open labor market (O'Brien & Dempsey, 2004).

For the sake of clarity, this book will provide three categories to describe employment for people with an intellectual disability, with the knowledge that what is described here as "integrated employment" will be identified in some countries as *supported employment* and in others as *open employment*. The three categories that describe the range of available employment options are

- Regular employment
- Integrated employment
- Specialized employment.

Regular employment is characterized as a situation in which the person is in the workforce under much the same conditions as any other employee. She reports to the same boss as other employees and has a similar job description to others. Her salary is usually the same as others doing the same work. She may have been assisted in finding the job through a specialist employment agency, and there may be minor adjustments to equipment or routines and initial salary subsidy. The agency may have provided some training before she started work and may have a process for monitoring her progress and satisfaction. Regular employment is sometimes described as open or competitive employment. However, the term *competitive* will sometimes be inaccurate as the person may have been employed in a regular position as part of a disability support scheme rather than through standard competitive advertisement.

Integrated employment is a situation where a person is able to work in a regular work situation under conditions that are somewhat different from those of the general workforce. The person may perform a role that is unlike those of other workers and that may have been designed specifically to fit his capabilities. The expectations on his productivity will usually be different from those of other workers, and there may be a special salary arrangement related to productivity. His work will be regularly supervised by an agency that will provide initial and ongoing training as required. He may have the help of a job coach. Sometimes a group of people with intellectual disability will work together in a supervised enclave or work crew within a regular employment situation (see Box 7.1). This is sometimes referred to as supported employment. The main feature of integrated employment is that the person's job is located in a regular workplace.

BOX 7.1 GARDENING AT THE UNIVERSITY OF NEWCASTLE

For the last 12 years, most gardening, mowing, and ground maintenance at the University of Newcastle, Australia, has been undertaken by about 20 adults with intellectual disability employed through the Delando Corporation, a community-based nonprofit organization. The University contracts the Corporation to provide its ground maintenance. In turn, the Corporation recruits and trains its workers, most of whom have a moderate degree of intellectual disability. The Corporation takes responsibility for the workers' occupational health and safety, and ensures that they are fully trained before they handle any equipment. Supervisors, employed by Delando, are on hand at all times to plan and supervise the daily schedule. The employees work in small groups on different sections of the grounds at any time. This integrated employment model could therefore be described as a "work enclave" or "work crew."

For the gardeners, the arrangement has provided ongoing integrated employment of a semipermanent nature. Some workers have been on the job for 12 years, since the contract started. Most workers travel independently to and from the University, using public transport. From the workers' perspective, they are employed full-time in a job that they enjoy as gardeners at the University. There is good camaraderie among the workers, and they also enjoy chatting with students and staff of the University as they go about their work. From the University's perspective, their ground maintenance is done in an effective and efficient way and employment of people with a disability is a goal of the University's equity plan. It is also beneficial for staff and students of the University to be able to observe the excellent work skills demonstrated by people with a significant intellectual disability.

DISCUSSION QUESTIONS:

1. Do you agree with the description of this program as "integrated employment?" Why or why not?
2. What impact is this program having on the lives of the workers?
3. What are the benefits to the University?
4. What other services could be provided through a work enclave?
4. What are the advantages and disadvantages of this model when compared with regular employment or specialized employment (such as a business service)?

Specialized employment describes the situation when people are working in a situation away from the regular workforce, primarily with other people who have a disability. The most common form of specialized employment is a business service (sometimes called a sheltered workshop), where people undertake routine contracted work such as packaging and assembly tasks and light industrial work. Workers usually receive a small wage, but their main income is a government benefits payment. While most governments have policies that encourage moves toward regular or integrated employment, specialized employment in the form of business services is still a very common provision for people with an intellectual disability (O'Brien & Dempsey, 2004). Disability-focused prevocational training programs and transition-to-work programs would also come under the category of specialized employment.

Many factors affect the likelihood of people with an intellectual disability gaining regular employment. Not the least of these is the general employment situation at the time. In times of high unemployment, people with disabilities, like all people, will find it much more difficult to obtain regular employment. Government policy is also very influential as it will determine the types of programs that are encouraged and financially supported (Wehman, 2006a). Such policies and the associated funding support vary greatly from country to country and even from state to state.

FOR DISCUSSION OR REFLECTION:

- Read Box 7.1 and discuss or reflect on the questions at the end.

Nonemployment Options

While the policy of many governments is strongly in support of moving as many people as possible toward some form of regular, integrated, or specialized employment option, this is often difficult to implement in practice. Some people have complex, multiple disabilities and/or severe intellectual disabilities, which require a high level of personal support. Others, for a variety of reasons, do not see employment as a realistic goal. These people and their families may choose alternative postschool options made available through government or government-sponsored organizations. The aim of these programs is to help people with a disability to lead an enjoyable and fulfilled life, and to provide relief to parents who have responsibility for full-time care of their adult or nearly-adult children.

Community access programs help people with disabilities to access services, facilities and resources of their choosing in the community. The aim is to provide leisure, recreational, and/or personal education opportunities that will enhance the person's quality of life. Access programs follow a philosophy that, wherever possible, people with a disability should access mainstream activities that already exist in the community, rather than have specialized, segregated centers created for them. Thus community libraries, swimming pools, gyms, movie theaters, and shopping centers are all typical sites for community access activities. Another aspect of community access philosophy is choice, so the person with a disability has a major role in deciding his activities, rather than having them thrust upon him. Some examples of activities offered through a community access service are provided in Table 7.2.

TABLE 7.2 Examples of Community Access Activities

Life Long Learning through Community Participation		
• Access Committees	• Hospitals	• Packaging
• Animals	• Ceramics	• Hospitality
• Art	• Propagation	• Trees in Newcastle
• Computers	• Oral Histories	• Worm Farming
• Communication	• Women with Disabilities	• Community Radio
• Conferences	• Nutrition	• Budgeting
• Committees	• Men's Business	• Wheelchair Maintenance
• Gardening	• Women's Business	• Car Detailing
• Meals On Wheels	• Peer support	• Internet
• RSPCA	• Gymnastics	• Fitness
• Paper Runs	• Sport	• Data Entry
• The Wetlands	• Travel Training	• Sailability
• Community Gardens	• Swimming	• Budgeting/Banking
• Aged Care	• Hydrotherapy	• Technical College
• Citizenship Workshops		

Source: Newcastle & Hunter Community Access
http://www.nhca.org.au/services.htm

Day programs also aim to provide leisure, recreation, and personal education for people with a disability, but these are usually provided for small groups of people, often in a specialized center. One reason for the continuation of this model is the relative cost. Community access programs are mainly one-on-one and are therefore very labor-intensive and costly to operate. Day programs can operate with groups of three or more people, and as a result, a person can receive more hours of service within a given budget. Thus a client may, for example, be offered 7 hours a week of community access or 20 hours of center-based day programs. Many would choose the extra hours.

Some disability advocates and researchers have been very critical of day programs as a continuation of segregated services. For example, Brown et al. (2006) have provided evidence that, given adequate support and instruction, people with a significant level of disability can function successfully in integrated vocational settings. Nevertheless, day programs can have a training and vocational focus, and may take place in community settings. An example of the range of activities offered through day programs in Victoria, Australia, is provided in Box 7.2.

BOX 7.2 EXAMPLES OF OFFERINGS IN DAY PROGRAMS

Disability—Day Programs

Day programs help adults with disabilities

Day programs help adults with disabilities to develop skills and increase their independence. Activities that increase independence include:

- Cooking and learning about health and nutrition
- Development of personal and social skills
- Learning to access community services—such as the bank, library and public transport

Getting ready for work

Day programs can help prepare adults with a disability for work. They offer:

- Development of literacy and numeracy skills
- Development or improvement of communication skills
- Pre-vocational training
- Physical care

Who can use day programs

Adults who can use day programs must:

- Be over 16 years of age
- Be better suited to day programs than aged care if they are over 65
- Have an intellectual, physical or sensory disability, or an acquired brain injury

Finding a day program

Day programs are offered at a number of community venues, including:

- Neighbourhood houses
- Technical colleges
- Day program centres
- Local clubs

Benefits of day programs

In addition to providing daytime activities and skills training, day programs offer:

- Improved confidence and self-esteem
- Improved skills for interacting with others
- A chance to take part in the local community
- A break (respite) for the person's carer
- Fun activities—such as arts and crafts and sports and leisure programs.

Source: Department of Human Services, Victoria. http://www.disability.vic.gov.au/dsonline/dssite.nsf?open

A possible disadvantage of community access and day programs, as well as of specialized employment programs such as sheltered workshops, is that, once in them, it becomes unlikely that people will move into a more open employment situation. There is evidence that people with an intellectual disability report a higher quality of life if they are in a regular or integrated employment situation as opposed to sheltered employment (Kober & Eggleton, 2005). Regular and integrated employment, in addition to possibly leading to an improved quality of life, have been found to be more cost-effective than sheltered employment (Cimera, 2007). Dempsey and Ford (2009) believe that further systematic studies of the impact of employment services on quality of life are needed.

FOR DISCUSSION OR REFLECTION:

- Reflect on your local community. What community activities could young adults with a disability access with support? What sort of support would be needed?

Teachers and Employment

There are many who would argue that even for students with severe disabilities, a realistic goal is regular employment or integrated employment (Brown, Shiraga, & Kessler, 2006; Rusch & Braddock, 2004; Wehman, 2006a). Rusch and Braddock see schools as having an important leadership role in preparing all students, including those with severe disabilities, for employment. They suggest that schools should partner with federal, state, and local services to ensure that all students find gainful employment. They also recommend that students receive long-term follow-up for at least 3 years to ensure that they make the transition into employment or postsecondary education, and they criticize adult day programs that, as they see it, "promote the segregation and marginalization of an entire population" (p. 242). Rusch and Braddock see schools as having a major role in the follow-up process.

We have come a long way in ensuring that the improved educational services received by school students lead into fulfilling and rewarding postschool experiences. Following principles of normalization discussed earlier in this book, the objective wherever feasible should be for as many students as possible to move into postsecondary education, leading to regular employment or integrated employment. Because of the complexity and variety of postschool education and employment support policies, teachers who are assisting students in transition from school programs need to seek local expert input and advice so that they can link their students to the best possible postsecondary education and employment opportunities. There are also some very useful specialized textbooks that will assist teachers in this important task (e.g. Getzel & Wehman, 2005; Wehman, 2006b).

The last 30 to 40 years have seen enormous changes in the lives of people with an intellectual disability. It is possible that someone who, 40 years ago, would have spent their entire life in an institution with minimal educational input, will now receive help through an early intervention program, will attend preschool, and will proceed through an educational program at a regular or special school into a supported, integrated, or regular employment situation. A person with an intellectual disability is now much more likely to live a life that is comparable to that of other people in the community. By the time the person leaves school, support will have been received from a large number of professionals, but the input of teachers will have been crucial at every stage. Teachers are the essential drivers of all phases of the journey of a student with an intellectual disability, from early intervention through to the transition into employment, and it is teachers who will be most influential in determining their successful outcome.

FOR DISCUSSION OR REFLECTION:

- What role could a school play in following up its students to ensure they are in an appropriate postsecondary program?

Summary

The end of formal schooling can be a difficult time for students with an intellectual disability. It is important that schools develop a comprehensive individualized transition plan that will lead students toward the best possible postschool outcome, and the last years of formal schooling should assist in the transition to postschool life. Good adaptive behavior skills appear to enhance employability, although employment also appears to improve adaptive skills. In addition to various forms of postsecondary and vocational education, people with an intellectual disability may go into competitive regular employment or a variety of supported options including regular, integrated, and specialized employment. Community access programs and day programs are alternatives for people who do not choose to access employment programs. However, there are arguments that all people, regardless of their level of disability, should have a goal of regular or integrated employment, and that schools should be helping all students work toward this goal.

References

Bambara, L. M., Wilson, B. A., & McKenzie, M. (2007). Transition and quality of life. In S. L. Odom, R. H. Horner, M. E. Snell, & J. Blacher (Eds.), *Handbook of developmental disabilities* (pp. 371–389). New York: The Guilford Press.

Brown, L., Shiraga, B., & Kessler, K. (2006). The quest for ordinary lives: The integrated post-school functioning of 50 workers with significant disabilities. *Research and Practice for Persons with Severe Disabilities, 31*(2), 93–121.

Cimera, E. V. (2007). The cumulative cost-effectiveness of supported and sheltered employees with mental retardation. *Research and Practice for Persons with Severe Disabilities, 32*(4), 247–252.

Cooney, B. F. (2002). Exploring perspectives on transition of youth with disabilities: Voices of young adults, parents and professionals. *Mental Retardation, 40,* 425–435.

deFur, S. H. (2008). Transition to postsecondary education. *Exceptionality, 16,* 175–177.

deFur, S. H., & Korinek, L. (2008). The evolution toward lifelong learning as a critical transition outcome for the 21st century. *Exceptionality, 16,* 178–191.

Dempsey, I. (2008). Transition to adult learning. In P. Foreman (Ed.), *Inclusion in action* (pp. 468–492). Melbourne: Thomson.

Dempsey, I., & Ford, J. (2009). Employment of people with an intellectual disability in Australia and the United Kingdom. *Journal of Disability Policy Studies, 19,* 233–243.

Drew, C. J., & Hardman, M. L. (2004). *Mental retardation: A lifespan approach to people with intellectual disabilities.* Saddle River, NJ: Pearson Education.

Garcia-Villamisar, D., & Hughes, C. (2007). Supported employment improves cognitive performance in adults with autism. *Journal of Intellectual Disability Research, 51*(2), 142–150.

Getzel, E. E., & Wehman, P. (Eds.). (2005). *Going to college: Expanding opportunities for people with disabilities.* Baltimore: Brookes Publishing Company.

Kober, R., & Eggleton, I. R. C. (2005). The effect of different types of employment on quality of life. *Journal of Intellectual Disability Research, 49*(10), 756–760.

Kraemer, B. R., & Blacher, J. (2001). Transition for young adults with severe mental retardation: School preparation, parent expectations, and family involvement. *Mental Retardation, 39*(6), 423–435.

Martorell, A., Gutierrez-Recacha, P., Perada, A., & Ayuso-Mateos, J. L. (2008). Identification of personal factors that determine work outcome for adults with intellectual disability. *Journal of Intellectual Disability Research, 52*(12), 1091–1101.

McDermott, S., Martin, M., & Butkus, S. (1999). What individual, provider, and community characteristics predict employment of individuals with mental retardation? *American Journal on Mental Retardation, 104*(4), 346–355.

Neubert, D. A., & Moon, M. S. (2006). Postsecondary settings and transition services for students with intellectual disabilities: Models and research. *Focus on Exceptional Children, 39*(4), 1–8.

Neubert, D. A., & Redd, V. A. (2008). Transition services for students with intellectual disabilities: A case study of a public school program on a community college campus. *Exceptionality, 16*(220–234).

O'Brien, J., & Dempsey, I. (2004). Comparative analysis of employment services for people with disabilities in Australia, Finland and Sweden. *Journal of Policy and Practice in Intellectual Disabilities, 1*(3/4), 126–135.

Rusch, F. R., & Braddock, D. (2004). Adult day programs versus supported employment (1988–2002): Spending and service practices of mental retardation and developmental disabilities state agencies. *Research and Practice for Persons with Severe Disabilities, 29*(4), 237–242.

Stephens, D. L., Collins, M. D., & Dodder, R. A. (2005). A longitudinal study of employment and skill acquisition among individuals with developmental disabilities. *Research in Developmental Disabilities, 26*, 469–486.

Su, C. Y., Lin, Y. H., Wu, Y. Y., & Chen, C. C. (2008). The role of cognition and adaptive behavior in employment of people with mental retardation. *Research in Developmental Disabilities, 29*, 83–95.

United States Congress. (2004). *Individuals With Disabilities Education Improvement Act of 2004*. Washington, DC: Author

Vila, M., Pallisera, M., & Fullana, J. (2007). Work integration of people with disabilities in the regular labour market: What can we do to improve these processes? *Journal of Intellectual and Developmental Disability, 32*(1), 10–18.

Wehman, P. (2006a). Integrated employment: If not now, when? If not us, who? *Research and Practice for Persons with Severe Disabilities, 31*(2), 122–126.

Wehman, P. (Ed.). (2006b). *Life beyond the classroom: Transition strategies for young people with disabilities* (4th ed.). Baltimore: Brookes Publishing Company.

Index

Note: "t" refers to table.

A

Education of Students with an Intellectual Disability, pages 223–237

B

C

D

E

J

K

L

M

R

S

T

X

www.ingramcontent.com/pod-product-compliance
Lightning Source LLC
Jackson TN
JSHW081026191125
94512JS00006B/513
9781607522140